FORGOTTEN HEROES
OF THE
BATTLE OF BRITAIN

This book is dedicated to those 'Forgotten Heroes' included in this book, in addition to the 'Forgotten Heroes' of the Battle of Britain today: the selfless and dedicated volunteers without whom so many museums and commemorative sites would not exist or function – not least the unique Kent Battle of Britain Museum at Hawkinge, from where Pilot Officer Dick Howley and Sergeant Albert Curley took-off in their Defiant on 19 July 1940 – to be slaughtered among the 'innocents'.

FORGOTTEN HEROES
OF THE
BATTLE OF BRITAIN

DILIP SARKAR MBE, FRHistS

AIR WORLD

AIR WORLD

FORGOTTEN HEROES OF THE BATTLE OF BRITAIN

First published in Great Britain in 2022 by
Air World
An imprint of
Pen & Sword Books Ltd
Yorkshire – Philadelphia

Typeset by SJmagic DESIGN SERVICES, India.

Printed and bound in the UK by CPI Group (UK) Ltd.

Pen & Sword Books Limited incorporates the imprints of Atlas, Archaeology, Aviation, Discovery, Family History, Fiction, History, Maritime, Military, Military Classics, Politics, Select, Transport, True Crime, Air World, Frontline Publishing, Leo Cooper, Remember When, Seaforth Publishing, The Praetorian Press, Wharncliffe Local History, Wharncliffe Transport, Wharncliffe True Crime and White Owl.

For a complete list of Pen & Sword titles please contact

PEN & SWORD BOOKS LIMITED
47 Church Street, Barnsley, South Yorkshire, S70 2AS, England
E-mail: enquiries@pen-and-sword.co.uk
Website: www.pen-and-sword.co.uk

Or
PEN AND SWORD BOOKS
1950 Lawrence Rd, Havertown, PA 19083, USA
E-mail: Uspen-and-sword@casematepublishers.com
Website: www.penandswordbooks.com

MIX
Paper from
responsible sources
FSC® C013604

Contents

Foreword

by Baroness Hodgson CBE of Abinger

Never in the field of human conflict was so much owed by so many to so Few.

Winston Churchill, 20 August 1940

In this book, *Forgotten Heroes of the Battle of Britain*, Dilip Sarkar sensitively reconstructs the lives and flying careers of six of The Few – five fighter pilots and an air-gunner – and a pilot killed in action during training. In these accounts we learn much about the Battle of Britain and, through Dilip's forensic descriptions, the dogfights over England and subsequent offensive operations over France are brought vividly to life. One cannot fail, in fact, to be moved by the enormous courage and dedication required to fly during the crucial Battle of Britain.

Although the men featured in this book did not become household names like some, they, along with many others, selflessly put their lives in great danger to help save our country in its time of need. Some of those whose stories are told here survived to lead full lives – but tragically others did not.

For me, this book has great personal resonance. My mother, Jean, married 'Billy' Burton when aged twenty – and was a widow at twenty-three, or, more accurately, a 'wife of the missing', Billy and other officers having been shot down over the Bay of Biscay whilst returning to North Africa from home leave in an unarmed Hudson; none were ever seen again. My mother stalwartly waited for years, hoping that Billy had been washed up and then incarcerated in a neutral Spanish alien internment camp. After nine years, she had to face the fact that Billy was not coming back; having accepted this, she later married my father, Keith Allom, who had served as an army officer in the Far East during the war, and I was born. For many years, my mother 'pressed the pause button' on her former loss – but once my father had died, all the unanswered questions came tumbling back to haunt her. It was not until she was in her eighties that she learnt what had happened to her beloved Billy. So I have witnessed first-hand the long-term trauma suffered by those left behind, and, of course, my mother was but one of millions who lost loved ones in the Second World War.

I am so grateful to Dilip for ensuring that Billy will not be forgotten, as I imagine the families of the other aircrew are. This book honours their memories and I hope that others will enjoy learning about the lives of these seven amazingly brave men, as I have done. In conclusion, my thoughts turn to the 'Airman's Hymn', sung annually at the Battle of Britain Memorial Trust's commemorative service at the National Memorial to The Few:

Strong son of man, save those who fly
Swift-winged across the unchartered sky;
Each anxious hour and lonely flight
Serenely challenged, day and night.
O'er land and ocean safely bear
All those in peril in the air.

Baroness Hodgson of Abinger, CBE, April 2022

Prologue

My intention here, from the outset, is to comprehensively contextualise *Forgotten Heroes of the Battle of Britain*, leaving no doubt as to why those featured within remain both relevant and important today, explaining the criteria for their selection. And I hope this causes the reader to reflect and think.

First, let us explore, briefly, why the Battle of Britain should always remain significant.

The Nazi dictator Adolf Hitler came to power in Germany in 1933. During the next few years, Hitler rejected the Versailles Peace Settlement of 1919, which, among other things, severely limited Germany's armed forces. Indeed, under the provisions of Versailles, Germany was prohibited from having an air force – but this, even before Hitler became Chancellor and subsequently Germany's tyrannical *Führer*, was being secretly rebuilt, far from prying western eyes beyond Russia's remote Urals. Having revealed his new *Luftwaffe* to a disbelieving world in 1935, the following year elements of this new and impressive air force saw action in support of the Fascist General Franco in the Spanish Civil War. It was there that Germany tested its new aircraft and other weapons under actual combat conditions, formulating effective strategies and tactics – which, in due course, would prove an immeasurable advantage.

As Germany rearmed, with the most modern military designs, elsewhere in Europe disarmament held sway, and it was only in 1936 that the small peacetime RAF, for example, began expanding and creating a substantial reserve of trained, part-time, amateur, airmen available for general mobilisation in the event of a crisis. Even so, it remained biplane equipped, whereas the *Luftwaffe* was already flying monoplanes; even Germany's new bombers were faster than the British frontline fighter, the Gloster Gauntlet. It was not until 1938, in fact, that RAF Fighter Command received the Hawker Hurricane and Supermarine Spitfire monoplane fighters, which began replacing the desperately obsolete biplanes. By the time war eventually broke out on 3 September 1939 therefore, two days after Hitler's invasion of Poland, Germany was leagues ahead in terms of modern weapons and tactics.

Despite valiant resistance, inevitably Poland soon collapsed against the overwhelming might of Hitler's modern forces; in the spring of 1940, Norway and Denmark followed. By this time, Germany's *Wehrmacht* had substantial, current, combat experience, whereas the Western Allies did not. Between the wars in Britain and France military thinking stagnated, there being an overriding expectation that another war would most likely follow the same pattern as the comparatively immobile First World War, and again be fought on the Continent. The British Expeditionary Force went out to France in September 1939, supported by the RAF's Advanced Air Striking Force. The latter's fighters were Hurricanes, the superior and less numerous Spitfire being preserved for home defence – and the exact nature of an aerial conflict remained a matter of conjecture.

On 10 May 1940, Hitler eventually attacked the West. On that fateful day, Winston Churchill succeeded Neville Chamberlain as Britain's Prime Minister – and lost no time pointing out to the House of Commons that all he could offer at that perilous and uncertain time was 'Blood, tears, toil and sweat'. If things looked bleak that day, much worse was to come a month later.

On the Continent, highly mobile *panzer* divisions negotiated the supposedly impassable Ardennes, outflanking the Maginot Line, paralysing the Allied command system and cutting off the British Expeditionary Force in a pocket around Dunkirk. The *Luftwaffe* enjoyed complete aerial superiority over the battlefield, making this lightning advance to the Channel ports possible – this largely due to the lethal Me 109 fighter, flown by highly experienced fighter pilots. While the subsequent evacuation of over 330,000 Allied troops from the flat beaches around Dunkirk was propagandised by Britain as a glorious victory, in reality the Fall of France was catastrophic.

Two days after the ignominious Dunkirk evacuation concluded, Churchill made Britain's stance very clear:

> Even though large tracts of Europe and many old and famous states have fallen, or may fall into the grip of the Gestapo and all the odious apparatus of Nazi rule, we shall not flag or fail. We shall go on to the end. We shall fight in France. We shall fight on the seas and oceans, we shall fight with growing confidence and growing strength in the air. We shall fight on the beaches, we shall fight on the landing-grounds, we shall fight in the fields and in the streets, we shall fight in the hills, we shall never surrender.

On 10 June 1940, Italy's Mussolini declared war on the Allies, extending the conflict to the Mediterranean and North Africa. When France asked for an armistice shortly afterwards, Hitler hoped that Britain would do likewise.

Although it has been convincingly argued that Britain stood on the shoulders of its Empire and Commonwealth, in military terms, in 1940, she really was alone, just as Poland, due to geography, had been in 1939. Only Britain's shores, not those of Commonwealth or Empire nations, were within range of German bombers and threatened by invasion. Although largely sympathetic, America, still smarting from casualties suffered during the First World War, steadfastly pursued its policy of isolationism from events in Europe, and given Hitler's breathtaking military success to date, there was little beyond Churchill's stirring rhetoric to suggest that David would beat Goliath in the battle ahead. After the Fall of France, described by Churchill as 'a colossal defeat', there was a further lull, while Hitler made plans and regrouped. The *Führer* now considered an unanticipated opportunity: a seaborne invasion of southern England. Hitler's infamous Directive Number 16 stated his aims clearly:

> As England, despite her hopeless military situation, still shows no sign of willingness to come to terms, I have decided to prepare, and if necessary to carry out, a landing operation against her. The aim of this operation is to eliminate the English motherland as a base from which war against Germany can be continued and, if necessary, to occupy completely.

Thirteen divisions of the German army, each some 19,000 strong, moved to the Channel coast as the vanguard of a landing force comprising thirty-nine divisions. Plans were made to disembark 125,000 men in Kent and Sussex during the first three days of the proposed invasion – codenamed 'Operation *Seelöwe*' (Sealion). To transport this force across the *Kanal*, the German navy assembled a makeshift invasion fleet of 170 large transport vessels, 1,500 barges, and several hundred tugs, trawlers, motor boats and fishing smacks. As the *Kriegsmarine* was hopelessly inferior to the Royal Navy in warships of every category, the German service chiefs agreed that the operation could only succeed if the *Luftwaffe* controlled the skies prior to the invasion fleet setting sail. Not unnaturally, *Reichsmarschall* Hermann Göring was supremely confident: 'My *Luftwaffe* is invincible… And so now we turn to England. How long will this one last – two or three weeks?'

PROLOGUE

On 18 June 1940, Churchill again stirred the British people – and made clear to Americans what was at stake:

> What General Weygand called the Battle of France is over. I expect that the Battle of Britain is about to begin. Upon this battle depends the survival of Christian civilisation. Upon it depends our own British life, and the long continuity of our institutions and our Empire. The whole fury and might of the enemy must very soon be turned on us. Hitler knows that he will have to break us in this Island or lose the war. If we can stand up to him, all Europe may be free and the life of the world may move forward into broad, sunlit uplands. But if we fail, then the whole world, including the United States, including all that we have known and cared for, will sink into the abyss of a new Dark Age made more sinister, and perhaps more protracted, by the lights of perverted science. Let us therefore brace ourselves to our duties, and so bear ourselves that, if the British Empire and its Commonwealth last for a thousand years, men will still say, 'This was their finest hour'.

Thus, the phrase 'Finest Hour' was coined – and so the rest of 1940, that most tempestuous year, would prove to be for Britain.

Officially, the Battle of Britain is considered to have begun on 10 July 1940, concluding sixteen weeks later on 31 October 1940 – by which date the *Luftwaffe* had failed to destroy Fighter Command and achieve aerial supremacy. Indeed, on 17 September 1940, Hitler had postponed *Seelöwe* 'indefinitely'. Moreover, just ten days later, Hitler ordered preparations be made for the invasion of Russia, Eastward expansion, of course, having always been Hitler's real war aim. Indeed, from Hitler's perspective, continuing to pursue the prospect of invading Britain at this time was pointless, because as a small island Britain had not the natural resources or living space required by his Nazi empire. Alone, without essential American military support, Britain appeared in no position to continue any significant resistance long-term – so could be left, isolated, without undue risk, while Russia, the infinitely greater prize, was conquered. Britain could be dealt with later. This strategy, however, would prove a fatal error.

Although 31 October 1940 represents the Battle of Britain's official conclusion, German bombers actually continued pounding Britain by night until May 1941, and fighters of both sides clashed until the weather finally brought the 'season' to a close in February 1941. Because of Fighter Command, however, Britain remained in the war. Importantly, this crucial

British victory, unexpected across the Atlantic, marked a new level of essential American commitment and closer support of the war effort.

On 22 June 1941, Hitler finally invaded Russia; on 7 December 1941, the Japanese made a devastating surprise air attack on the American Pacific fleet at Pearl Harbor. That night, Churchill wrote of how he had been 'saturated and satiated with emotion and sensation, I went to bed and slept the sleep of the saved and thankful'. On 11 December 1941, Hitler, already fighting on two fronts, sealed the fate of Nazi Germany: the *Führer* declared war on the United States of America. Ultimately, America poured men and materiel into Britain, from where, on 6 June 1944, the Allies eventually launched the liberation of enemy-occupied Europe. With the Russians investing Berlin, on 30 April 1945 Adolf Hitler committed suicide in his underground bunker. On 8 May 1945, Germany surrendered – unconditionally. In the Far East, the war against Japan continued until the Emperor surrendered on 15 August 1945 – by which time the United States had avenged Pearl Harbor by dropping atomic bombs on Hiroshima and Nagasaki.

Without Fighter Command's victory in the Battle of Britain, however – make no mistake – this Total Victory would not have been possible. Had Britain fallen, there would have been no island base from which the liberation of Europe could be launched, or pressure on Hitler from the West maintained. That being so, the Second World War's outcome would have been entirely different, the Western democracies – and possibly even the United States – ground to dust, and a new, Nazi-dominated world order, based upon murderous racist policies, imposed.

That is why Fighter Command holding out and giving Hitler his first reversal of the war remains Britain's greatest contribution to defeating Nazi Germany – because without the Battle of Britain, there could have been *no* other battles, not even the subsequently crucial Battle of the Atlantic. Rightly, therefore, the Battle of Britain story remains a matter of great national pride and a crucial part of the national narrative.

Some argue that the Battle of Britain's outcome was not a decisive victory over the *Luftwaffe*, because the enemy air force was not destroyed. The essential point, however, is that it was never Fighter Command's job or intention to destroy the *Luftwaffe* – whereas the *Luftwaffe*'s aim *was* to annihilate Fighter Command. Fighter Command's role was to defend Britain, which it did – successfully. During the summer and autumn of 1940, that defence continued, robustly, until the enemy could no longer sustain such heavy losses by day, thereby being forced to abandon invasion plans, and the weather became unfavourable to aerial operations. This bought time, during which Britain was able to bolster its forces and defences, and better prepare for the war ahead. True, the bombing of British cities by night continued until May 1941, but that campaign had not the same war aim as the daylight bombing attacks during the Battle of Britain. So, without doubt, Fighter Command did indeed achieve a victory, which was decisive, because Hitler never again threatened to invade Britain – a valid point rarely mentioned.

Nearly 3,000 aircrew of Fighter Command and other officially accredited units fought in the Battle of Britain. Of those men, 544 lost their lives during the Battle; 791 more would perish before the war was won. On 20 August 1940, Churchill immortalised the aircrew concerned, who at the time were still fighting this decisive battle:

'Never was so much owed by so many to so Few'.

A master of the English language, in that speech Churchill cleverly identified Dowding's aircrews with Henry V's disease-ridden and outnumbered army, which had defeated the might of France at Agincourt on 25 October 1415. In Shakespeare's play *Henry V*, in his morale-boosting speech before the great battle, Henry refers to his army as 'We few, we happy few, we band of brothers' – hence Churchill's description and association with what was an important English victory, centuries before, against apparently overwhelming odds.

Again, it has been argued by some that the 'Few' were not actually so few in fact, and that the opposing air forces were pretty evenly matched numerically. Again, this is largely true, and Air Chief Marshal Dowding far-sightedly arranged his Command so that fighter squadrons were not concentrated just in the south-east. Instead, they covered the whole country, which from a Fighter Command perspective was divided into groups. Battered squadrons in the south, therefore, could be withdrawn to rest and refit away from the main combat zone, replaced by squadrons at full-strength from northern groups. Although the supply of replacement pilots became potentially critical at one stage, it was never actually acute – although what those pilots lacked was combat experience, which was a disadvantage. Moreover, the supply of aircraft was never an issue either. So is all of this a myth?

It must be understood that before the Second World War, owing largely to a lack of experience on the new monoplane fighters and the limitations of the TR9 radio set fitted to RAF aircraft, most training revolved around the flight of six aircraft, rather than the squadron of twelve as a whole. This provided, in the event, for small, flexible, formations to be deployed against enemy air attacks – notwithstanding 12 Group's 'Big Wing' of first three, then five, squadrons, which was wholly impractical and a story in itself, covered in my *Bader's Big Wing Controversy: Duxford 1940* (Pen

& Sword, 2021). In order to preserve limited resources while executing maximum damage to the enemy, Air Chief Marshal Dowding and Air Vice-Marshal Park largely chose to fight the Battle of Britain with small formations. In this way, Fighter Command's strength was never purely concentrated in the south-east, the main battle area, or committed to battle en masse. Consequently, a single flight or squadron of Hurricanes or Spitfires could, and often did, find itself intercepting and engaging large German formations of bombers with their fighter escorts over the 10 and 11 Group areas. This, then, is what gives the impression of a handful of fighter pilots facing overwhelming odds. While on paper, Fighter Command's overall strength supports the argument that the two sides were evenly matched, the way in which the Battle was fought over southern England – and that is where it mattered – was very much a case of comparatively few Fighter Command pilots engaging a numerically superior enemy. So, the 'Few', facing overwhelming odds in this context, is entirely correct. The broader myth, therefore, is that Britain was entirely defended by a just handful of Fighter Command aircrew, which was not the case, but within that, like all myths, is a truism – and that is what matters.

Having explained and argued why the Battle of Britain is of such importance to modern history, and contextualised the Few, what is a hero?

According to the Cambridge Dictionary, a hero is 'A person who is admired for having done something very brave or having achieved something great.'

Considering Fighter Command's experience and achievement during the Battle of Britain, collectively the Few 'achieved something great', so all are heroes by virtue of being there, prepared to play their part – to the death if necessary – whether or not an individual saw action or destroyed an enemy aircraft. Indeed, it was not just about 'aces', which is to say fighter pilots who claimed five enemy aircraft destroyed, but, as Dowding said, the 'team'. Patrolling a potentially hostile sky, miles above the earth, is in itself 'something very brave', and engaging an enemy aircraft or formation represents courage beyond the comprehension of most of us. So yes, by definition, the Few are *all* heroes.

Today, there are various commemorative sites and memorials connected to the Battle of Britain, not least the atmospheric and dignified National Memorial to the Few on the white chalk cliffs overlooking Folkestone and the English Channel, and the impressive London Battle of Britain Monument on Westminster's Embankment; various museums bring us closer to the Battle of Britain story, none more so than the Kent Battle of Britain Museum at Hawkinge, where the remains of over 700 aircraft destroyed during the conflict can be seen, among a vast collection of appended artefacts;

social media has also helped create a 'Battle of Britain community' and raise awareness of the Few. Even so, the point is that through memorials, museums, social media, anniversaries, air shows and the like, the Few collectively are remembered – but not so much on an individual basis, which is the focus of my research.

We often hear about 'human interest' stories, which appear of great interest to the media. Well, the Few represent the best part of 3,000 such stories. Every individual is a separate story, of background, family life, education, motivation, interests, route to the cockpit, subsequent service and ultimate fate. Just because, at the time of writing, all but one known Battle of Britain pilot have passed from us, does that make their lives and experiences less relevant? Some stories were cut short – like that of Pilot Officer Dick Howley and Sergeant Albert Curley, a Defiant crew featured in this book and killed in action on 19 July 1940. Others, like Group Captain Tom Gleave, survived traumatic events during the Battle of Britain and went on to live a successful and productive life. We can learn from all of these stories, I believe, the facts and events of which can influence how we behave and inform our decisions today, and both media and general public alike are more likely, in my experience, to engage with a personal story, rather than that of the colourless strategy involved. And that is what is important: raising awareness beyond the narrow world of the enthusiast.

While the Few are a collective, to me it is the individual, personal, stories that reflect the greatest 'human interest' – and these can easily be forgotten, while commemorated as a whole. To me personally, the recording and sharing of individual stories, working closely alongside the families concerned, is the way forward. The Battle of Britain, the ins and outs and strategy of which is now a well-trodden path by historians and would-be authors, and will continue to receive media coverage at significant anniversaries, the next being the 85th in 2025, which is as it should be, but if 'human interest' stories on a more individual basis is what is required to sustain a wider and more prolonged interest, there are plenty like those featured here which still require researching, recording and sharing. The micro is equally, if not more, fascinating than the macro story, and whereas the macro story is well-told, much micro work remains – possibly of wider interest owing to the 'human interest' element.

All of that said, those featured in this book are far from entirely forgotten. Each and every one is remembered by their family first and foremost, and within the wider collective of the Few. Their individual stories, however, have never been told before, certainly not in as much detail, and in several cases not at all. This book did not arise through reviewing the Few and selecting a cross-section for commercial or comprehensive appeal, focusing upon, say, pilots and aircrew of all participating aircraft types and nationalities. The difficulty with such an approach is that an individual may be selected for inclusion on the basis of exploits and service record, only to find that little or no previously unshared material exists – leaving nothing new to say. The key is both an affinity with the subject, for whatever reason, and the appended existence of previously unpublished material, be that the written word, official documents, photographs, family recollections, or preferably all of those things combined.

The first story in this book concerns Wing Commander 'Billy' Burton, the 1936 Cranwell Sword of Honour recipient, fighter ace and, after the Battle of Britain, pioneer of close air support in the western desert – a man of enormous ability and potential, whose story is unknown even among enthusiasts. The same is so of Wing Commander Eric Thomas, one of the RAF's first ever Spitfire pilots and later a fighter ace leading the Biggin Hill Wing. In recent years, much attention has been paid to the contribution made by the Poles of 303 Squadron during the Battle of Britain, and the story of Wing Commander Johnny Kent, a flight commander on 303, is well-known, not least because of his published memoir, *One of The Few* (see bibliography); the squadron's English-speaking commander, Ronald Kellett, who also survived the war, is less well-known however, although there is a memorial commemorating him in his local parish church in Kent. Kellett's story is of great interest, not just from an RAF perspective but equally from the angles of social and political history – and here, for the first time, we have that story in full, drawing upon Wing Commander Kellett's personal and previously unshared memoir. Similarly, Group Captain Tom Gleave – possibly an ace in a day – who suffered disfiguring burns during the Battle of Britain, also survived, becoming a post-war historian; his story too appears here, in detail, for the first time, drawing upon both the original and unedited manuscript of his 1941 memoir *I Had A Row With A German*, and a later unpublished 500+ page broader memoir. From across the Atlantic, Tina Howley Harney contacted me about her brother, Pilot Officer Dick Howley, a Defiant pilot lost with his air gunner, Sergeant Albert Curley, during the massacre of 141 Squadron on 19 July 1940; certain material had previously been shared online, but here we have the much wider context. Finally, the story of Sergeant Bruce Hancock which was initially researched many years ago by my old friend Allan White, who – moved and concerned by the fact that although Hancock had given his life, he is not one of the Few – initiated a memorial. That story is retold here, in more detail than has been possible before, because it too is an important one to keep alive.

All of those included in the book are heroes and to varying degrees comparatively unknown today, which, in certain cases, considering their achievement, is surprising. Hopefully, this book redresses the balance for those found among its pages – although clearly there could be countless such volumes. Indeed, going forward, I very much doubt that this will be a lone beacon…

* Unless otherwise indicated, all photographs are Dilip Sarkar Archive.

Author's Note & Glossary

The aviation-minded reader will notice that I have referred to German Messerschmitt fighters by the abbreviation 'Me' (not 'Bf', which is more technically correct), or simply by their numeric designation, such as '109' or '110'. This not only reads better but is authentic: during the Battle of Britain, Keith Lawrence, a New Zealander, flew Spitfires and once said to me 'To us they were just "Me's", "109s" or "110s", simple, never "Bf".'

In another attempt to preserve accuracy, I have also used the original German, wherever possible, regarding terms associated with the *Luftwaffe*, such as:

Adlerangriff	'Attack of the Eagles'
Adlertag	'Eagle Day'
Eichenlaub	The Oak Leaves, essentially being a bar to the Ritterkreuz.
Erprobungsgruppe	Experimental group, in the case of *Erprobungsgruppe* 210, a skilled precision bombing unit.
Experte	A fighter 'ace'. Ace status, on both sides, was achieved by destroying five enemy aircraft.
Freie hunt	A fighter sweep.
Gefechstand	Operations headquarters.
General der Jagdflieger	General of Fighter Pilots.
Geschwader	The whole group, usually of three *gruppen*.
Geschwaderkommodore	The group leader.
Gruppe	A wing, usually of three squadrons.
Gruppenkeil	A wedge formation of bombers, usually made up of vics of three.
Gruppenkommandeur	The Wing Commander.
Jagdbomber ('*Jabo*')	Fighter-bomber.
Jagdflieger	Fighter pilot.
Jagdgeschwader	Fighter group, abbreviated JG.

Jagdwaffe	The fighter force.
Jäger	Hunter, in this context a fighter pilot or aircraft.
Kampfflieger	Bomber aircrew.
Kampfgeschwader	Bomber group, abbreviated KG.
Kanal	English Channel.
Katchmarek	Wingman.
Lehrgeschwader	Literally a training group, but actually a precision bombing unit, abbreviated LG.
Luftflotte	Air Fleet.
Oberkanone	Literally the 'Top Gun', or leading fighter ace.
Oberkommando der *Wehrmacht* (OKW)	The German armed forces high command.
Ritterkreuz	The Knight's Cross of the Iron Cross.
Rotte	A pair of fighters, comprising leader and wingman, into which the *Schwarm* broke once battle was joined.
Rottenführer	Leader of a fighting pair.
Schwarm	A section of four fighters.
Schwarmführer	Section leader.
Seelöwe	Sealion, the codename for Hitler's proposed seaborne invasion of England.
Seenotflugkommando	*Luftwaffe* air sea rescue organisation.
Stab	Staff
Staffel	A squadron.
Staffelkapitän	The Squadron Leader.
Störflug	Harassing attacks, usually by lone Ju 88s.
Stuka	The Ju 87 dive-bomber.
Sturkampfgeschwader	Dive-bomber group, abbreviated StG.
Vermisst	Missing.
Wehrmacht	Armed forces.
Zerstörer	Literally 'destroyer', the term used for the Me 110.
Zerstörergeschwader	Destroyer group, abbreviated ZG.

Each *geschwader* generally comprised three *gruppen*, each of three *staffeln*. Each *gruppe* is designated by Roman numerals, i.e. III/JG 26 refers to the third *gruppe* of Fighter Group (abbreviated 'JG') 26. *Staffeln* are identified by numbers, so 7/JG 26 is the 7th *staffel* and belongs to III/JG 26.

Rank comparisons may also be useful:

Gefreiter	Private 1st Class
Unteroffizier	Corporal, no aircrew equivalent in Fighter Command.

Feldwebel	Sergeant
Oberfeldwebel	Flight Sergeant
Leutnant	Pilot Officer
Oberleutnant	Flight Lieutenant
Hauptmann	Squadron Leader
Major	Wing Commander
Oberst	Group Captain

RAF Abbreviations:

AAF	Auxiliary Air Force
AASF	Advance Air Striking Force
A&AEE	Aeroplane & Armament Experimental Establishment
AC1	Aircraftsman 1st Class
AFC	Air Force Cross
AFDU	Air Fighting Development Unit
AI	Airborne Interception radar
AOC	Air Officer Commanding
AOC-in-C	Air Officer Commanding-in-Chief
ATA	Air Transport Auxiliary
ATS	Armament Training School
BEF	British Expeditionary Force
CAS	Chief of the Air Staff
CFS	Central Flying School
CGS	Central Gunnery School
CO	Commanding Officer
DAF	Desert Air Force
DES	Direct Entry Scheme
DFC	Distinguished Flying Cross
DFM	Distinguished Flying Medal
DSO	Distinguished Service Order
E/A	Enemy Aircraft
FAA	Fleet Air Arm
EFTS	Elementary Flying Training School
FIU	Fighter Interception Unit
FTS	Flying Training School
GPC	Guinea Pig Club
ITW	Initial Training Wing
LAC	Leading Aircraftman
MC	Military Cross
MRAF	Marshal of the Royal Air Force

MSFU	Merchant Ship Fighter Unit
MTB	Motor Torpedo Boat
NCO	Non-Commissioned Officer
OR	Other Ranks
ORB	Operations Record Book
OTC	Officer Training Corps
OTU	Operational Training Unit
PDC	Personnel Distribution Centre
RAFVR	Royal Air Force Volunteer Reserve
RFS	Reserve Flying School
RN	Royal Navy
RNAS	Royal Navy Air Service
R/T	Radio Telephone
SASO	Senior Air Staff Officer
SHAEF	Supreme Headquarters Allied Expeditionary Force
SOO	Senior Operations Officer
SSC	Short Service Commission
TAF	Tactical Air Force
UAS	University Air Squadron
U/S	Unserviceable
WDAF	Western Desert Air Force

Also:

'Angels' refers to height measured in thousands of feet, hence 'Angles One-Five' means 15,000ft. A 'vector' is a compass course, measured in degrees, a 'Bandit' is a confirmed enemy aircraft while a 'Bogey' and an 'X-Raid' are as yet unidentified but potentially hostile radar plots. 'Tally Ho!' was shouted when the enemy were sighted and the leader was ordering an attack.

Chapter One

Wing Commander Howard Frizelle 'Billy' Burton DSO DFC* Croix de Guerre

Howard Frizelle Burton – known universally as 'Billy' – was born in Letchworth Garden City, Hertfordshire on 21 June 1916, the youngest son of Major Louis Burton and his wife, Edith Jane Burton. Time would prove Billy to be an exceptional individual, no doubt destined for great things – but sadly it was not to be. War, however, had touched the Burton family very early on in young Billy's life – rather setting the scene for subsequent, tragic, events…

The Burtons lived in a large and substantial semi-detached house at 32 Broadwater Avenue, in a comfortable Letchworth suburb, but on 9 June 1917, during the First World War, 42-year-old Major Burton, a professional soldier and one-time gunnery instructor at both Shoeburyness and Larkhill ranges, was killed on active service in France with 'D' Battery, 70 Brigade, Royal Artillery. This unprecedented global conflict, of course, represented Europe's first head-on collision with industrialised warfare, generating some 27 million casualties, mainly sustained in Europe, where vast military cemeteries were created after the Armistice in 1918. While the Americans, who had arrived late to battle and consequently suffered substantially fewer casualties than Britain, undertook to return, upon request, the dead for burial back home, Britain's stance was contrary: the Imperial War Graves Commission, constituted by Royal Charter in 1917, recognised that only the wealthy could afford such repatriation, which was discriminatory and therefore contrary to the Commission's ethos of equality. Instead, the Commission declared that 'A higher ideal than that of private burial at home is embodied in these war cemeteries in foreign lands, where those who fought and fell together, officers and men, lie together in their last resting place, facing the line they gave their lives to maintain.' Consequently, Major Burton was buried at St Hilaire Cemetery, Frevent, to the west of Arras, so for the Burtons there was no grave at home to visit. As Major Burton had been killed shortly before his third son's first birthday, growing up fatherless

The grave of Major Louis Burton RA, Billy Burton's father, at St Hilaire Cemetery, Frevent (Kevin Barnes).

was the normal way of things for Billy and countless others whose fathers had fallen in battle. Billy's mother, Edith, never remarried, and chose the following epitaph on her husband's headstone: 'Only goodnight, beloved, not farewell.'

Fortunately, although now a war widow, Mrs Burton remained of sufficient means to provide a private education for her children – which was the essential key to so many professions. Most pupils at these so-called 'public' schools boarded, were between thirteen and eighteen years, and had previously attended a preparatory school between the ages of eight and twelve. Collectively, such public schools were considered 'training grounds for leaders of the nation'. Indeed, in 1931 it was estimated that of 691 holders of 'high office' in the church, state and industry, 76 per cent were educated at public schools, the top three being Eton, Harrow and Winchester. In 1930, Billy went up to Bedford School, where he became a member of the Officer Training Corps (OTC), which provided a grounding in military training and encouraged pupils to consider taking a Commission in one of the services – something impossible without a public-school background and indicative of such an education's crucial importance. It was not towards the army or his late father's old regiment that Billy felt drawn, though, but to a still comparative new service: the Royal Air Force.

During the First World War, British military aviation had been served by two forces, the Royal Flying Corps, associated with the army, and Royal Naval Air Service. In 1918, the General Staff decided that, going forward, so important was military aviation that a new air force should be formed, independent of both the army and navy. The man chosen to oversee the creation of this junior service was Major General Hugh Trenchard, who became the first Chief of the Air Staff. Trenchard, a former army and RFC officer, found himself responsible for building an air force with aerodromes and necessary logistics, absorbing both the RFC and RNAS. Although rank titles and structure were more similar to the RN, Trenchard otherwise modelled his new force, the RAF, which came into being on 1 April 1918, on the army – particularly regarding commissions. Since 1905, all public schools had OTCs, delivering a specific military syllabus and examination; those who passed were awarded Certificate 'A', armed with which, together with a good school report and an application endorsed by any colonel, guaranteed a commission. Trenchard adopted this process for the RAF, his vision being that all RAF officers would be pilots. The training of the new service's officers was solely undertaken at the RAF College Cranwell, an old airship station near Sleaford in Lincolnshire.

The selection process to become a flight cadet at Cranwell, in terms of medicals and interviews, was not rigorous; in truth, the RAF College was an extension of the public-school system and required fees paying. A former inter-war flight cadet once described Cranwell and its traditions thus:

> The life of the College is resumed with alacrity and care at the beginning of term. One day the place will be wearing a wan and neglected air, while the next day everything will be bustle and confusion. The night seems to bring forth cadets in the same way a conjurer produces rabbits from a hat. But as they come, so they depart, yielding place for others in a never-ending stream: each one, however, leaves his impression for good or bad on the College. Some may be forgotten; others will be talked of by terms of the distant future. Yet one and all will retain indelible memories of their sojourn at Cranwell, and will regard the College with an esteem and affection which is of more value than the cosmopolitan camaraderie of greater seats of learning. For the associations of Cranwell are enjoyed only by a privileged few, who are closely bound together by their careers.

The Cranwell course was of two years duration. Appendix III of Air Publication No 121 described the syllabus thus:

Year One
English language and literature, General ethnology, The British Empire, Applied Mathematics, including mechanics and draughtsmanship, Elementary physics, History of the RAF, Theory of flight and rigging, Air pilotage and map reading, Drill and physical training, Air Force Law and administration, Hygiene and sanitation, Workshops and engines, Wireless telegraphy, Radio telephony and signal procedure, and Practical flying.

Year Two

Theoretical and practical instruction in internal combustion engines, Aerodynamics, Practical instruction in rigging, Advanced work in the wood and metal workshops, Outline of wireless telegraphy and telephony, Armament, Practical flying, Air pilotage and airmanship, Meteorology, Outline of the organisation of the Navy and Army, War, strategy and tactics.

Cranwell, therefore, aimed to provide a broad education for its flight cadets; that legendary legless airman Group Captain Sir Douglas Bader, recalled that the RAF College:

> was half a university for us. It gave us time to read, to think, to listen, to talk and make friends. We drank it all in – the flying, the intimacy of the place, the gaiety, the walks, the messing about on motor bikes, the games, the discipline, the leadership. It was all there. And there seemed to be time for everything and this was reflected in our flying. We absorbed the instruction rather than learnt it.

After the First World War, however, disarmament held sway and the size of all three services were vastly reduced. Indeed, the RAF at that time has often been described as similar to a small and elite flying club, through which Cranwell was able to train the required number of officers. All were 'Permanently Commissioned', which is to say they were professional airmen and career officers. It was into this world that Flight Cadet H.F. Burton stepped in June 1935. Fortunately for Mrs Burton, Billy had won a coveted King's Cadetship with outstandingly high marks, meaning that the service met all fees. This was the first indication of Billy Burton's exceptional ability. Without doubt Billy thrived at Cranwell, playing in the College's cricket, rugby and squash teams, serving as President of the Debating Society and sub-editor of the College Journal, in addition to being a member of the dramatic society.

Then, there was the flying. Flight cadets gained initial flight experience on the two-seater Avro Tutor and de Havilland Tiger Moth biplanes, before progressing to more advanced single-engine biplane types including, as recorded in Billy's personal pilot's flying logbook, the Hawker Hart light-bomber and its army cooperation derivative, the Hawker Audax, in addition to the Hawker Fury fighter. On 7 October 1936, shortly before the end of his course, Flight Cadet Burton was flying Hawker Fury K5681 and engaged on an air-firing exercise with Flight Lieutenant Roy James Oliphant Bartlett, a

4

The RAF College Cranwell (Sylvia Lewis).

28-year-old instructor. For some reason the pair collided. Both pilots baled out, but Flight Lieutenant Bartlett was killed when struck in mid-air by his aircraft, K5682, which crashed at Navenby, eight miles south of Lincoln. Billy landed safely by parachute, and no blame was apportioned to either pilot by the subsequent Court of Inquiry.

Ultimately, Flight Cadet Burton passed out of Cranwell in December 1936 – having been awarded the highly prized 'Sword-of-Honour'. This great trophy, a Wilkinson's blade, was awarded by the Air Ministry to the flight cadet on each course having demonstrated 'outstanding ability, officer qualities and the potential to progress in the Service'. Billy's sword would prove unique, in fact, as the only blade inscribed 'Edward VIII', the sole such sword awarded during that somewhat controversial monarch's short reign. Clearly, Billy had lived up to all expectations of a King's Cadet and, as a commissioned pilot officer, was now on the second leg of his service career.

The year 1936 was also a significant one for the RAF on the wider stage, because the service had started expanding and preparing for war. It was clear that when war came, Cranwell and the small professional air force alone could not provide the number of replacement pilots required to make good losses. True, the service was already supported by the Auxiliary Air Force of squadrons based around the territorial principle, but this was not enough. Trenchard, therefore created the RAF Volunteer Reserve of citizen volunteers who remained in their civilian occupations while learning to

1935

JOURNAL OF THE ROYAL AIR FORCE COLLEGE

CRICKET TEAM.

[Photo : Gale & Polden, Ltd.

Standing.—F./C. U./O. D. W. Balden.   F./C. H. E. Burton.   F./C. H. R. Goodman.   F./C S. P. Coulson.
    F./C. L. Wilson.   F./C. G. S. H. Powell,   F./C. P. B. Chamberlain.
Seated.—F./C. Cpl. N. M. Hall.   F./C. M. P. Skinner,   F./C. Cpl. R. I. Jones.   F./C. W. A. A. de Freitas.
    F. /C. R. M. Longmore.

Flight Cadet HF 'Billy' Burton (back row, second left) in the Cranwell cricket team, 1935 (courtesy Jean Allom Estate [JA Estate]).

fly at weekends and, with the Civil Air Guard providing subsidised flying lessons in return for an undertaking to volunteer for the RAF in time of crisis, thereby provided a trained reserve available in an emergency. Moreover, Trenchard also changed tack from his original vision that all pilots would be officers (and all officers pilots) by allowing a small number of serving Non-Commissioned Officers to become pilots and fly for several years before reverting to their original trades and again increasing the trained reserve available. Until this point, as we have seen, the RAF's officers were all Permanent Commissions, professional career officers and Cranwell-trained. Another far-sighted Trenchard feature of the 1936 Expansion Plan 'F' was the Short Service Commission initiative, providing an opportunity for young men from Britain and the Commonwealth to take a commission and fly for four years only, before going onto the reserve. SSC officers could only attain the rank of flight lieutenant, preserving more senior appointments for Cranwellians, but in peacetime it was unlikely that an officer would achieve that rank in so short a time. The SSC appealed to

RUGGER TEAM.

[Photo: Gale & Polden, Ltd.

Standing.—F./C. U./O. H. F. Burton. F./C. Cpl. I. S. Soden. F./C. Sergt. S. W. B. Menaul. F./C. C. W. M. Newman. F./C. D. G. Heaton-Nicholls. F./C. J. T. Wilkins. F./C. R. H. McConnell. F./C. B. P. Young. F./C. P. G. St. G. O'Brian. F./C. G. H. D. Evans. F./C. P. R. Hatfield.
Seated.—F./C. E. H. Lynch Blosse. F./C. J. A. Pitcairn-Hill. F./C. G. V. W. Kettlewell. F./C. U./O. G. S. ff. Powell (Captain). F./C. U./O. H. E. Button. F./C. J. M. N. Pike. F./C. R. Lloyd.

Flight Cadet Burton (standing, extreme left), Cranwell rugger team (JA Estate).

young men across the globe, attracting adventurous young men like the South African Adolph Gysbert Malan, a former mercantile marine officer known universally as 'Sailor', who would become one of the most outstanding RAF fighter leaders of the war. It must be said, however, that all of these men were white. The Air Force Act of 1917, which provided the legal mechanism to create the RAF, specifically prohibited people of colour – and women – from serving, this being reinforced by the Recruiting Regulations of 1923. Nonetheless, as the prospect of war with Germany increased, the elite identity of the small pre-war RAF was changing. More squadrons were also created, many of which were stood-down after the First World War and now re-formed. Pilot Officer Burton's first posting was to one of these new squadrons, 46, at Kenley.

46 Squadron had a proud First World War history and had re-formed at Kenley shortly before Pilot Officer Burton's arrival from a flight of 17 Squadron. For a young fighter pilot, Kenley was a dream come true; an established and famous fighter station in Surrey, to the south-west of, and so essential to the defence of, London. There, Billy found his new squadron operating what was at the time the RAF's frontline operational fighter: the Gloster Gauntlet biplane. Pretty though it was, the type was already outclassed by Germany's new monoplanes. Whereas the Gauntlet's top speed was 230 mph, for example, its German counterpart, the Me 109

SIXTH TERM, WINTER, 1936.

[Photo: Gale & Polden,]

Back Row.—F./C. R. S. J. Edwards. F./C. D. Weston Burt. F./C. A. R. Vaughan-Williams. F./C. M. H. Cox.
Third Row.—F./C. D. A. ffrench-Mullen. F./C. D. E. Bennett. F./C. K. Ault. F./C. P. E. S. F. M. Browne. F./C. W. A. Harris. F./C. S. P. Coulson. F./C. Cpl. B. Barthold.
Second Row.—F./C. G. P. Robinson. F./C. Cpl. T. D. Calnan. F./C. K. M. B. D. Duke-Woolley. F./C. Cpl. M. C. Pearson. F./C. I. J. Fawdry. F./C. Cpl. L. W. Lowden.
F./C. R. H. McConnell. F./C. Cpl. N. C. Harding. F./C. J. G. Fraser. F./C. Cpl. L. D. Wilson.
Front Row.—F./C. Cpl. A. D. Jackson. F./C. Cpl. L. F. Cooper. F./C. Sergt. C. D. Milne. F./C. U./O. G. S. ff. Powell. F./C. U./O. H. F. Burton. F./C. U./O. H. E. Bufton.
F./C. Sergt. S. W. B. Menaul. F./C. Sergt. I. T. B. T. Rowland. F./C. Cpl. I. S. Soden.

Flight Cadet Billy Burton (seated, centre) at Cranwell, 1936. Several of his colleagues would go on to fight in the Battle of Britain, and Flight Cadet D Weston Burt (second from left, back row) would later command a squadron of tank-busting Hurricanes in Billy's Wing in the western desert – the pair would both receive DSOs for their devastating attack on German armour in March 1943 (JA Estate).

fighter, reached 354 mph. Moreover, the Gauntlet's only armament was two rifle-calibre machine-guns, whereas the 109 would soon boast two similar weapons and a pair of hard-hitting 20mm cannon. It was now that the folly of what Churchill famously called the 'Years of the Locust', that period of disarmament, was apparent; the Gauntlet was actually only marginally faster than the German Do 17 bomber, but markedly slower than the He 111 and Ju 88, these being the bomber types it could be called upon to defend Britain from. Indeed, as one RAF pilot lamented, 'Our Gauntlets were not even fast enough to run away!' A solution, however, was at hand: on 6 November 1935, the Hawker Hurricane monoplane fighter had flown for the first time, and had been ordered in numbers by the Air Ministry. Likewise on 6 March 1936, the Supermarine Spitfire made its maiden flight and was likewise ordered for the RAF. Nonetheless, neither aircraft would actually enter service until 1938, and so for now, the Gauntlet, in which Pilot Officer Burton looped and rolled over the Surrey hills, represented Britain's primary fighter.

When Britain belatedly began rearming in 1935, air defence was coordinated by the Air Defence of Great Britain (ADGB), but in 1936 it

Whilst at Cranwell, Flight Cadet Burton was flying a Hawker Fury and engaged on a gunnery exercise when he collided with his instructor, Flight Lieutenant RJO Bartlett. Both pilots baled out, but Bartlett was struck by his aircraft and killed. His grave can be found at St Andrew's, Cranwell.

was sensibly decided to separate this unwieldy command into two: Fighter and Bomber Commands. Thus, Fighter Command was created on 6 July 1936, with its headquarters at Bentley Priory, to the North of London. On 14 July 1936, Air Chief Marshal Sir Hugh C.T. Dowding was appointed the first Commander-in-Chief. This reorganisation provided an unprecedented opportunity to overhaul and revise the nation's air defences – giving Dowding freedom to harness sophisticated science and techniques into the mix. Having been Air Member for Research & Development, involved in the commissioning of both new monoplane fighters and Radio Direction Finding (RDF, better known as 'radar'), there could have been no better choice for this task. Unlike many of his peers, Dowding had always been a champion of air defence – arguing against Trenchard's obsession with offence, steadfastly maintaining his unshakeable belief that:

> security of the base must come first … The best defence of the country is fear of the fighter. If we are strong in fighters we should probably never be attacked in force. If we are moderately strong we shall probably be attacked and the attacks will gradually be brought to a standstill … If we are weak in fighter strength, the attacks will not be brought to a standstill and the productive capacity of the country will be virtually destroyed.

Here, then, was a man with the experience and vision necessary to prepare Britain to resist determined air attack; it was just in the nick of time.

Fighter Command was organised into groups: 13 Group defending Scotland, 12 Group the industrial Midlands and the North, and 11 Group

After Cranwell, Pilot Officer Burton was posted to fly Gloster Gauntlet fighters with 46 Squadron at Kenley – this is a similar aircraft of 43 Squadron.

London and the south-east (with 10 Group, responsible for the West Country, added in July 1940). Before the war, it was assumed that any air attack on Britain would be made from Germany, by unescorted bombers approaching the east coast from the North Sea. This, therefore, made 12 Group the potential frontline, and it was to the 12 Group Sector Station of Digby, in Lincolnshire, that 46 Squadron was posted in November 1937. Still flying Gauntlets, from there 46 Squadron, by now commanded by Squadron Leader Philip 'Dickie' Barwell, a highly experienced Cranwellian, continued training for war by day and night. On 19 June 1938, Billy was promoted to flying officer, by which time he was an established member of 46 Squadron.

When war broke out, Flight Lieutenant Burton was posted to command a flight of 66 Squadron's Spitfires at Duxford, this being an airborne 'Clickety-Click' Mk I from that time.

Flight Lieutenant Burton relaxing at the Red Lion Hotel, Whittlesford, near Duxford in Cambridgeshire (JA Estate).

In February 1939, 46 Squadron received the new Hawker Hurricane – a very different machine to the dainty Gauntlet biplanes. The top speed of the Rolls-Royce Merlin-powered Hurricane was 328 mph – nearly 100 mph faster than the Gauntlet, but slower than the Me 109's 348 mph. The Gauntlet's maximum ceiling, however, was a surprising 33,500ft, the Hurricane adding only another 1,500ft, whereas the 109 achieved 36,500ft. The Hurricane was a much-needed step in the right direction, but was outclassed in many respects by the German fighter from the outset. Nonetheless, this was a modern fighter with an enclosed cockpit, retractable undercarriage (unlike the Gauntlet's fixed 'undercart'), and, most importantly, eight Browning .303 machine-guns. The first Hurricanes were fitted with a two-bladed, wooden, fixed-pitch, propeller, which would eventually be changed, first for the three-bladed two-pitch airscrew and finally the Constant Speed propeller, enabling the pilot to select the correct pitch (angle of bite into the air and therefore similar to changing gear in a car) by rotating the blades through nearly 360°, all of which developments helped increase performance; needless to say, though, the 109 already had a variable pitch airscrew.

Flying Officer Burton first flew a Hawker Hurricane Mk I, L1792, on 20 February 1939, the flight comprising 'Local flying and circuits and landings'. By this time, Billy was commanding 'A' Flight, the squadron being divided into two flights, 'A' and 'B', and so in addition to converting to and mastering the Hurricane himself, he also had to checkout his pilots on the Miles Magister monoplane trainer before authorising them to fly the new machine. On the afternoon of 20 February 1939, for example, Billy checked out and passed Pilot Officer Peter Lefevre (who would also later fight in, and survive, the Battle of Britain, only to be reported missing in 1944). In between these check-flights, Billy trained on the Hurricane, practising battle climbs, formation flying, mock interceptions, and

Billy Burton (right) boating on the Broads, June 1940, with his great friend Flying Officer Frankie Rimmer, also of 66 Squadron – who would later be killed in action with 29 Squadron during the Battle of Britain (JA Estate).

night-flying. The Hurricane, like the Spitfire, was designed as a day-fighter, and although a better night-flyer than the Spitfire, owing to its wider track and more forgiving undercarriage, it was still not an easy aircraft to fly at night because of the two banks of glowing exhausts in front of and either side of the pilot, ruining his night vision. These aircraft were equipped with the TR9 radio, facilitating communication with other pilots of the same squadron and the ground controller, but there were none of the computerised flying aids available today, and night-flying was particularly dangerous. Billy took all of this in his stride and was promoted to flight lieutenant in March 1939. By 1 June 1939 he was an experienced 'chap', having accumulated a total of 529.05 flying hours. On 20 June 1939, Squadron Leader Barwell assessed Flight Lieutenant Burton's ability as a fighter pilot and navigator as 'above the average', and in air gunnery 'Exceptional' – the highest possible endorsement and rarely given. The training for war, now on Hurricanes, continued relentlessly, with firing practice out to sea off the east coast, and squadron formation climbs to 25,000ft. On 26 June 1939, however, Billy's time with 46 Squadron came to an end when he was posted to 12 Group HQ at Hucknall on 'Operations Staff Duties'.

Exactly what Flight Lieutenant Burton's staff role was at Hucknall at that time is unknown, but he did have sufficient freedom to continue flying in his new appointment, largely from station to station in various Magisters, either solo or occasionally with a passenger. On 3 September 1939, Britain and France declared war on Nazi Germany following Hitler's refusal to remove his troops from Poland, which Germany had invaded two days previously. The waiting was over, and so too was Billy's brief tour as a staff officer. With experience on Hurricanes and as a flight commander, Flight Lieutenant Burton was just the young and promising officer required to take

WING COMMANDER HOWARD FRIZELLE 'BILLY' BURTON

Having fought over Dunkirk, on 27 June 1940, Flight Lieutenant Burton married Miss Jean Maxwell Robertson, only daughter of Air Commodore EDM Robertson, in Ashtead Parish Church, Surrey (JA Estate).

over 'B' Flight of 66 Squadron, based at Duxford – another famous fighter station – near Cambridge in 12 Group. 'Clickety-Click' had been the RAF's second Spitfire-equipped squadron and still operated Mitchell's fighter; Billy arrived to take up his new appointment on 7 September 1939.

'B' Flight's new commander first flew a Spitfire Mk I, K9988, on a thirty-five-minute familiarisation flight on 8 September 1939, and thereafter many more flights over the next few days while converting to type. It was a busy time. Almost overnight the pre-war service disappeared forever, with mobilisation of the AAF and RAFVR. The prevalent aerial doctrine of the period was built around the concept that the 'bomber would always get through', and that the way to win a modern war was for the bomber force to deliver a 'knockout blow', aimed squarely at destroying the enemy's manufacturing capacity and, by bombing civilian populations, not only crush morale but thereby encourage a rising against their own government. The Spanish Civil War of the mid-thirties had provided Germany a unique opportunity to test its new weapons and tactics, and one word struck terror into the hearts and minds of all: Guernica, a small Basque town wasted by German bombers on 26 April 1937. Then, at the start of the Second World War, Warsaw suffered terribly. Consequently, the fear of bombing was almost tangible. Everyone was keyed up, anticipating a huge German air attack – just how anxious was tragically demonstrated on 6 September 1939, when Spitfires of 74 Squadron mistook Hurricanes of 56 Squadron for enemy fighters, shooting two down and killing one pilot. Also based at Duxford at that time was 19 Squadron, the RAF's first and premier Spitfire squadron, with which Flying Officer James Coward was serving and who recalled the outbreak of war and feverish activity:

> From my log book I see that on 3, 4 and 5 of September 1939, we were scrambled at night, on one occasion as a squadron,

but of course no enemy aircraft were sighted. I believe that the 'enemy' turned out to be our own aircraft returning in the wrong places. Night flying in a Spitfire was always a little bit tricky, with a bright exhaust flame on either side, a narrow undercarriage, and uneven grass strips of limited length, but after war started on a dark night one was on instruments as soon as one passed the last dim Glim Lamp on take-off, as the whole country was blacked out. One pilot … displayed a remarkable feat of airmanship by forced-landing a Spitfire at night in a field, which was too small for a subsequent take-off – his engine had cut-out on take-off, at about 500ft. He dropped a flare and glided safely down with no damage to the aircraft. Most pilots would have been hard pressed to do it in daylight.

Once war started, we were called to Readiness as a squadron and stayed at Readiness right through the night. We slept on our camp beds under the wings of the aircraft in our flying gear, ready to go. Each night we were sent off and the first night we intercepted some of our aircraft returning in the wrong places along the coast. Same thing on the second sortie when I nearly shot one down. It gets very exciting when you have a controller telling you one bandit three miles ahead, now two miles ahead, gets you all keyed-up for this great attack. I just saw this aircraft silhouette and luckily recognised it as a Blenheim. I could so easily have shot it down.

Although Germany was expected to attack from the North Sea, the air defences of East Anglia were sparse. New aerodromes near Norwich, at Horsham St Faith and Coltishall, were incomplete; 12 Group's Debden Sector spread east over Essex, guarding the northern approach to London, and Wittering protected Duxford's northern flank. The area between Debden and Wittering sectors was Duxford's responsibility. Immediately war was declared, therefore, 19 and 66 Squadrons sent flights of Spitfires daily to the Advanced Landing Ground at Watton, a bomber station near Thetford. This was to afford those stations fighter protection in case the *Luftwaffe* unleashed an all-out offensive against RAF bombers based in East Anglia – which were clearly a threat to Germany. Consequently, the Wellington and Blenheim bombers concerned withdrew to stations further west, but it was considered that more fighters than those supplied by Duxford's squadrons were required, leading to 73 Squadron's Digby-based Hurricanes reinforcing the Duxford Sector. 19 Squadron also assumed initial responsibility for night readiness, hence the intensive night-flying

Above left: Flight Lieutenant Burton off-duty at his in-laws' home, 'Tain' – his brother-in-law, Flying Officer Duncan Maxwell Robertson relaxes in the background (JA Estate).

Above right: In September 1940, Billy was promoted to command 616 Squadron, which had been badly battered at Kenley, continuing to fly Spitfires (JA Estate).

activity, although on the day Flight Lieutenant Burton arrived, 66 Squadron relieved 19 of the nocturnal commitment, which was thereafter shared by the two Duxford squadrons, which did a week about.

In addition to operational commitments by day and night, the squadrons also continued training, practising attacks, cine-gun firing, and cooperation exercises with bombers and searchlights. No 'knockout blow' materialised however, the truth being that neither side was in a position to deliver such a decisive air attack. Winter weather curtailed flying, although the enemy continued probing Britain's defences and harassing shipping. Consequently there was a little excitement for 66 Squadron on 11 January 1940, when Yellow Section of 'A' Flight intercepted a He 111 attacking a trawler off Cromer. With smoke pouring from its port engine, the raider managed to escape, shooting-up Sergeant Stone in the process, who managed to reach land and safely put down his damaged Spitfire. Information was later received, though, that the enemy bomber subsequently forced-landed in Denmark, where the aircraft was destroyed by its crew.

Squadron Leader Burton took 616 Squadron to Kirton, receiving and training new pilots around a small cadre of combat experienced men, where this photograph was taken in early 1941. Squadron Leader Burton is standing with pipe and wearing forage cap; others identified are: 2nd left, standing – Sergeant Bob 'Butch' Morton; fifth left: Flight Lieutenant Ken Holden; sixth left: Pilot Officer 'Nip' Hepple; fifth from right: Flight Lieutenant Colin MacFie; Sergeants Syd Mabbett and 'Chem' Le Cheninent. Kneeling with dog is Flying Officer Lionel 'Buck' Casson.

For the first three months of 1940, little happened. The Soviets finally overwhelmed the Finns, and U-boats continued attacking Britain's North Atlantic shipping, but elsewhere the 'Phoney War' persisted. With the exception of the Czechs and Poles, few people had thus far suffered unduly from the conflict. The truth was, neither the British nor French favoured early military action against Germany. In an unfortunately pronounced confirmation of his astonishing and ongoing naivety, the British Prime Minister, Neville Chamberlain, clung desperately to the forlorn hope that Hitler could still be persuaded to abandon his European territorial ambitions, thereby avoiding a 'hot' war. Intelligence reports suggested that Germany's intensive rearmament programme had actually weakened the internal economy and created shortages of essential raw materials. Britannia, of course, had long ruled the waves, so Chamberlain believed that a naval blockade could strangle Germany and engineer Hitler's downfall. The French agreed. While this strategy was pursued, Britain and France concurrently continued rearming and preparing defences. In October 1939, in fact, Germany had offered to discuss peace, various world leaders then encouraged Britain to continue exploring options for a compromise peace. As far as Britain and France were concerned however, no deal could be brokered without the restoration of Czechoslovakia and Poland – and

WING COMMANDER HOWARD FRIZELLE 'BILLY' BURTON

Flight Lieutenant
Colin MacFie,
one of Squadron
Leader Burton's two
experienced flight
commanders at
Kirton.

the precondition that the Nazi government was eliminated. Naturally the Germans refused to give up any territory, and there was no question of Hitler relinquishing power. So, after the fall of Poland, Hitler paused for the winter, while the British Expeditionary Force dug in along the Franco-Belgian border – and awaited Germany's next move.

During the winter of 1940, both sides recognised the strategic importance of Scandinavia. Swedish iron-ore was essential to German industry, and the occupation of Denmark and Norway would provide German ports from which the *Kriegsmarine* could access the Atlantic and further threaten Britain's essential maritime supply lines. Conversely, if Britain and France could obstruct the supply of iron-ore to Germany, Hitler's economy and industry might be irrevocably damaged. The improved weather of spring 1940, therefore, saw both camps focused on Scandinavia. German troops landed on 9 April 1940. Britain sent a task force steaming to Narvik, but British land forces were evacuated just two weeks later. In fact this unsuccessful British campaign highlighted the problems ahead owing to the lack of a long-range fighter. Flying from aircraft carriers, air cover for the British task force had been provided by a handful of obsolete Gloster Gladiator biplanes and just one squadron of modern Hurricanes. Losses indicated the disparity in performance between the British and German aircraft in actual combat – which bode not well for the fight ahead. Then, at last, 'the balloon went up'…

At 0405 hrs on Friday 10 May 1940, disbelieving Belgian sentries saw, in the dawn half-light, troop-carrying German gliders silently approaching their huge concrete fortress at Eben-Emael (commanding the Albert Canal's all-important bridges and considered the strongest defensive position in

17

Squadron Leader Burton ready to go, sporting black pre-war flying suit and squadron leader's pennant painted on his Spitfire.

existence). Confused, Belgians failed to react until 0420 hrs – by which time it was too late. Achieving complete surprise, at 0435 hrs, 136 German divisions crashed into Belgium and Holland. Overhead, 2,500 German aircraft streamed westwards to attack Allied airfields, while 16,000 German paratroopers seized Rotterdam, Leiden and The Hague. At 0700 hrs, the British government received desperate pleas for help from both the Dutch and Belgians; the great and long-awaited storm had at last broken.

In the British sector, Lord Gort, the BEF commander, now left carefully prepared defences along the Franco-Belgique border, pivoting forward sixty miles into previously neutral Belgium across unreconnoitred ground and without prepared supply dumps. To some extent there was a party atmosphere west of the front line, with Belgian civilians cheering on their British champions, showering the advancing troops with flowers and pressing refreshment upon them. The reality of *Blitzkrieg* had (literally) yet to hit home – it rapidly would, because the calculated process of completely dislocating and unhinging the Allied defences and command was already well underway. While the Allies' attention was diverted by events on the Belgian-German border, the way was clear for XIX *Panzer Korps* to negotiate the supposedly 'impassable' Ardennes and deliver the *Schwehrpunkt* (point of main effort), some forty miles further south. This was a military masterstroke. Believing the main attack to be coming through the Netherlands and Belgium, as it had in the First World War, the Allies focused their attention in that direction – completely missing this cleverly disguised armoured sickle-cut, which would by-pass the Maginot Line and race for the Channel ports.

On the day Germany's Blitzkrieg struck the West, Flight Lieutenant Burton received a new pilot for 'B' Flight: Pilot Officer H.R. 'Dizzy' Allen, who reported straight from operational training at Shawbury. Having first presented himself to the Squadron Commander, another Cranwellian,

Squadron Leader Burton at Kirton, sometime between 16 October 1940 and 26 February 1941 – the Spitfire is a presentation aircraft, X4617, QJ-K, 'Falkland Islands III', one of ten aircraft donated by the Falkland Islanders under the auspices of the Spitfire Fund (JA Estate).

Squadron Leader Rupert 'Lucky' Leigh, Pilot Officer Allen made his way to 'B' Flight, located a mile across Duxford aerodrome from the hangars and other buildings. Allen found that 'B' Flight's operational area comprised two long wooden huts, one for the pilots, the other for administration and use by airmen. Flight Lieutenant Burton's office was located in an adjacent bell tent, into which Allen stepped, saluted his seated flight commander and presented himself for interview, later remembering Billy as:

> quite short, tough, erect, a gentleman, a product of public school and the RAF College Cranwell … Billy took me along to the pilots' hut to introduce me and give me my bearings. There were only a dozen or so pilots in the shack, which contained beds, a dartboard, a tea urn, trestle tables, a cabinet for maps, and a dozen large, steel flying-clothing lockers. The walls of the room were covered with charts showing silhouettes of aircraft … Magazines were scattered around on the tables, and some pilots were giving them a cursory glance while others played darts or snoozed on their beds … Nearly half the pilots were of senior NCO rank, the rest were officers. Billy introduced me, and they gazed at me languidly

… Billy Burton asked Hugh Kennard to take me under his wing and attempt to turn me into a fighter pilot… then took me along to meet some of the NCOs, who were the backbone of the squadron… That afternoon, Billy accompanied me to a Spitfire… told me all about the layout in the cockpit, how to start the engine, what the Spitfire's flying characteristics were, what her maximum speed was on the dive, and so on … After a few weeks, Billy gave me a flight commander's checkout, beat me hollow in a dogfight but declared me operational.

Allen would go on to become a decorated ace (and a controversial writer post-war, critical of anyone and everything connected with the Battle of Britain).

The Air Officer Commanding 12 Group, wherein Duxford Sector Station lay, was Air Vice-Marshal Sir Trafford Leigh-Mallory, who had been an army cooperation pilot during the First World War – but had no fighter experience. He was also intensely ambitious and extremely jealous of Air Vice-Marshal Keith Park, a more junior air vice-marshal in the Air Force List, who had been recently given command of the prestigious 11 Group, defending London and the south-east. Like Dowding, however, Park had been a fighter pilot and leader, and previously served as Dowding's Senior Air Staff Officer at Fighter Command HQ. Together, Dowding and Park had built and perfected the System of Fighter Control, and outside Germany were arguably the two most experienced fighter leaders in the world. In May 1940, Dowding faced considerable challenges in trying desperately to preserve sufficient fighters to guarantee the aerial defence of Britain, instead of wasting them in a battle already lost in France. However, Britain's new Prime Minister, Winston Churchill, was under pressure from the French to provide more fighters. Dowding was unmoved and eventually won the day; no more fighters would be sent across the Channel. In any case, while the Advanced Air Striking Force had gone to France, wisely Dowding only sent Hurricanes across the water, preserving his precious Spitfires for home defence.

The Spitfire was a more modern design than the Hurricane, with high-altitude performance enabling it to take on the lethal Me 109 – which would prove crucial in the dark months ahead and hence why the type was so carefully preserved by Dowding. The problem was that because the Hurricane had flown and been ordered by the Air Ministry first, and because the Supermarine factory near Southampton was a comparatively small facility struggling to produce Spitfires in the large quantities now required, Dowding had at his disposal two-thirds more Hurricanes than the superior

Squadron Leader Burton's brother-in-law, Flying Officer Duncan Maxwell Robertson – killed on 27 October 1940 in a flying accident, whilst training to be an air gunner at Manby (JA Estate).

Spitfires. Both Dowding and Park knew, therefore, that it was vital to carefully shepherd their limited resources, especially Spitfires, while simultaneously exacting maximum damage to the Germans. It was very much a defensive battle that lay ahead – exactly what both the Spitfire and Hurricane, as short-range daylight interceptors, had been designed for. Air Vice-Marshal Leigh-Mallory, however, saw things very differently. Leigh-Mallory, or 'LM' as he was commonly known, was desperate to get 12 Group into battle, if necessary even by sending 19 Squadron, 66's sister unit, to France. His was an offensive outlook, the first evidence of which emerged on 12 May 1940 in an operation Flight Lieutenant Burton and 66 Squadron were involved in.

What the RAF lacked at this time was a long-range offensive fighter. It was originally intended that the twin-engine Bristol Blenheim would fulfil this role, but with advances in German aircraft it proved too slow. Then there was the Boulton-Paul Defiant, a single-engine fighter accommodating a pilot and gunner, the latter in a rear turret armed with four Browning machine-guns. The type lacked forward-firing armament operated by the pilot and therefore the split-second eye-to-hand coordination required for fast, modern, fighter combat. Although the turret could swivel round to fire forwards, this was at an elevation to avoid hitting the pilot's canopy, making the whole process impractical. Moreover, powered by the same engine which propelled the lighter Spitfire and Hurricane, the Defiant also lacked performance, and had not the range of a truly offensive fighter. Nonetheless, LM moved the newly Spitfire-equipped 222 Squadron from Duxford to Digby, its place at the former station taken by the Defiants of 264 Squadron. LM then lost no time in arranging an offensive patrol involving both 66 and 264 Squadron.

A Fairey Battle light-bomber preserved at the RAF Museum, Hendon – it was during a gunnery exercise on this type that Flying Officer Robertson was killed, when the aircraft stalled and crashed into the North Sea off Donna Nook.

After practising tactics together, on 12 May 1940 Squadron Leader Leigh led six Spitfires of 66 Squadron up from Duxford to support five 264 Squadron Defiants on a patrol off the Dutch coast. Squadron Leader Leigh led Blue Section, while Flight Lieutenant Burton led the three Spitfires of Green Section. Passing close to RN destroyers off the Hague, a bomb was seen to splash into the sea nearby. Squadron Leader Hunter of 264 Squadron then sighted a Ju 88, and ordered his Defiants to attack. Chasing the raider to ground-level, the Defiants fired at the enemy machine from both sides. A Spitfire attacked from astern, sealing the enemy bomber's fate, which crashed into a field of cows, surrounded by water, ten miles south-west of Rotterdam's Waalhaven airfield. According to the after-action report:

> The Ju 88 was deceived into thinking that he was dealing with
> Spitfires only. By turning and diving he actually played into
> the hands of the Defiants because their initial acceleration in
> the dive proved greater than the Ju 88. Turning only wasted the
> Ju 88's time and played into the Defiant's hands.

Above left: Flying Officer Robertson's grave at Manby – his loss was a devastating blow to the family (Nick Willey).

Above right: The grave of Flying Officer Robertson's pilot at Manby, the Polish Kapral Franciszek Skrzypczak (Nick Willey).

Flight Lieutenant Burton's personal combat report:

> Took off with Blue Section for The Hague at 1320 hrs. At 1400 hrs crossed the Dutch coast. At 1403 hrs sighted enemy aircraft, probably a He 111 at 7,000ft. Gave chase but enemy climbed into cloud and disappeared. Later noticed large explosion 400 yards to port of destroyers steaming south. Sighted enemy aircraft (E/A) with our machines chasing it. Dived down and carried out two deflection attacks from port quarter. Enemy eventually crashed fifteen miles east of The Hague.

The Defiants were credited with the Ju 88 destroyed, while Squadron Leader Leigh, Flight Lieutenant Burton, Flying Officers Campbell-Colquhoun and Rimmer, and Pilot Officer Kennard, shared destruction of the He 111. The after-action reported concluded that 'The pilots of both squadrons are extremely enthusiastic about this scheme of patrolling as a composite flight or squadron and unanimous in their desire always to carry out patrols of this description in this formation.' It was certainly a significant day for Billy Burton – who had fired his guns in anger for the first time, but optimism would shortly prove unfounded.

Early the following morning, 'A' Flight of 66 Squadron escorted 264 Squadron's Defiants back to the Dutch coast, hoping for a similarly successful engagement while attacking enemy troop transports north of Den Haag. Inland, south-east of Rotterdam, a formation of Ju 87 Stuka dive-bombers was successfully engaged – then Me 109s rained down on the RAF fighters. 66 Squadron lost Flying Officer Brown, who forced-landed in Belgium and evaded, but 264 Squadron was literally massacred: five out of six Defiants were shot down, during what was the Defiant's first encounter with Me 109s – proving the Defiant's total unsuitability as a day-fighter. There was also arguably no need for 12 Group to be prowling around the Dutch coast at this critical time, wasting resources for no apparent good purpose, and responsibility for the fiasco lay firmly with LM.

On 14 May 1940, Flight Lieutenant Burton moved with 66 Squadron from Duxford to operate from the new airfield at Horsham St Faiths in Norfolk. There, life went on much the same as before, routinely patrolling and training – without any further offensive sorties across the North Sea. On the Continent, however, the Allies were facing disaster.

By 21 May 1940, German troops had reached the seaside resort of Le Crotoy, on the Channel coast, at the mouth of the Somme – cutting the Allied armies in half. This astonishing German thrust to the Channel changed everything; overnight, the BEF was now in grave danger of being driven back against the North Sea coast, enveloped and destroyed. Although under political pressure to counter-attack to the south, the crumbling Belgian front to the north dictated no option for Lord Gort but to withdraw behind the Ypres-Comines Canal. Significantly, on 24 May 1940, Hitler – who believed that the war would be over in six weeks and the way clear for an agreement with Britain – agreed to General von Rundstedt's request that the German advance be halted east of the Lens-Bethune–St Omer-Gravelines line, in order to preserve armour for operations against the French. Both Hitler and Von Rundstedt were confident that the Allied forces could be destroyed from the air. Indeed, the Germans enjoyed complete aerial supremacy over France, the Stukas operating with impunity, and allowing ground forces to advance unhindered by air. While the Germans paused, however, the evacuation of British troops started – a thousand embarked from Boulogne that day, on which Hitler's air assault began. It was now clear to Lord Gort that evacuation was the only option to prevent the BEF's destruction, even if that meant losing all transport and heavy weapons. By 25 May 1940, there was clearly no option but for the BEF to withdraw further still, towards the sea.

Also killed in the crash was another trainee air gunner, Pilot Officer Eric Wright Blackwell, buried at South Leigh (St James) churchyard, Oxfordshire (Gordon Lawley).

A perimeter now formed with the port of Dunkirk at its base, a corridor which the Allies had to maintain at all costs to facilitate the retreat of troops to the coast; the battle for France was lost. A day later, it was decided that the BEF was to retire on, and evacuate from, the beaches around Dunkirk; the unthinkable had happened.

Air Vice-Marshal Park was the man in charge of the air component of Operation DYNAMO, the Dunkirk evacuation. For what he had to do, there was no precedent. Even when reinforced with fighter squadrons from 12 Group, Park lacked the aircraft necessary to provide cover from dawn to dusk. Significantly, though, indicating the urgency of the hour, Spitfires were committed to battle across the Channel for the first time. At first, Park's squadrons patrolled individually – only to meet Me 109s sweeping the French coast in *gruppe*-strength – thirty-six aircraft. Sensibly, the Spitfire squadrons operated from 11 Group airfields close to the coast, thereby reducing the range, and thereafter flew in 'wings' over the Channel of up to four squadrons strong. The lack of aerial resources, however, ultimately led to the evacuation being suspended in daylight, which greatly assisted Park, who could now patrol in strength at dawn and dusk.

By 1 June 1940, certain Fighter Command squadrons had suffered sufficient losses to be pulled out of 11 Group, to rest and refit. On that day, 66 Squadron, fresh to the battle, flew south, to Gravesend, from where Flight Lieutenant Burton participated in an uneventful patrol over Dunkirk. 'Clickety-Click' then returned to Duxford, and at dawn the following day was off to operate from Martlesham Heath. Flight Lieutenant Billy Burton was in the 66 Squadron formation led by Squadron Leader Leigh across to Dunkirk's blazing oil tanks, 'Clickety-Click' arriving over the battered

French port at 0745 hrs and patrolled at 29,000ft. Billy, flying his usual Green 1 spot and leading Green Section, reported that at 0845 hrs:

> Sighted one Ju 88 at about 11,000ft. Dived on him and got in a short burst, but could not observe results as windscreen misted up. Cleared this and then went through a lower bank of cloud. On coming out I found I was over Dunkirk. Enemy aircraft were everywhere. Attacked two Me 109s with short bursts but could see no results owing to ice on inside of my screen. Then carried out attack from dead astern on right-hand aircraft of formation of three He 111s. Broke sharply away to right and saw aircraft begin to lose height with smoke pouring from it. I was about to continue attack when noticed smoke pouring from the starboard side of my engine. Radiator temperature increased, so re-formed and landed at Manston.

Billy's attack on the He 111 was solo and therefore the result unconfirmed. This was, in fact, 66 Squadron's first major engagement of the Second World War, with all pilots engaged, claiming three Me 109s and a Ju 88 destroyed. Sergeant Douggy Hunt was shot down and safely baled out, but Sergeant Hayman was reported missing. In his log book, Billy noted that during combat the 'header tank' of his Spitfire (N3043) had been 'punctured', referring to the glycol coolant system. While the pilot enjoyed the benefits of sheet-steel armour plating behind his head and back, and between his body and the main fuel tank, situated immediately behind his instrument panel, and a thick 'armoured glass' windscreen, the rest of the Spitfire was surprisingly unprotected. Vital organs, such as the radiator and coolant system, were covered only by thin aluminium airframe skinning, and therefore vulnerable. All it took to bring a Spitfire, or any other fighter, down was a single bullet piercing a fuel line or damaging the engine-cooling system. Billy was lucky that his engine kept going and did not dangerously overheat, enabling him to return to land in Kent. Another interesting point about his report is the very high altitude at which the Spitfires patrolled – 29,000ft – and that this was above banks of cloud. These combats so high above and over cloud were invisible to watchers on the ground, giving rise to the wholly unfair slur that the 'Brylcream Boys' had failed to protect the soldiers on the beaches. German aircraft certainly got through to attack shipping and the defenceless troops – but many more were kept away from the beaches through the gallantry of Park's Spitfire pilots.

At 2330 hrs that night, the Senior Naval Officer Dunkirk, Captain Tennant, reported that the BEF had been successfully evacuated. Although

WING COMMANDER HOWARD FRIZELLE 'BILLY' BURTON

On 26 February 1941, Squadron Leader Burton led 616 Squadron to Tangmere, in 11 Group, where a month later the legless Wing Commander Douglas Bader arrived to become the Station's first Wing Leader. Bader based himself with 616 Squadron at Westhampnett (Goodwood), and exclusively led the Tangmere Wing at the head of Burton's unit. This snapshot was taken at Westhampnett before a sweep during the summer of 1941; from left: Squadron Leader Burton, Flying Officer Hugh 'Cocky' Dundas, Flight Lieutenant Colin MacFie, Wing Commander Bader, and Pilot Officer Johnnie Johnson. Both MacFie and Bader would in due course be captured whilst Dundas went on to become one of the RAF's youngest group captains and Johnson emerged the RAF's official top-scoring fighter pilot of the conflict.

over the next two nights a further 28,000 men were brought home; essentially, Operation DYNAMO was over. Initially, it had been hoped to save 45,000 men – the actual number rescued was 338,226, the operation continuing for nine days, as opposed to the originally expected two. Although Churchill, still haunted by the Gallipoli fiasco of the First World War, was quick to point out that 'wars are not won by evacuations', the combined efforts of the Navy, RAF and civilian 'Little Ships' had famously snatched a victory from the jaws of a catastrophic defeat – creating a legend, the 'miracle' of Dunkirk. The BEF had, however, left behind 68,000 men, 40,000 of whom were prisoners of war, and 200 ships had been sunk.

Essential to the evacuation's success was the contribution made by Air Vice-Marshal Park and his fighter squadrons – but the RAF effort was much criticised at the time. Admiral Ramsay, Flag Officer Dover in overall charge of the naval side, complained that efforts to provide air cover were 'puny'. Clearly there was no appreciation of the Fighter Command strength available for the operation, or the limitations due to aircraft performance. While German bombers had got through to the beaches, without Fighter Command's presence many more would have been able to wreak havoc upon the virtually defenceless troops below. Indeed, more than half of Dowding's fighters had been lost fighting over France – 453 fighters destroyed or abandoned and 435 pilots failed to come home – before the evacuation began. Upon conclusion of DYNAMO, his squadrons were exhausted – with only 331 Spitfires and Hurricanes left; indeed, as Churchill wrote to the French Prime Minister on 5 June, 'British fighter aviation has been worn to a shred and frightfully mixed up by the demands of Dunkirk.' The RAF had lost 106 precious fighters and eighty even more valuable pilots over Dunkirk (*Luftwaffe* losses were heavier but benefited from the release of 400 captured aircrew after France surrendered). DYNAMO had, in fact, provided Spitfire pilots with their first taste of aerial combat against the Me 109, and Air Vice-Marshal Park decided that it was better to spoil the aim of many enemy aircraft than to just destroy a few – which became the basis for how he would soon defend England. Any criticism of the RAF contribution to DYNAMO is, therefore, unfounded – and the experience gained over the bloody beaches would prove significant tactically, technically and strategically.

On 4 June 1940, 66 Squadron, having returned to Duxford after DYNAMO, was sent to operate from Coltishall, in Norfolk. There, life continued much the same as it had before Dunkirk, with routine patrols and training, flying by day and night. On 17 June 1940, the French sued for peace. The following day, Churchill addressed the House of Commons, concluding with these powerful and prophetic words:

> What General Weygand called the Battle of France is over. I expect that the Battle of Britain is about to begin. Upon this battle depends the survival of Christian civilization. Upon it depends our own British life, and the long continuity of our institutions and our Empire. The whole fury and might of the enemy must very soon be turned on us. Hitler knows that he will have to break us in this island or lose the war. If we can stand up to him, all Europe may be free and the life of the world may move forward into broad, sunlit uplands. But if we fail, then the whole world, including the United States, including all that we have known and cared for, will sink into the abyss of a new Dark Age made more sinister, and perhaps more protracted, by the lights of perverted science. Let us

therefore brace ourselves to our duties and so bear ourselves that, if the British Empire should last a thousand years, men will still say, 'This was their finest hour'.

The Fall of France was a catastrophe, the enormity of which for the Western democracies is perhaps difficult for people to grasp today. In June 1940 however, the British people were in no doubt of their perilous position – facing the undefeated Germans alone across just twenty-two miles of the English Channel. A version of Churchill's speech was broadcast – leaving the British people in no doubt that fighting on, alone, for their very survival now lay ahead.

After Dunkirk, the *Luftwaffe's* new-found access to airfields in the Pas-de-Calais, just over twenty miles across the English Channel from Dover, changed the whole strategic picture. This unexpected geographical shift put the entire British Isles within range of German bombers, which could now be escorted to London by the lethal Me 109 fighter. This unanticipated and unprecedented military success was as big a surprise to Hitler as everyone else – the Führer now suddenly presented with an unexpected opportunity to mount a seaborne invasion of southern England. First, though, aerial supremacy, at least over the invasion area, was prerequisite, and very soon the Battle of Britain would decide the issue. Before assaulting Britain, however, the *Luftwaffe* needed to regroup and refit, so a lull followed the Battle of France and Dunkirk evacuation. By night, though, the Germans maintained a degree of pressure, lone raiders prowling over Britain, dropping bombs and causing a general nuisance. On the night of 18/19 June 1940, the greatest attack to date on mainland Britain was launched, with over seventy intruders attacking a wide range of targets. That night, the South African 'Sailor' Malan of Hornchurch's 74 Squadron scored the Spitfire's first nocturnal victory, followed by a second shortly afterwards. Other pilots were also successful, but the attack indicated that the enemy was now firmly focused on the British Isles – every inch of which was now within the range of German bombers.

For Flight Lieutenant Burton, action came on the evening of 19 June 1940, when he led Blue Section off from Coltishall, scrambled to intercept a suspected raider off the east coast. At 1930 hrs, forty miles off Yarmouth, Billy sighted a Ju 88, flying south at 12,000ft:

> I turned and gave chase from astern. Climbed into cloud on same course as bandit, and came down twice to make sure he was still on same course. When about half a mile behind, climbed above cloud layer and continued same course. Cloud cleared

and sighted E/A, 500ft below on my port beam. Commenced attack from port beam and got about a three second burst with deflection up to very close range. On breaking away, I noticed cannon firing for the first time. I attacked again with three second burst from port quarter and twice more from starboard, my numbers 2 and 3 following. After third attack I did not notice any further cannon fire. After fourth attack was down to about 2,000ft and lost sight of E/A and numbers 2 and 3. After searching, I failed to pick them up and returned to base. Had no difficulty in catching E/A and did not need 12lb boost. I also kept up with him in dive, but he kept turning in towards me at the start of the attack.

Although the combat was inconclusive, the Ju 88 had obviously been damaged and the gunner either wounded or killed. It was all experience – but dangerous work, fighting over the cold sea at a time when air sea rescue was in its infancy and pilots relied more upon rescue by a passing trawler than by a formal organisation.

On 22 June 1940, France formally surrendered. Britain was now alone. In more recent years some historians have argued that this was a myth, because Britain enjoyed the benefits of its Empire's resources in men and materiel. True though that was, it misses the essential point: it took time for those resources to reach the beleaguered island, and Britain – and Britain alone – lay beneath the much-feared German bombers. The British people, however, did not falter or fail in their resolve to stand up to Hitler – and in that respect, Britain truly was alone – the scene set for an epic contest.

Billy's last flight that month was on 27 June 1940, 'Attack practice' in Spitfire N3032, bringing his total solo flying hours to 731.55, 182.30 being on the Spitfire by day, 18.35 by night. He did not fly again until 5 July 1940, the reason being a happy occasion; Flight Lieutenant Howard Frizelle Burton got married on 29 June 1940, to 20-year-old Miss Jean Ferelith Maxwell Robertson, the only daughter of Air Commodore E.D.M. Robertson CB DFC, and Mrs Evelyn Jane Robertson, of 'Tain', Greville Park Road, Ashtead, Surrey.

The bride's father had a distinguished service record, having begun his service life as a Midshipman, RN, in 1902, before being promoted to lieutenant in just four years, later commanding HMS *Riviera* during the Cuxhaven Raid of Christmas 1914. In June 1918, having subsequently become a service pilot, he was the pilot of a flying boat attacked and shot down by five enemy aircraft – pilot and crew were fortunately rescued after eight hours clinging to their aircraft's wreckage. A DFC followed, and after

Shopwyke House became the Tangmere Officers' Mess, Squadron Leader Burton pictured on the terrace there in 1941 (2nd left) with (from left) the Station Commander, Group Captain AB 'Woody' Woodhall, Wing Commander Bader, and the Canadian Squadron Leader Stan Turner (JA Estate).

commanding various flying boat and other stations in the new RAF, by 1931, having also served as Director of Personnel, Robertson was appointed Air Aide de Camp to the King. Retiring in 1935, he became Superintendent at Croydon Airport, and would soon be recalled to the RAF, serving until 1945. The bride's brother, Duncan Maxwell Robertson, who was an usher and to whom Jean was close, had, understandably, been inspired by his father's august record and had joined the RAF himself; a flying officer, Duncan was training to be an air gunner. The bride's younger brother, Struan, was also an usher.

Billy's best man was another serving RAF officer and an interesting character, for sure, although somewhat older: Squadron Leader Hubert Williams, who had flown fighters with the RFC during the First World War and recently returned to the air force to work in training (he died in 2002, aged 106, and was the last surviving RFC pilot). Wearing a dress of silver and white brocade, the bride was given away by her father, the ceremony taking place at Ashtead parish church, while the reception was held at 'Tain', the Robertson's family home; the wedding cake was, naturally, according to the *Dorking and Leatherhead Advertiser*, 'decorated with aeroplanes and a model of a Spitfire was on top'. Afterwards, the newlyweds left to spend

Squadron Leader Burton walking in at Westhampnett after a sweep during the summer of 1941. Behind him is a cannon-armed Spitfire Mk IIB of 616 Squadron, about to be re-fuelled and re-armed. Interestingly, Billy is wearing a highly prized German lifejacket, which was far more efficient than the RAF 'Mae West', very likely taken as a souvenir from the Me 109 pilot he shot down near Manston on 21 June 1940, and who was captured (JA Estate).

their honeymoon at the Oatlands Park Hotel, near Weybridge. With, as the Prime Minister famously said, the Battle of France over and 'the Battle of Britain about to begin', a most uncertain future lay ahead – not just for Billy and Jean, but for the whole world.

For 66 Squadron at Coltishall, the same routine continued, of interception and convoy patrols, and training. Now though, having met the enemy, Fighter Command's pilots had a better idea of what to expect in modern air combat – and had already resigned the Fighter Command Book of Tactics to the bin. Before the Second World War, as any air attack on Britain was expected to come from bases in Germany itself, across the North Sea, it was assumed that enemy bombers would be unprotected by Me 109s, which lacked sufficient range. Consequently, Fighter Command's tacticians had devised set-piece attacks, based around the section of three aircraft flying in a tight vic formation. These fighters would attack in formation, simultaneously, bringing twenty-four guns to bear instead of a single fighter's eight. As the lead section broke away, the following section would

Squadron Leader Burton and Wing Commander Bader prepare for a sweep during the summer of 1941, removing anything able to provide the enemy intelligence (JA Estate).

attack, and so on; all of this providing enemy bombers simply plodded along, taking no evasive action. With the *Luftwaffe* now ensconced in air bases in the Pas-de-Calais, German bombers would actually be escorted, changing everything.

The Germans had worked everything out during the Spanish Civil War, their fighter pilots knowing full-well that the factors governing First World War fighter tactics – height, sun and surprise – still applied. Moreover, their fighter formation was based not on close formation flying, requiring far too much concentration and too little time searching for the enemy, but on a section of four aircraft – the *Schwarm* – spread out 200 metres apart, in line abreast, stepped up, each aircraft protecting its neighbour and pilots, without fear of collision, able to search the sky. In combat, the *Schwarm* broke into two fighting pairs or *Rotte*, comprising leader, whose job it was to get the shot, while his number 2 or wingman – *Rottenhund* – protected his leader's tail. Having now met these fluid and flexible fighter formations it was clear that the vic was totally unsuitable for modern air fighting – but there was no guidance from the Air Ministry or Fighter Command HQ as to an alternative tactical formation. Instead, RAF fighter squadron commanders aware of this significant deficiency experimented with their own formations, Malan, for example, favouring the section of four in line astern, but there was no consistency and little or no provision for information sharing between squadrons. Training took on an even more urgent note and new exercises crept into the programme, such as Billy practising 'Head-on attacks' on 21 July 1940.

From the beginning of July 1940, the *Luftwaffe* began attacking shipping in the Channel, probing British defences. Later, Air Chief Marshal Dowding, in his despatch, decided that the start-date of what became known as the 'Battle of Britain' was 10 July 1940, although in truth the fighting had been ongoing for a week previously. Nonetheless, the lull was over, and the

Billy's wife, Jean (left) and friend running the NAAFI wagon at Tangmere, summer 1941 (JA Estate).

German air force was now to mount a sustained aerial assault on southern England, with a view to mounting a seaborne invasion. 11 Group would bear the brunt of this attack, while 10 and 12 Group's squadrons, in addition to observing their own defensive commitments, would reinforce 11 Group upon request and provide a protective aerial umbrella over Air Vice-Marshal Park's airfields while his fighters were engaged further forward. That, at least, was the plan. Before the war, most operational training was based around the section or flight, not the whole squadron flying collectively. Furthermore, limitations of radio communications prevented squadrons speaking with each other in the air, only able to communicate with pilots in their own unit and ground control. This made it impossible for an airborne leader to control several squadrons in the air, once battle was joined. During DYNAMO, Air Vice-Marshal Park had sent multiple squadrons across the Channel together, in a 'wing', but this was more a convoy system in strength, providing for many fighters to arrive over the battle area together. Afterwards, squadrons patrolled independently – with assistance not far away, if required. Given the pre-war training, limitations of communications and need to carefully preserve resources, Air Vice-Marshal Park decided that it was 'better to spoil the aim of many, rather than destroy a few', and fight the forthcoming battle with small formations, or at most two squadrons operating together. However, the evidence confirms that Air Vice-Marshal Leigh-Mallory was not only lacking in fighter experience, but was arguably obsessed with mass fighter formations. On 21 July 1942, for example, Flight Lieutenant Burton recorded in his log book that he and 66 Squadron had flown 'Wing formation practice with 242 Squadron', and again three days later. This would, in due course, prove significant.

Wing Commander Burton whilst serving in the western desert, 1942 (JA Estate).

242 Squadron was a Canadian Hurricane unit badly battered in France. Suffering from poor morale, LM needed a very special new commander to rebuild the squadron and inspire it; he chose a Cranwellian, unique in the service for having no legs: Squadron Leader Douglas Bader. Like Billy Burton, Bader had been a King's Cadet, and excelled at sport – and aerobatics. Posted to 23 Squadron at Kenley, he was soon representing the service as an aerobatic pilot, but, although frequently warned regarding the perils of unauthorised low-flying, one day went too far and, in his own words, 'Made a balls of it', when his Bulldog crashed, slow-rolling at Woodley. Bader was so seriously injured that to save his life both legs had to be amputated. A lesser man would have thrown in the towel or died, but Bader, as brave as a lion and with an indomitable spirit, overcame his disability, mastering 'tin legs', and had every intention of returning to the cockpit. Unfortunately, King's Regulations failed to provide for disabled pilots. Unprepared to accept a ground commission, Bader left the service, forlorn, in 1933 – but, assisted by Cranwell connections, argued his way back into the service and in a flying capacity when war broke out.

Initially, Flying Officer Bader flew Spitfires with 19 Squadron at Duxford, but ultimately found it intolerable serving under his old Cranwell and 23 Squadron friend Squadron Leader Geoffrey Stephenson, and in terms of experience on new monoplane fighters, being the most junior pilot on the squadron in spite of his age. Fortunately, 222 Squadron, also at Duxford, was commanded by a Cranwell chum, Squadron Leader H.W. 'Tubby' Mermagen,

35

Conditions in the desert were harsh. Wing Commander Burton led 239 Wing, flying the P-40 Kittyhawk, the presence of which had a great influence on the desert air war.

who agreed for Bader to fill a flight commander's vacancy on his Spitfire squadron. This was more like it. In a matter of months Bader had risen from lowly pilot officer to flight lieutenant, and was happy now that he had a team to lead. Over Dunkirk, on 2 June 1940, he made his first combat claim, and, having no legs, was enormously newsworthy, a propagandist's dream. Naturally, given his background and ability, he was also well-known to, and a favourite of, both LM, his Air Officer Commanding 12 Group, and Wing Commander A.B. 'Woody' Woodhall, Station Commander at Duxford. With Mermagen's recommendation, supported by Woodhall, LM agreed to Bader being promoted further still and given command of 242. The arrival of a legless squadron commander, however, initially failed to impress the disgruntled Canadians – until an angry Bader gave a breath-taking aerobatic display over Coltishall, much of the time *inverted*. Here, then, was no passenger, but a real war leader, like Churchill, and on 10 July 1940, the day the Battle of Britain started, Squadron Leader Bader signalled 12 Group and Fighter Command HQs to the effect that 242 Squadron was again fully operational. The introduction of this swashbuckling, fearless, character into the mix adds another dimension to Billy Burton's story, as we will explore.

On 29 July 1940, Billy was in action again, at 1515 hrs, 9,000ft, fourteen miles east of Hammond's Knoll:

> Enemy (He 111) sighted at 1512 hrs about ten miles due east of us … we approached head-on … E/A flew below us at 9,000ft and saw crosses on upper wings. Section formed line astern and turned around and pursued E/A, which commenced turning to port. Section closed in and gave a burst about 350 yards

with quarter deflection and then closed into range 300 yards, closing to 80 yards. Broke away to starboard and waited for numbers 2 and 3 to carry out attacks. Repeated attack from astern and closed into 150 yards with one long burst, finishing ammunition. Enemy appeared then to be slowing down and heading towards land. Waited on port side while numbers 2 and 3 finished their ammunition. Large plume of white vapour poured back from port engine. Little return fire experienced and not accurate. Enemy fired at about 1,000 yards. Enemy gradually lost height and made for cloud at Yarmouth, his port engine was stopped and he could not make height. After approaching Yarmouth he turned slowly to port and made off ESE at about 130–140 mph, losing height slowly. Enemy jettisoned about six bombs when ten miles off Yarmouth. I left enemy gradually losing height. Whenever I approached within about 1,000 yards, he kept shooting, but most inaccurately.

Again, the outcome of the combat was inconclusive, but the He 111 was clearly damaged. The ranges at which fire was opened is of interest, being too great – pilots would soon learn to get in as close as possible before letting fly. That Billy put his section into line astern, rather than attacking in a vic, suggests a tactical awareness and rejection of approved tactics.

August 1940 continued much the same for Coltishall's squadrons, chasing about after unescorted lone reconnaissance or nuisance bombers, while the Battle of Britain hotted up over 11 Group. On 15 August 1940, 66 Squadron from Coltishall and 19 from Fowlmere, Duxford's satellite, were called upon to reinforce 11 Group and defend Martlesham Heath

A snapshot taken by Wing Commander Burton of one of his Kittyhawks formating on him over the desert (JA Estate).

aerodrome. Unfortunately, the 12 Group Spitfires arrived too late to prevent Martlesham being bombed. Air Vice-Marshal Park was furious, but 12 Group countered that they had been requested too late, and considering time and distance, it was then impossible for LM's Spitfires to arrive in time. It was the start of major friction between the two groups which would ultimately have far reaching consequences for Fighter Command as whole, as we will soon see.

On 3 September 1940, Billy Burton recorded in his log book, 'Promoted to Acting Squadron Leader and posted to command 616 (Fighter) Squadron.'

616 'South Yorkshire' Squadron was a Spitfire-equipped AAF unit which, until 19 August 1940, had been based at Leconfield in 12 Group. Although it had participated in the so-called 'Junkers Party', when a German attack on north-east England made from Scandinavian bases was routed, up until that point the squadron's experience was similar to that of 66, having fought over Dunkirk but otherwise undertaking routine patrols, intercepting the odd lone raider, and training. On the day in question, 616 had been sent south to Kenley, in 11 Group. The change in the tempo of combat, owing to the presence of Me 109s, was traumatic. By 3 September 1940, in fifteen days the squadron had lost eleven Spitfires destroyed and three damaged. Five pilots had been killed, six wounded and one captured. It was no exaggeration to say that 616 Squadron had been virtually annihilated; 616 Squadron's exhausted CO, Squadron Leader Marcus Robinson, was relieved of his command when the unit was pulled out of Kenley and flew to Coltishall. Like 242 Squadron, LM needed a special leader to rebuild this fighter squadron and it is no surprise that Billy was chosen – an exceptional young officer, with combat experience, in whom 616 Squadron could trust. Acting Squadron Leader Burton's job was now to rebuild 616 Squadron into an effective fighting unit.

On 7 September 1940, the day on which the Germans began round-the-clock bombing of London, cost the *Luftwaffe* forty aircraft, but Fighter Command lost twenty-seven, with fourteen more pilots killed – and casualties were now an increasing concern at Fighter Command HQ. That afternoon, Dowding called an urgent meeting at Bentley Priory to decide measures for 'going downhill' in an economical manner, providing for a rapid climb back. When losses decreed, depleted squadrons in 11 Group were replaced by those from other groups, which were at full-strength, 616 being a case in point; having suffered such heavy losses at Kenley it had been relieved there by 64 Squadron withdrawn to Coltishall in 12 Group, under Billy Burton's command, there to refit and train new pilots before returning to the combat zone. The problem was that while squadrons like 616 could provide new pilots with further operational training, and perhaps

Group Captain HA 'Jimmy' Fenton, who had commanded a Hurricane squadron during the Battle of Britain, before a Wing in the desert and commanding 212 Group (JA Estate).

even limited action, these replacements lacked combat experience – and that was the problem. In any case, there were insufficient pilots, trained, combat experienced or otherwise. Dowding's Senior Air Staff Officer, Air Vice-Marshal Evill, provided the meeting figures confirming that in the four weeks ending 4 September 1940, casualties totalled 338, whereas during that period the Operational Training Units had only converted 280 pilots. Air Vice-Marshal Park pointed out that in 11 Group, casualties were approaching 100 a week. The solution – arrived at by Dowding and Park – was the 'Stabilising Scheme'.

This categorised fighter squadrons as 'A', 'B' or 'C' units. 'A' were those in the frontline, maintained with a minimum strength of sixteen operational pilots; 'B' were those being rested, with up to six combat-ready pilots, who could be called upon if necessary; 'C' were those currently rebuilding after suffering losses and unlikely to be called to battle. With a minimum quota of three combat-ready pilots, the latter units were to provide operational experience to pilots fresh from OTU, away from the combat zone. Once these new pilots were considered combat ready, they could be posted to 'A' or 'B' squadrons further south. Initially, 616 Squadron became a 'C' unit, but just six days later moved to Kirton-in-Lindsay, in Lincolnshire, and was recategorised a 'B' squadron. Fortunately, while receiving and training replacement pilots, Squadron Leader Burton had the advantage of a small cadre of Kenley survivors around whom to build his new team; men like the solid and reliable Flying Officer Ken Holden, and Pilot Officers Hugh Dundas and Lionel 'Buck' Casson. Among the replacement pilots arriving direct from OTUs and fighter squadrons too busy with operational commitments to provide them further training was one Pilot Officer James Edgar 'Johnnie' Johnson – destined to become the RAF's official top-scoring fighter pilot of the Second World War; Johnnie recalled his arrival at Coltishall, before the squadron moved to Kirton, on 6 September 1940:

> I did not like the atmosphere. The veterans kept to themselves and seemed aloof and very remote. Even to my inexperienced eye it was apparent that the quiet confidence of a well-led and disciplined team was missing from this group. There was a marked difference between the bunch of aggressive pilots I had [previously] met at Fowlmere [19 Squadron] and these too silent, apprehensive, men.

Clearly, Squadron Leader Burton had work to do, to raise the spirits of these demoralised men.

Johnnie's new CO, however, immediately impressed:

> Billy Burton, being a regular officer who had won the Cranwell Sword-of-Honour in 1936, was an outstanding product of the Cranwell system. Exacting in his demands, he was always full of vitality and enthusiasm. I liked him at first sight and have never served under a better or more loyal officer.

Half an hour after this initial interview, Johnnie was airborne for fifty minutes in Spitfire X4055, being put through his paces by Squadron Leader Burton. Afterwards, the CO concluded that Johnson's performance was 'Not bad', but emphasised the need to keep a constantly good look-out. Johnnie:

> No one, so far, had really talked to us about tactics. We were, of course, very keen to know what it was like fighting the Me 109, and how to best shoot one down. At training school we

virtually had to cajole instructors into imparting knowledge, and while at Duxford had listened keenly to what the Spitfire pilots of 19 Squadron and the Czech Hurricane pilots of 310 had to say – but this was all in the informal environment of either dispersal or the Mess. After that flight with Billy, though, he talked to me about the difficulties of deflection shooting and the technique of the killing shot from the line-astern or near line-astern positions; the duty of the number two whose job was not to shoot down aircraft but to ensure that the leader's tail was safe; the importance of keeping a good battle formation and the tactical use of sun, cloud and height. Here was a man, I thought, who knew what he was about, and under whose leadership we might actually get somewhere.

There was, however, a problem; an old rugby injury to a shoulder caused Johnnie great pain and discomfort during the very physical experience that flying a Spitfire entailed, threatening to end his flying career. He was given two choices: be posted away to fly a desk, or go under the knife. Without hesitation, Johnnie chose the latter, and before he left Kirton for surgery, Squadron Leader Burton agreed to take him back once fit: 'It was a second chance. All I wanted was to live and fight with men like Billy Burton and Ken Holden, so I was very grateful and happy indeed to return to 616 Squadron on 28 December 1940.' It was a wise decision on Squadron Leader Burton's part, considering Johnnie's subsequent RAF career.

Various old friends found their way to the desert, including Flight Lieutenant Roy Marples, who had served under Billy Burton in 616 Squadron but was destined to lose his life as a wing leader later in the war (JA Estate).

Among the demoralised Kenley survivors of Burton's Squadron was 20-year-old Pilot Officer Hugh Spencer Lisle Dundas – universally known as 'Cocky', given his love of cocktails. On 22 August 1940, Dundas had been shot down by the 'Father of Modern Air Fighting' himself – Major Werner 'Vatti' Mölders, Kommodore of JG 51. Wounded in the leg and shoulder, Dundas successfully took to his parachute but remained traumatised by what had been a terrifying experience. Of Billy, Dundas later wrote that his new CO was:

> a Regular officer with impeccable credentials – not only a Cranwell man, but a Cranwell Sword-of-Honour man … not a man to tolerate a situation or an atmosphere where there was any brooding over the past. He sent for me and asked me straight out whether I felt in every way fit to go back to flying. It was a critical moment. The memory of my terrifying experience on 22 August was overpowering … reinforced by the absence of so many old friends and knowledge of what had happened to them … The inner conflict between wanting to stay alive rather than engage the enemy was very much to the fore at that moment. But I had myself saying that yes, I did indeed feel in every way fit and ready, whereupon Burton very sensibly ordered me into the air without further delay or discussion … When I landed I was able to tell Burton in good faith that I really did feel fine and ready for anything.

Again, this is an example of Squadron Leader Burton's sound judgement and natural leadership: Dundas would go on to become a decorated ace and one of the service's youngest Group Captains with a distinguished war record.

At Kirton, 616 Squadron began an intensive period of flying training, including interception practice with 264 Squadron's Defiants, and operational commitments such as scrambling after unidentified radar plots – 'bogeys', otherwise known as 'X-Raids'. It was all good experience. It was also to Squadron Leader Burton's enormous credit that on the morning of 19 September 1940, only a fortnight since 616 Squadron had been pulled out of Kenley, Billy led no less than fourteen Spitfires from Kirton to operate from Fowlmere, the Duxford satellite airfield. This, however, requires explanation.

While previously based at Coltishall, Squadron Leader Burton had met Squadron Leader Douglas Bader, who, as previously explained was the legless, extraordinary, swashbuckling leader of 242 Squadron and a fellow Cranwellian. Bader thirsted for action, and found it intolerable that he should be left waiting at the side-lines in 12 Group while 11 Group got all the fighting. Bader was exasperated that 242 Squadron were not called into action further south. Then, on 30 August 1940, the chance came when 11 Group requested reinforcements from 12 Group to deal with a large raid aimed at aircraft factories near Watford. Scrambling from Duxford, 242 Squadron successfully intercepted the Germans, a formation of bombers escorted only by the twin-engine Me 110. After the battle, 242 Squadron claimed seven Me 110s destroyed and three 'probables', and three He 111s destroyed, generating congratulatory signals from the Chief of the Air Staff, LM, and even the Under-Secretary of State for Air.

Three days later, Bader submitted a report outlining his impressions of the action, concluding that had he had more fighters under his command, then even more damage to the enemy could have been achieved. LM agreed and arranged for 242 to operate from Duxford with the Hurricanes of the Czech 310 Squadron, and the Fowlmere-based Spitfires of 19 Squadron, in a three-squadron-strong 12 Group Wing – led by Bader. Such a formation was contrary, however, to how Dowding wanted the battle fought, but the C-in-C had given his group commanders sufficient autonomy for LM to try out this idea – and LM had already given indications in favour of

Primitive conditions for 239 Wing in the western desert (JA Estate).

239 Wing's mobile operations caravan (JA Estate).

aggressive patrolling by large formations of fighters. In any case, the whole concept was flawed from the outset because, contrary to 242 Squadron's perception that it alone had intercepted the enemy on 30 August 1940, various 11 Group squadrons were simultaneously engaged, around fifty fighters in fact, immediately negating Bader's assertion that had more than a single squadron of fighters been involved, the execution would have been greater. The fact is, they had been.

The 'Duxford Wing' first went into action on 7 September 1940 over London, but the engagement was not entirely successful owing to the wing being ambushed by Me 109s while still climbing. Over the next few days,

The WDAF AOC, Air Vice-Marshal Harry Broadhurst, famously used a captured German Storch as his personal transport – snapped here by Billy Burton at Alamein, October 1942 (JA Estate).

WING COMMANDER HOWARD FRIZELLE 'BILLY' BURTON

Air Vice-Marshal Sir Arthur 'Mary' Coningham, a primary architect of close air support, visiting 239 Wing (JA Estate).

however, the wing saw plentiful action and made comparatively staggering combat claims, which were accepted with little or no scrutiny by 12 Group HQ. The impression given was that the Duxford Wing was incredibly successful, achieving far greater success than 11 Group's penny-packet formations, thus calling into question the tactics employed by Dowding and Park, all of which became, ultimately, a dark political intrigue aimed squarely at removing these two fine commanders. Today, we know that the more fighters are engaged the greater the confusion and consequently, although made in good faith, the more exaggerated are pilots' combat claims. Consequently, the evidence actually confirms that the Duxford Wing consistently and substantially overclaimed by a ratio of 7:1, and was not, therefore, anywhere near as successful as 12 Group promoted at the time. Nonetheless, back then, the wing provided an opportunity for 12 Group and Squadron Leader Bader especially, to get into the battle – and it was then arranged for the Hurricanes of 302 (Polish) Squadron and Spitfires of 611 to be added to the Duxford Wing – making for a five-squadron 'Big Wing'. On 15 September 1940, the Germans made their greatest effort against London, on what became known as 'Battle of Britain Day' and a clear turning point in the defenders' favour. That afternoon, some sixty fighters of the Big Wing appeared over the capital, which was undoubtedly a morale-boosting sight for the hard-pressed and outnumbered 11 Group pilots – and this has to be the Big Wing's greatest contribution and moment.

When Squadron Leader Burton and 616 Squadron arrived at Fowlmere on 19 September 1940 for operations with the Big Wing, it was to relieve 611 Squadron of further Wing commitments. Between then and the end of the month, 616 would share the wing commitment with Kirton's other Spitfire squadron, Squadron Leader 'Sailor' Malan's 74 'Tiger' Squadron.

Air Vice-Marshal Coningham (left) with Wing Commander Burton and a Group Captain Carter, whilst visiting 239 Wing – a Kittyhawk fighter can be seen in the background (JA Estate).

Billy would lead 616 Squadron on a number of largely uneventful Big Wing patrols, but on 27 September 1940 the wing was engaged by Me 109s, 616 losing Pilot Officer Don Smith, its last casualty of the Battle of Britain. The following day, Billy led the squadron on two more Wing patrols, after which it too was released from further Wing commitments.

Back at Kirton, 616 Squadron, now with operational experience over London and the south-east, continued training, while Squadron Leader Burton and his two excellent flight commanders, Flight Lieutenants Colin MacFie and C.A.T. 'Jerry' Jones, continued moulding the squadron into the highly efficient fighting unit it became.

On 28 October 1940, there was a tragedy for Squadron Leader Burton's family: his brother-in-law, Flying Officer Duncan Maxwell Robertson, was killed in a flying accident; 27-year-old Duncan was undergoing final training to be an air gunner at 1 Air Armament School, Manby, in Lincolnshire, and on the fateful day was engaged on aerial gunnery practice at the Donna Nook ranges with another trainee, Pilot Officer Eric Wright Blackwell, in a Fairey Battle light-bomber (L5027) flown by Polish Kapral Franciszek Skrzypczak, when the aircraft stalled and crashed into the North Sea. Billy's wife, Jean, was close to her brother, and according to family Duncan's loss was something their mother never entirely recovered from. It was a sad loss indeed.

Hurricane tank busters over the desert (JA Estate).

With the Battle of Britain officially considered over on 31 October 1940, and the threat of invasion past, 616 Squadron settled down to a comparatively dull routine at Kirton, training and more training punctuated by the odd chase and engagement with one raiders – which also visited Kirton airfield on several occasions, causing damage. The winter weather soon severely restricted flying, and in February 1941 deep snow completely prevented it. On 25 February 1941, though, there was great excitement when Squadron Leader Burton received a long-awaited signal: 616 Squadron was to fly south the following day, to Tangmere, near Chichester, in 11 Group, and there relieve 65 Squadron. Under Billy's leadership and example, the battered and depleted 616 Squadron had been returned to full-efficiency and enjoyed great morale; Johnnie Johnson: 'Oh yes, we were incredibly keen to get down there and have a proper crack at the Germans.' And 'a proper crack' 616 Squadron would certainly have, throughout the forthcoming 'season' of 1941.

After the Battle of Britain, the evidence suggests almost entirely due to the controversy and political intrigue over the 'Big Wing' argument, Air Chief Marshal Dowding had been replaced as C-in-C Fighter Command by Air Marshal Sholto Douglas, and Air Vice-Marshal Park at the helm of 11 Group by Air Vice-Marshal Leigh-Mallory. Both new men lacked the experience of their predecessors, and believed that mass formations of fighters should become standard practice in both defence and offence. Consequently, in the spring of 1941, Fighter Command was reorganised so that each sector station became home to a three-squadron-strong Spitfire wing, the type having replaced the Hurricane as the RAF's primary frontline fighter. To lead these new formations the unprecedented post of 'Wing Commander (Flying)' was created, with responsibility for his wing's operational performance.

The Hurricane IID was armed with two 40mm cannons – able to penetrate the armour of any panzer in the western desert.

Among the first Wing Leaders, needless to say, was Wing Commander Douglas Bader, who chose to lead the Tangmere Wing, comprising 145, 610 and 616 Squadrons. As Sergeant 'Butch' Morton, a pilot of 616 Squadron, said, 'When Douglas Bader arrived in March 1941, we knew that something big was in the offing.' It was indeed: Fighter Command's new broom had decided on an aggressive stance for the forthcoming 'season', 'reaching out' and 'leaning into France', taking the war across the Channel to the Germans in north-west France, the objective being 'to establish air superiority over the enemy in his own country'. New operations were devised, including 'Rhubarbs', low-level nuisance raids which ultimately generated heavy losses and which the pilots hated; and the more complex 'Circus', involving a small number of bombers attacking a target such as an enemy airfield, transport and communications centre, port or factory, escorted by literally hundreds of Spitfires. Considering that less than a year before Fighter Command was on the back foot, fighting a critical defensive battle, it was optimistic indeed – but nonetheless inspiring, and the new wings eagerly looked forward to action, their morale high.

At Tangmere, Bader found 145 Squadron, commanded by Squadron Leader Jack Leather, and Squadron Leader Billy Burton's 616 Squadron, while Squadron Leader John Ellis's 610 Squadron was dispersed to the nearby Westhampnett satellite airfield. Pilot Officer Johnnie Johnson:

> Bader based himself with us at Westhampnett, and led the wing with us, because he already knew us and there was the Cranwell connection with Billy, the bond of which cannot be underestimated … Because Douglas always flew at the head of our Squadron, our CO, Billy Burton, was unhappy as he never

got to lead his own Squadron. I do not think it was necessary for Douglas to do this. Later in the war, when I was a Wing Leader, I flew with all of my squadrons in rotation, although I'd keep the same Number Two in each one. It would definitely have been better for the Tangmere Wing had Douglas done this too.

All of that said, there was no antipathy between Wing Commander Bader and Squadron Leader Burton, who understood each other perfectly and worked together well.

The day after Wing Commander Bader arrived at Tangmere, the 'Wingco' was aloft at the head of 616 Squadron, leading the wing on a 'Channel snoop', looking for trouble. Afterwards, Squadron Leader Burton recorded in his log book 'Wing patrol with 610, led by Wing Commander Bader. "Johnno" gave alarm: "Look out!"'. Pilot Officer Johnnie Johnson:

> Suddenly I spotted three lean 109s only a few hundred feet higher than our formation and travelling in the same direction … I should have calmly reported the number, type and position of the 109s to our leader, but I was excited and shouted "Look out, Dogsbody!" The other pilots … weren't waiting for further advice from me. To them, "look out" was a warning of utmost danger – of the dreaded "bounce" by a strong force of 109s. Now they took swift evasive action and half-rolled, dived, aileron-turned and swung out in all directions … In far less time than it takes to tell, a highly organised Wing was reduced to a shambles and the scattered sections could never be re-formed in time to continue the planned flight. I was the last to land, for I had realised the error and knew the consequences would be unpleasant. They were all waiting in the dispersal hut.

"Close the door, Billy", ordered Bader. And then:

"Now who's the clot who shouted 'look-out'?"

I admitted being the guilty party.

"Very well. Now tell us what we had to 'look-out' for?", demanded the angry Wing Commander.

"Well, sir, there were three 109s a few hundred feet above…"

"*Three* 109s!" interrupted Bader. "We could have clobbered the lot. But your girlish scream made us think there were fifty of the brutes behind."

This public rebuke hurt deeply, but it was well justified, for our first operation had been a complete failure, thanks to my error. Bader went on to deliver an impromptu lecture on tactics ... since he was quick to forgive, he gave me an encouraging grin when he stomped out of the dispersal hut. I never forgot this lesson.

Without doubt, Bader was a true war leader, this legless dynamo who booked squash courts over the radio while sallying forth to engage the enemy over France, and exuded total fearlessness. As Pilot Officer Johnson later recalled, he was very 'salty', you know, always 'effing and blinding'. Our Controller, Woodhall, would shout up and say "Come on, Douglas, I've got WAAFs down here!", and Bader would just reply "Oh, it's alright, Woody, I'll just come and see 'em later and apologise!"

Even Squadron Leader Burton, according to Paul Brickhill in *Reach for the Sky*, was:

appalled by Bader's uninhibited comments. Like Bader, he nearly always had a pipe in his mouth, and sometimes in the privacy of the pilots' room he would take it out and say "D'you know what the Wingco called me this morning? He called me a ____ !" He used to repeat these things in a voice of wonder as though they could not really have happened, then break into a puzzled laugh.

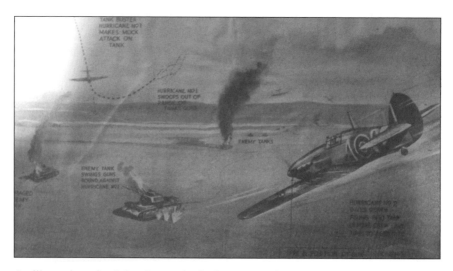

An illustration of tank busting tactics in the western desert.

WING COMMANDER HOWARD FRIZELLE 'BILLY' BURTON

Pilot Officer Johnnie Johnson:

> Bader would come stomping into dispersal and say to Billy
> Burton, "What are we doing today, then, Billy?"
>
> And Billy might respond "Well, the Form 'D', the
> Operational Order, has come through, sir, but we're not on it.
> The other wings are but not us".
>
> Bader would explode! "Right, we'll bloody well see about
> that, I'll have a bloody word with Leigh-Mallory!" And then
> he'd call up the AOC himself, remonstrate, and, lo and behold,
> we'd be on ops!'

Group Captain 'Woody' Woodhall, Tangmere's Station Commander and
'Boss Controller':

> From June 1941 onwards, the Tangmere Wing was carrying
> out two or three sweeps a day over enemy occupied territory.
> Douglas Bader always led the wing himself. He never spared
> himself, and by this time was a legendary figure.
>
> These sweeps required such accurate briefing, involving as
> they did such large numbers of Spitfires in addition to the bombers
> they were escorting, that it became necessary for Leigh-Mallory
> to hold a conference of sector commanders, Wing Leaders and
> squadron commanders at Group HQ several times a week.
> After the last mission of the day, on these occasions, Douglas
> Bader and I, and perhaps the wing's squadron commanders,
> and I would climb into our Spitfires and fly to Northolt, where
> we were met by car and taken to Uxbridge. These briefing
> conferences were most rewarding. Leigh-Mallory, with his
> usual courtesy, encouraged everyone to express his opinions,
> listened to arguments, and then laid down his plan of further
> action. After the conference, we visitors to 11 Group HQ would
> then have a quick cup of tea in the Mess, before flying back to
> our sectors. Shortly after landing at our aerodromes, complete
> and detailed instructions, implementing decisions made, for the
> next operation would arrive by teleprinter, headed "Operational
> Order for Circus No *".

The pressure was relentless.

On the morning of 21 June 1941, the longest day of high summer,
the Tangmere Wing along with the Hornchurch Wing, provided Forward

A Panzer Mk IV destroyed by 239 Wing's tank-busting 6 Squadron, commanded by Billy Burton's Cranwell contemporary, Squadron Leader D Weston Burt (JA Estate).

Support to Circus 16, attacking the airfield at St Omer–Longuenesse, where a big fire was started in a wood. Between St Omer and the French coast, 610 Squadron was attacked by a *Rotte* of Me 109s; Flight Lieutenant Lee-Knight (White 1) engaged these enemy fighters in a dogfight just inland of Calais, leaving the rearmost machine 'smoking violently and apparently on fire'. He then turned north but was chased down to sea level by three more Me 109s, which opened fire as the Spitfire pilot broke hard to port. One of the Germans overshot, White 1 blasting the 109 at point blank range, sending it crashing into the sea. White 1 was then pursued by two more 109s, which he lost, but Pilot Officer Gaze (White 2) was bounced by a *Schwärm* of 109s over Dunkirk. Making a head-on attack, White 2 was unable to see the results of his fire because his windscreen became smothered in oil, probably from a damaged 109.

'Captured German 205mm gun, El Hamma' (JA Estate).

WING COMMANDER HOWARD FRIZELLE 'BILLY' BURTON

Air Vice-Marshal Broadhurst briefing pilots at 239 Wing at their desert base, 26 March 1943, prior to the Anglo-American assault on the Mareth Line (JA Estate).

Sergeant Macbeth became separated from 145 Squadron over St Omer – codename the 'Big Wood' – and came under attack from a 109, which he managed to evade and fire a fleeting burst at. *Oberfeldwebel* Luders of 6/JG26 was attacked by Flying Officer Machacek of 145 Squadron, and Squadron Leader Burton; the latter reported that:

> Just after take-off my hood came adrift and I landed, had it fixed in about ten minutes and endeavoured to catch up the wing. Climbed to 20,000ft over Dungeness, could see no sign of Wing so dived and patrolled speedboat with two other Spitfires, about ten miles east of Dover. About 1220 hrs our fighters started to come in and I suddenly noticed two Me 109s crossing the coast NE of Dover. I then saw one Spitfire attacking. I joined in and we cut off one Me 109; the other one quickly disappeared. We dived and zoomed for several minutes overland between Dover and Manston, alternately engaging E/A with quarter and beam attacks. Finally, E/A opened hood and baled out. His machine crashed into a railway embankment and blew up. Pilot landed safely and was made prisoner by a civilian. I personally cannot be sure which Spitfire pilot was responsible for destroying the E/A. It appeared that he was hardly damaged at all when he baled out. The other Spitfire attacking was of 145 Squadron, SO-D.

Wing Commander Burton walking in, carrying parachute, after his forced-landing in the desert (JA Estate).

Churchill's aircraft during the Prime Minister's visit to the western desert, February 1943 (JA Estate).

The enemy fighter was confirmed as destroyed and shared between the two Spitfire pilots.

Three days later, the Tangmere Wing participated in a Circus raid to Lille, Billy later commenting in his log book: 'Odd squirt here and there at 109s which disappear downwards at fantastic speeds. Majority appear to be 109Fs.'

Many years later, Squadron Leader Burton's young wife, Jean (the now late Mrs Jean Allom), reflected upon those heady days of high summer:

> Now, looking back over half a century later, I realise that there is always the temptation to view the events of summer through rose-tinted spectacles, but even allowing for this and the undisputed effect of time on one's memory, I cannot

Churchill meeting WDAF personnel – Wing Commander Burton in forage cap (JA Estate).

reflect upon the summer of 1941 as anything but a succession of beautiful English sunny days, such as one would long for in peacetime.

However, in wartime, from the RAF wife's point of view, it would prove to be the reverse. After the gallant defensive fighting of the previous summer, 1941 was the start of Fighter Command taking the war to the enemy, so those sweeps over France and occupied territories were mostly conducted from airfields in southern England, including Tangmere. Thus, nearly every day the wonderful weather presented yet another chance of risk to life or limb for my husband, so for me bad weather, a day without flying, was always something to be thankful for.

Wing Commander Douglas Bader chose to lead the Tangmere Wing and fly with 616, Billy's Squadron. They were great friends despite the gap in age and seniority, but no doubt their mutual Cranwell background played a part in this. On 9 May 1941, 616 Squadron moved to Westhampnett. I had spent a very cold and snowy winter up at Kirton, so I was delighted to be back in warmer climes and to find lodgings in a large country house in Lavant; from the bottom of the garden, I had a ringside seat of the squadron taking off and landing. I could thus approximately gauge the time 616 would return from a sweep and station myself in the garden anxiously and hopefully awaiting the safe return of Billy's Spitfire, QJ-K. Although this was to prove a somewhat stressful occupation, the relief when I saw those familiar aircraft letters on landing was well worth it.

I was, of course, liable to be called up for war work, but as luck would have it I was invited to drive a mobile canteen in the Goodwood area. The canteen catered for the needs of the many army units in the area, largely ack-ack posts, and Westhampnett airfield, which of course meant visiting 616 Squadron, which I would otherwise have been unable to do!

I had already met Douglas Bader and his wife, Thelma, the previous summer in Norfolk, and during the summer of 1941 got to know then really well, largely due to their generous open-house entertaining at the Bay House, Aldwick, in the evenings, to which Billy and I, together with other members of the wing, were often invited. It was a friendship which lasted until the Baders' deaths, and one I valued greatly.

Owing to the demanding routine of operational flying day after day, organised social events were a rarity. Only one such evening stands out in my memory, a dance held at Shopwyke House, the Officers' Mess, when hospitality was of a pre-war standard. I recall thinking that as the band played *We'll gather lilacs* that the atmosphere was reminiscent of the famous ball in Brussels on the eve of Waterloo; behind all the glitter, the reality of war was uncomfortably close as the wing would soon be in action again.

The rest of the summer passed swiftly by, Billy with little respite from ops, me driving the mobile canteen and snatching what little time we could together.

On 4 July 1941, Circus 32 targeted the chemical plant at Chocques, the Tangmere Wing orbiting St Omer. Pilot Officer Johnson and Sergeant Morton, both of 616 Squadron, each damaged a 109. Wing Commander Bader reported that he had:

Intercepted one Me 109F some miles south of Gravelines at 14,000ft, while with a section of four. Turned on to its tail and opened fire with a short, one second burst at about 150 yards.

Right: Wing Commander Burton (left) in the western desert with Prince Bernhardt of the Netherlands, himself a trained Spitfire pilot, and Air Vice-Marshal Broadhurst (JA Estate).

Below: Officers of the WDAF at Castel Benito, Tripoli, in January 1943 with Air Chief Marshal Sir Keith Park (seated, third left, AOC Egypt), Air Vice-Marshals Sir Arthur Coningham (seated, centre), and Air Vice-Marshal Broadhurst. Wing Commander Burton is back row, extreme left (JA Estate).

I found it very easy to keep inside him during the turn and closed quite quickly. I gave him three more short bursts, the final one at about twenty yards range; as he slowed down very suddenly, I nearly collided with him. I did not see the result except one puff of smoke half way through. Squadron Leader Burton in my Section watched the complete combat and saw the Me 109's airscrew slow right down to ticking over speed. As I broke away the 109 did not half-roll and dive but just sort of fell away in a sloppy fashion, quite slowly, as though the pilot had been hit. Having broken away I did not again see the 109 I attacked, since I was trying to collect my Section together. I am, however, satisfied that I was hitting him and so is Squadron Leader Burton, from whose evidence this report is written.

On the second operation of 23 July 1941, Squadron Leader Burton led the Tangmere Wing, escorting bombers attacking a tanker off Ostend. II/JG 26 intercepted the Beehive, and in the whirling combat, Squadron Leader Turner and Sergeant Grant of 145 Squadron claimed 109s destroyed, and over the target 610 Squadron drove off several Me 109s. Three Blenheims were shot down over France, however, and a fourth, which was lagging behind on the return journey, crashed into the sea off Deal. Wing Commander Bader reported that:

Took off from Manston with Squadron Leader Burton at approximately 1340 hrs, after 242 Squadron on the expedition to bomb ship off Dunkirk. The weather was very hazy from about 1,000ft upwards but clearer below. We flew from North Foreland and near Gravelines were attacked by a Me 109 out of the sun. We countered and Squadron Leader Burton had a shot at it. It flew low over the water to the French coast. We carried on up to Dunkirk and slightly past where we saw some flak and then a Spitfire (squadron markings XT) flying straight for home in a dive, being attacked by a Me 109. We immediately turned on the Me 109 which saw us and did a left-hand climbing turn back to France, but I got a very close short burst (half a second) at him from underneath and behind him. It definitely hit him and produced a puff of white smoke under his cockpit. I turned away immediately as I had no idea how many were about and did not want to lose Squadron Leader Burton. I claim this Messerschmitt as damaged but would like information from 242 Squadron who told me on landing back at Manston that they had seen two Me 109s go into the sea in that area. We flew back to Manston after this and landed among 242 Squadron, who arrived back at the same time. I claim a damaged aircraft just around Dunkirk out to sea, which may be a destroyed one. I never saw this Messerschmitt after breaking away because visibility was poor.

Squadron Leader Burton's log book records of that sortie, 'Two squirts. Found 109 beating up a Spitfire. Sent 109 quickly back to France.'

By now, the pressure was beginning to tell, even on the Tangmere Wing's swashbuckling leader. Towards the end of July 1941, Wing Commander 'Sailor' Malan, Biggin Hill's Wing Leader, recognised in himself the signs of exhaustion, and, realising the negative implications for those he led, asked to be rested. At Tangmere Wing Commander Bader's wife, Thelma, and friends urged this human dynamo to take a break from operations, but in his thirst for continual action this he would not do. Inevitably, on 9 August 1941, it all went wrong. During another escort sortie, the Tangmere Wing was led into a trap and ambushed by a large force of Me 109s. In the ensuing combat, involving over seventy fighters at close-range, Wing Commander Bader was shot down, the evidence suggests accidentally, by 616 Squadron's Flight Lieutenant 'Buck' Casson, and captured. It was a body-blow to the Tangmere Wing, which continued daily sweeps over France under the leadership of Wing Commander C.A. 'Paddy' Woodhouse.

On 5 September 1941, there was cause for celebration when Squadron Leader Burton's DFC was gazetted, the citation for which read:

> This officer has led his squadron with commendable skill and coolness. He has participated in fifty-four sorties over enemy territory during which he has assisted in the destruction of two Messerschmitt 109s, probably destroyed a Heinkel and damaged a further two enemy aircraft. Squadron Leader Burton has on all occasions proved an inspiration to his unit.

It was a well-earned award, and due recognition for Billy's efforts in transforming 616 Squadron into one of the most confident and combat experienced squadrons in Fighter Command.

Jean Allom:

> On 1 October 1941, Billy was at last taken off operations and posted to 11 Group HQ as 'Squadron Leader Tactics'. He hated leaving 616 Squadron, but it was obvious to all that he was desperately tired, and after that long summer of operational flying, he badly needed a rest.
>
> I piled our few worldly goods into his little Morris Minor [sic] and set off for Uxbridge to try and find us somewhere to live. Tangmere was now in the past, but that summer remains among my most vivid memories, perhaps because it was the first and last that Billy and I were ever to spend together.

Although now a staff officer, Squadron Leader Burton still flew regularly. On 2 October 1941, for example, he was at Boscombe Down, testing Spitfire W3228, which, his log book records, was 'Fitted with negative "G" carbs'. Two days later, he flew Spitfire R7120 from Boscombe Down to Northolt, 'Testing pressure cabin, reached 39,000ft without trouble.' On 12 October 1941, Billy flew a Bell Aerocobra American fighter, which he concluded was 'quite a pleasant machine'. The Hurricane features prominently in his log book throughout this period, flying 'liaison trips' around England from Northolt. On 11 February 1942, however, Billy was posted to command RAF Hawkinge, near Folkestone; Fighter Command's closest airfield to the enemy, just twenty-two miles away across the Channel. On 16 February 1942, he flew a Tiger Moth for thirty minutes on an unspecified sortie, and two days later

Above and below: Wrecked German aircraft in Tunisia after the Anglo-American victory (JA Estate).

recorded being 'Posted overseas to Java.' Things were going very badly indeed for Britain in the Far East, this being at the time of the fall of Singapore – the greatest defeat in the proud history of the British Army. On 14 March 1942, however, the posting was cancelled, and instead Billy was 'Posted to command Hunsdon', an airfield in Hertfordshire where he flew a twin-engine Boston III bomber, a Defiant and a Spitfire on an 'air test'. That posting was also short-lived, though, as a few days later, Squadron Leader Burton was posted to HQ RAF Middle East. It would prove a significant posting.

The 'Middle East', so far as the military were concerned, stretched from the western Libyan desert to the Red Army's left-flank in Persia, north to the Balkans and south to Central Africa – and being oil-rich and providing shipping access via the Suez Canal from the Indian Ocean to the Mediterranean, was of great strategic importance. The war arrived in these lands when Mussolini's Italy entered the war as an Axis Power on 10 June 1940. Thereafter it became a matter of advance and retreat in the Libyan desert as territory was gained but lost, and British forces were driven from Greece and Crete. The British, however, held the tiny island of Malta, between the North African coast and Sicily, providing a crucial base in the Mediterranean from which enemy supply routes could be harassed by sea and air. An Italian air force and army had been destroyed in Cyrenaica, another in Abyssinia, and the British controlled the Red Sea and, therefore,

Wing Commander Burton (seated, centre) with his officers of 239 Wing HQ, March 1943. Squadron Leader O.V. 'Pedro' Hanbury DSO DFC is front row, second right (JA Estate).

the vital Suez Canal. The region was the responsibility of HQ, RAF Middle East, based in Cairo, to which Squadron Leader Burton was now posted.

When war broke out in the Middle East, RAF squadrons in theatre remained there, reinforced by units of Commonwealth air forces, Free French and Hellenic squadrons, and the Royal Yugoslav Air Force. Ultimately, this collectively represented a powerful air force under overall RAF control – and control of the air was vital. The campaign became, therefore, a battle for airfields – and while the RAF remained in Egypt, there were great swathes of the Mediterranean it was unable to cover, leaving shipping vulnerable to attack. That is why it was vital for the Allies to advance westwards, through the western desert, and eventually seize Tunisia. By early February 1942, however, the British had been driven back by Rommel's Afrika Korps to Gazala, half way between Cairo and Tunisia. One of the problems faced by the Desert Air Force at this time was that its fighters were largely Hurricanes and other obsolete types, although the Curtiss Tomahawk had started re-equipping DAF fighter squadrons from June 1941 onwards. This was an American-built, single-seater, single-engine, all-metal fighter, which, lacking a two-stage supercharger, lacked real high-altitude fighting ability and therefore unsuitable for the air war in north-west Europe. By February 1942, the more powerful Curtiss P-40 Kittyhawk was increasingly equipping DAF squadrons, although this too lacked high-altitude ability. The P-40 was, however, effective against the Axis air forces over the western desert and became the DAF's primary fighter. It was a stable gun platform and of rugged construction, performing well in the harsh desert conditions – and the sand, of course, got absolutely everywhere. From 26 May 1942, however, the Kittyhawk squadrons began operating as fighter-bombers – 'Kittybombers' – in the close support role. It was now that the work of the DAF AOC, Air Vice-Marshal Sir Arthur Coningham, paid off in creating, according to the official history, 'a new kind of air power, trained in cooperation with land and sea forces, flexible for attack and defence, designed to control the air over North Africa and the Mediterranean'. Such tactical air power was, of course, central to Germany's Blitzkrieg tactics, which it had perfected by 1940. Despite having previously neglected the art, the nature of the war in the western desert meant that by 1942, the RAF had rapidly risen to equal the *Luftwaffe's* delivery of close air support. It was at the sharp end of this, in fact, that Billy Burton would soon find himself.

Squadron Leader Burton reached Cairo, via India, on 30 June 1942. The following month, serving on Coningham's staff as a liaison officer, Billy flew communications aircraft, including the Audax, Anson, Lysander, Proctor, and even a Blenheim Mk IV bomber, around the command. The pattern continued into September 1942, Billy flying a Kittyhawk for the first time (AL638) for an hour on 22 September, from Helwan to Ballah. On 7 October, he spent another hour aloft in a Kittyhawk (AK741), during which he 'Tried out two spins from which I had no trouble in recovering. Also tried out loop, but stalled on top.' On 22 October 1942, Billy flew a Hurricane Mk IIC, 'and fired cannons for practice'. That month, promoted to Acting Wing Commander, Billy had been posted to the recently formed 212 Group, commanded by Battle of Britain survivor Group Captain H.A. 'Jimmy' Fenton, who had previously commanded 243 Wing. In August 1942, Fenton had formed his new Group 'from scratch', which comprised two Hurricane-equipped wings, 243, a SAAF wing, and a Greek squadron, the intention being that the 212 Group would participate in the forthcoming British Eighth Army's break-out and advance from the Alamein Line. Based in the desert near Alex, Fenton had to:

> assemble staff, design and build a mobile operations room, acquire the necessary equipment, establish operational procedures, and ensure that the twelve squadrons, some newly arrived from England, were 'genned-up' and trained in the tactics we had developed. It was the first time such training was possible, as until then it had developed directly from operations. In my Group HQ, the Signals Officer occupied a key position, and I was given three experienced Wing Commanders, all of whom I knew already, to take turns in directing the day's operations. They were Billy Burton, Dudley Honour and Gerry Edge. They arrived in time to help turn the Ops Room into a going concern.

It was good experience.

In November 1942, Wing Commander Burton was posted away from 212 Group HQ and given command of 243 Wing, based at Gambut. This formation comprised 1 Squadron SAAF, and 33, 213 and 238 Squadrons RAF, all equipped with the Hurricane Mk IIC, armed with four 20mm cannon – and very much focused on the ground-attack role. Having flown over Dunkirk, during the Battle of Britain, and on the relentless offensive operations over France in 1941, this was beyond Wing Commander Burton's experience to date. Typically, he lost no time in familiarising himself with this new weapon and tactic, practising cannon-firing on 'an old car', 'a ship', and 'strafing practice with 213'. With 238 Squadron, the new Wing Leader practised 'flight formation', and 'jumping' these Hurricanes. Just one month later, however, Billy moved on again, succeeding Wing Commander G.D.L. Haysom DFC in command of 239 Wing, based at Marble Arch. This

One of the two Hudsons flying a group of senior RAF officers home on leave in May 1943, snapped by Wing Commander Burton (JA Estate).

was 212 Group's other fighter wing, equipped with P-40 Kittyhawks and formed of 3 and 450 Squadrons RAAF, 5 Squadron SAAF, and 112, 250 and 260 Squadrons RAF. The wing had been heavily engaged in the desert campaign, and Billy was immediately leading his new command on bomber and fighter-bomber escort sorties, and operating in the fighter-bomber role.

After the second Battle of El Alamein (23 October – 11 November 1942), the siege of Tobruk was lifted and the Axis forces began a fighting retreat west to Tunisia. Among the battered enemy formations after Tobruk was the Italian 132nd Armoured Division 'Ariete', which had been all but destroyed, the name thereafter applying to a rag-taggle task force. There was no respite, however, because on 9 January 1943, Wing Commander Burton recorded in his log book that he had flown a 'Kitty II' twice that day, 'Bombing Ariete Division with 500lbs', three more identical sorties following over the next three days. On 13 January 1943, 239 Wing, led by Billy, attacked a German landing ground in the desert, escorted Bostons the next day and flew an 'offensive sweep' on the next. Further sweeps followed, with Billy leading Kittyhawk fighters on 18 January 1943, covering the 'Kittybombers' of 250 and 260 Squadrons, which were 'bombing and strafing enemy motor transport concentrations near Tarhuna'. During that operation, Billy recorded in his log having destroyed an Me 109, the pilot of which was seen to bale out, and on 21 January 1943, while leading the wing on a sweep, attacked four Italian Macchi 202 Folgore fighters. Two days later, the Eighth Army entered Tripoli after an advance of over 1,400 miles, possibly the greatest single advance in military history – made possible through tactical air power. By 24 January 1943, 239 Wing was based at Castel Benito, from where Billy led the wing's 'first Kitty fighter-bomber raid on Tunisia', an attack on Ben Gardan airfield.

The pursuit, however, went on, as the Axis forces continued west, towards the Mareth Line, Billy leading his 239 Wing on numerous further 'bombing', 'strafing' and 'road attacks'. On 30 January 1943, for example, air support was called for by army units to deal with a German 88mm gun located in a 'strong point', which Billy led 'Kittybombers' to successfully destroy. On 3 February 1943, Billy bombed barges and strafed a seaplane, attacking dispersed enemy vehicles two days later, on which sortie the Wing Leader 'Encountered one Me 109. No result'. On that day's second operation, 'Bombing Motor Transport in Ben Garden area, jumped by six 109s. No luck.' Such attacks, on retreating panzer formations, were a daily occurrence – and Billy led all of them – leading to a Bar for Billy's existing DFC, the citation for which, gazetted on 23 February 1943, read:

> Since he assumed command of the wing in December, 1942, this officer has taken part in nearly all its sorties. On one

Gibraltar snapped by Wing Commander Burton during his final homeward bound flight. (JA Estate)

occasion, the formation was attacked by a very large force of enemy fighters, 1 of which Wing Commander Burton shot down. He has displayed great keenness and devotion to duty.

On 26 February 1943, Wing Commander Burton destroyed a 109 during another bombing commitment – which, according to the 239 Wing ORB, 'flew into a hill, in flames'. It would be Billy's final combat claim, bringing his tally to two and four shared destroyed, one probable, one and one shared damaged. By now, Billy had substantial experience of air fighting and close air support, having led a flight, squadron, and a wing, in addition to having served tours on headquarters' staffs. This marked him out as one of the most experienced and able young officers in the service.

The Allied success in North Africa brought about structural changes to the DAF. What was now known as the 'Western Desert Air Force' became a sub-command of Coningham's Northwest African Tactical Air Force, and in February 1943, Air Vice-Marshal Harry Broadhurst, a highly respected and accomplished fighter pilot and leader, arrived in North Africa to become the WDAF's first commander. That month also saw creation of Mediterranean Air Command, with that exemplary airman and officer Air Chief Marshal Sir Arthur Tedder in overall command of all Allied air forces in the Mediterranean Theatre. Wing Commander Burton and 239 Wing, though,

Air Vice-Marshal Broadhurst sleeping during the long flight home (JA Estate).

remained more concerned with continually flying operations, bomber escorts, bombing and strafing the retreating enemy. Now, Allied air forces were flying in support of Operation PUGILIST, the Eighth Army's frontal assault on the Mareth Line, a defensive position constructed by the French in southern Tunisia, behind which the Axis forces had withdrawn, which began on 19 March 1943. On 26 March 1943, the British attacked again, breaking through the Tebaga Gap during Operation SUPERCHARGE, forcing the exhausted enemy to withdraw a further thirty-seven miles to the North.

On 30 March 1943, *The Times* reported that:

> Two Western Desert fighter pilots have been awarded the DSO in recognition of brilliantly executed attacks on German tanks and armoured vehicles which were holding up the advance of troops attacking the Mareth Line. Both officers – Wing Commander H.F. Burton of Ashstead, Surrey, and Squadron Leader Weston Burt, of Southampton, are twenty-six years old and both were cadets at Cranwell in 1935.
>
> Wing Commander Burton led a flight of Spitfires against the *Luftwaffe* during the Dunkirk evacuation and again in the Battle of Britain. Later, he commanded a fighter squadron under Wing Commander Bader. He came to the Western Desert just before

the battle of El Alamein, and in December took over the largest fighter wing in the desert. 'The most interesting feature of our work', he said, 'has been the ever closer and more direct support we are giving the army. What began as patrols over our forward troops and bombing targets well behind the enemy lines has gradually come to include similar attacks in the course of battle, when opposing ground forces are sometimes almost on top of each other. Our job is getting more specialised every day. We must be able to distinguish at a glance silhouettes of our own and enemy tanks and armoured cars. We must be familiar with military formations and tactics: we must be able to spot well dug-in enemy gun emplacements and then destroy them.'

Squadron Leader Weston Burt joined his present squadron early this month. He went to the assistance of the Fighting French post at Ksar Ghilane and led the squadron in an attack which left the ground strewn with flaming enemy tanks and vehicles.

The Runnymede Memorial, on which Wing Commander Burton is commemorated.

WING COMMANDER HOWARD FRIZELLE 'BILLY' BURTON

The late Mrs Jean Allom, photographed in 1996, with the flying jacket of her late first husband, Wing Commander HF 'Billy' Burton, reported missing on 3 June 1943.

It had been on 22 March 1943, during a 'Bombing and strafing' commitment, that Billy's Kittyhawks 'Located Hun tanks'. Later that day, Billy flew a Kittyhawk, 'Leading Tank Busters' to attack the enemy armour. These were Squadron Leader Weston Burt's Hurricane Mk IIDs, fitted with a pair of 40mm Vickers cannon, weighing 320lbs apiece and firing a shell weighing 2½lbs – able to penetrate the armour of any panzer in the desert. With the Kittyhawks providing aerial cover, the 'Flying Can Openers' went to work, pulverising German armour threatening to overrun the French garrison. Afterwards, Wing Commander Burton received a signal from the WDAF AOC, Air Vice-Marshal Broadhurst: '6 Squadron's effort today was magnificent and there is no doubt that your contribution was of the first importance. Please accept my thanks and congratulations.'

Billy's DSO followed immediately, the citation reading: 'Wing Commander Burton is the commanding officer of an exceptionally successful wing. Recently, he has taken part in several sorties involving low level attacks on heavy armoured fighting vehicles. His brilliant leadership has contributed in a large measure to the great success achieved.'

The French were equally appreciative, Air Chief Marshal Bouscat, Chief of the Free French Air Staff, mentioned Wing Commander Burton DSO DFC* in dispatches:

> Wing Commander Burton personally led his Wing's operations over Kasr Ghilane with his customary skill and decisiveness. His squadron conducted a very low-level attack on enemy forces to devastating effect, confronting a potent and accurate anti-air defence. During one sortie, one element of the forces at Wing Commander Burton's disposal, operating without cover, attacked and destroyed a large number of enemy planes. He lost six of his pilots during these operations. Through his

leadership and personal example, Wing Commander Burton made a significant contribution to his Wing's success in these operations.

The citation included the award of the Croix de Guerre with Etoile de Vermeil.

It was great recognition, but the fighting continued; on both 23 and 24 March 1943, Billy's log records: 'Strafing. Hit by flak'. On 29 March, on another ground-attack sortie, Billy's 'Kitty' was again hit by flak, this time forcing him to land near El Kamma – fortunately without injury.

In April 1943, the Allied air forces unleashed Operation FLAX, which severed Rommel's supply line into North Africa. Wisely, the 'Desert Fox' believed that the remnants of his once much-vaunted Afrika Korps should now be evacuated to Italy, and made ready to fight again. Hitler rejected this and so, after the Allied ground offensives, Operations VULCAN and STRIKE, on 13 May 1943 Axis forces in Tunisia finally surrendered unconditionally, bringing the fighting in North Africa to an end. Without doubt, the Allied air forces had been the primary factor in achieving that victory, preparing the way for what followed in Sicily, Italy and north-west Europe. With that kind of experience behind him, equally beyond question is the fact that Wing Commander Billy Burton could look forward to playing a key role in the continuing air war. Sadly, it was not to be.

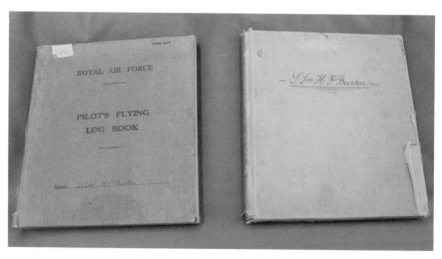

Wing Commander Burton's log books, preserved at the RAF College, Cranwell.

WING COMMANDER HOWARD FRIZELLE 'BILLY' BURTON

The 1936 Cranwell Sword-of-Honour presented to Flight Cadet Burton, now preserved at RAF Cranwell and displayed in the library – the only such blade inscribed with the name of Edward VIII.

After the Allied victory in Tunisia, on 18 May 1943, Wing Commander Burton left 239 Wing at El Adem, and with other officers, including Air Vice-Marshal Broadhurst and Squadron Leader Osgood 'Pedro' Hanbury DSO DFC, another Battle of Britain survivor and fighter ace, returned to England aboard an unarmed Lockheed Hudson transport aircraft, via Gibraltar. The journey was for a well-deserved home leave, during which Squadron Leader Hanbury and Wing Commander Burton attended a luncheon at RAF Kenley, now commanded by Group Captain Jimmy Fenton, formerly of WDAF 212 Group. The occasion was to celebrate the first DSO for Kenley's Wing Leader – none other than Wing Commander Johnnie Johnson, who had previously served under Billy as a lowly pilot officer in 616 Squadron. Afterwards, it was back to North Africa…

Early on 3 June 1943, Wing Commander Burton and the following officers, all returning from home leave, gathered at RAF Portreath, in Cornwall, ready for their return flight to North Africa:

Wing Commander Paul Temple Cotton DFC, a reconnaissance pilot and staff officer attached to 216 Group (31).

Wing Commander Jack Goodhead, an operations officer with 117 Squadron (27).

Squadron Leader Osgood Villiers 'Pedro' Hanbury DSO DFC, also on the staff of 216 Group (25).

Squadron Leader John Kenneth Young MBE, an Ops 'B' Controller with No 1 Overseas Aircraft Delivery Unit (37).

Squadron Leader Eric Paul of the RAAF, an Air Observer with 216 Group (33).

Flight Lieutenant John Bowyer Buckley RCAF, a pilot in 216 Group (21).

The aircraft concerned, Hudson VI FK386 of No 1 OADU, 44 Group, Transport Command, was to be flown by the CO of 117 Squadron,

Group Captain Robert Gordon Yaxley (31) a pre-war officer who had been awarded the MC for his actions during the Arab revolt in Palestine during 1936. During the Second World War he had first commanded a squadron, then a wing, of Beaufighters engaged in anti-shipping strikes, earning a DFC, before receiving the first DSO awarded during the campaign in Libya. Yaxley's navigator was Flying Officer James McSherry (23), a New Zealander, his Wireless Operator/Air Gunner Pilot Officer Dennis Victor Edwards (23).

Jean Allom: 'In actual fact, there were unofficially two Group Captains aboard, as while Billy was in England, Broadhurst had told him of his promotion and to put up his fourth stripe.'

The problem, though, was that since 1 May 1943, there had been increased enemy fighter activity over the Bay of Biscay, as the Ju 88Cs of V/KG 40 provided cover for U-Boats entering and leaving their bases on the French Atlantic coast – making the Bay dangerous airspace indeed. Especially in daylight. And for some unfathomable reason, Group Captain Yaxley decided to make the trip by day. The first leg was to refuel at Gibraltar, which meant passing over the Bay in daylight, before continuing to 249 (Transport) Wing's base at Castel Benito, Tripoli. Wing Commander Burton DSO, DFC and Bar, Croix de Guerre, was the most decorated officer aboard – but as he was officially an acting Group Captain, Yaxley was the senior officer; Jean Allom:

> I understand that Billy tried to do everything possible to dissuade Yaxley, but the latter, the more senior man, insisted upon doing so – with disastrous consequences. It is impossible to understand why such an experienced officer as Yaxley took such a foolhardy course of action.
>
> In retrospect, there seems to have been doom hanging over this flight as the Hudson should never have been flying that day – it was due to return several days earlier. The delay was caused by those servicing the aircraft discovering some desert insects therein, and so it had to be fumigated. Of course, the date on which the flight was to return to Gibraltar was then scheduled to take place, 3 June 1943, was one on which there was maximum *Luftwaffe* activity over the Bay of Biscay. Only two days before, in fact, a Dakota had been shot down over the Bay – all aboard were lost, including the actor Leslie Howard.

Yaxley took off from Portreath at 0737 hrs on the day in question, and, perhaps inevitably considering the high level of enemy air activity, was

Wing Commander Burton's impressive medal group, preserved and displayed at RAF Cranwell, his logs, sword and medals having been presented to the RAF College by his widow, the now late Mrs Jean Allom.

intercepted and shot down over the Bay of Biscay by a 14/KG 40 Ju 88C, flown by *Leutnant* Heinz Olbrecht. The defenceless and doomed Hudson crashed into the Atlantic – with the loss of all aboard: two fighter aces, one a Wing Leader, and officers between them decorated with three DSOs, six DFCs, a MC, an MBE and a Croix de Guerre. It was a dreadful loss and blow to the WDAF. Perhaps saddest of all is the fact that Squadron Leader Hanbury, one of the Few with over ten aerial victories, had got married while on leave – and would never meet his son, born nine months later.

It was not until 7 June 1943 that Jean received the official telegram notifying her that Billy was missing, although a subsequent letter from the Casualty Branch pointed out that 'This does not necessarily mean that he is killed or wounded, and if he is a prisoner of war he should be able to communicate with you in due course.' That was, however, a forlorn hope.

On 10 July 1943, Air Vice-Marshal Broadhurst wrote to 'My Dear Mrs Burton':

> I will report what little I know of this affair.
> First of all I would like to say how dreadfully sorry I am about the whole business and to offer you the deepest sympathy of all of us in the Desert Air Force.
> Billy had done a magnificent job of work with us and there is no doubt that he was cut out to be a 'Big Chief' in the RAF.
> I left in the first of the two aeroplanes to go … The other arrived at their departure aerodrome and from all the evidence

I have it was Yaxley who decided to go through in daylight. Had I been with them I would never have allowed it. At first, I thought as you did, that they had been routed by day but I have been assured since that it was Yaxley's decision and I am not at all sure that he did not insist. It really is a deplorable business, and much as I would like to tell you otherwise, I cannot hold out any hope of Billy being alive. It sounds a dreadful thing to say but I think it would be cruel to give you any hope when I have none myself.

I hope you will believe me when I say how sorry I am. I counted myself a friend of his and had a great admiration for him, as indeed the whole Force had. I'm so glad that you

Wing Commander Burton's flying jacket.

had that time at home with him – I know he had enjoyed every moment of it and by God he had earned it. I hope we meet when I am at home.

On 13 June 1944, Jean, now a war widow, attended an investiture at Buckingham Palace to proudly receive her late husband's DSO and Bar to his DFC. Putty medals were little consolation, however, for a life so nobly lived but lost in such foolhardy circumstances. By that time, the Allied armies had landed in Normandy and were advancing eastwards to Germany itself. The groundwork for the Allied close air support that characterised the successful Normandy campaign had been worked out in North Africa – and Wing Commander Billy Burton was at the forefront of that pioneering and dangerous flying. Indeed, after the German surrender in North Africa, the Allies looked to Sicily and Italy, both of which, in due course, were invaded and taken. Again, close air support played a huge part in these similarly successful campaigns, and so the work of the DAF and WDAF cannot be underestimated. Had Billy Burton not been lost over the Bay of Biscay that fateful day, ironically to a comparatively inexperienced German pilot, as a Group Captain he would have become a group commander and continued climbing the ladder to become, as Air Vice-Marshal Broadhurst wrote, a 'Big Chief' – perhaps even Chief of the Air Staff.

In 1947, the authorities officially concluded that those reported missing aboard Group Captain Yaxley's Hudson had been 'lost at sea'. All are commemorated on the Air Forces Memorial at Runnymede, which records the names of over 20,000 men and women of the British and Commonwealth air forces who have no known grave.

Although Jean later found happiness and remarried, it is true to say that the tragic losses of both her beloved brother, Flying Officer Duncan Robertson, and husband, Wing Commander Billy Burton – who was 26 years old – were never far away. Indeed, as Jean wrote in 1996, 'Even after more than fifty years I can hardly bear to think of them trapped in an unarmed aircraft with no means of defence, when one considers the many deeds of gallantry those aboard had performed.'

Further words would be superfluous.

Chapter Two

Group Captain
Thomas Percy Gleave CBE FRHistS

Thomas Percy Gleave was born on 6 September 1908 in Liverpool, the second son of Arthur and Amy Catherine Gleave, joining elder brother Howard and three sisters, Amy, Olive and Adeline. The family owned a tannery, which provided well enough for 'Tom' to be privately educated at Westminster High School and Liverpool Collegiate School. Indeed, in 1924 he joined the Sefton Tanning Company, which was the family owned business, although more out of loyalty than desire. Many years later, in 1991, Tom's sister Amy, by then his only surviving sibling, recalled Tom's boyhood fascination with aeroplanes and that aviation was always his first love. It was no surprise, therefore, that as a young adult Tom pursued this passion, and in 1927 became a founder member of the Merseyside Flying Club. On 6 July 1929, Tom was awarded his 'A' Licence, his mother having funded the lessons necessary to turn his lifelong dream of being a pilot into reality. Aviation remained a hobby though, and as Tom himself later wrote, he spent 'six years of his life making leather, with flying as a side-line'.

In the summer of 1929, the adventurous and intrepid young Tom travelled to Canada, joining the Beardmore Tanning Company in Ontario and continuing to fly, with the Toronto Flying Club. Although Tom wanted to become a full-time pilot, his father considered flying too dangerous, encouraging his son to remain in the family business, but eventually relented when Tom applied to join the Canadian air force – with one condition: that he return home and join the Royal Air Force. Consequently, Tom returned to England in 1930, successfully applied for a Short Service Commission and in September that year became Acting Pilot Officer T.P. Gleave. After a three-week induction at RAF Uxbridge, Tom was off to No 5 Service Flying Training School at Sealand in Flintshire, there to convert to service types. Having successfully completed the course with a rare 'Exceptional' assessment, Pilot Officer Gleave joined No 1 (Fighter) Squadron at Tangmere in September 1931.

This was, of course, the between-the-wars period when the RAF was comparatively small and resembled an elite flying club, the daily routine

Right: Pilot Officer Tom Percy Gleave shortly after joining No 1 Squadron at Tangmere in 1931 (courtesy Thomas Percy Gleave Estate [TPG Estate]).

Below: A young Tom (second left) in sailor suit and with siblings (TPG Estate).

being training flights and inter-squadron competitions in such things as gunnery and aerobatics. At Tangmere, Pilot Officer Gleave joined 'A' Flight, flying such aircraft as the Armstrong Whitworth Siskin and Hawker Fury, which were single-seater, single-engine biplane fighters similar to those of the First World War, and was again given an 'Exceptional' rating. Soon becoming a member of the aerobatic team, on 11 October 1933 the ever-adventurous Tom attempted to become the first man to fly from England to Ceylon. Taking-off that day from Lympne in a civilian registered Simmonds Spartan biplane (G-AAMH), four days later he was 'forced down by a down-draught in the mountains east of Kutahya and Anatolia, Turkey'.

Years later, Tom elaborated on the story, explaining to presenter Michael Aspel on the popular TV show *This Is Your Life* (recorded 7 November 1990), that the record attempt ended when he:

> had to land in a tree! I was in a ravine and had the choice of crashing straight ahead, which would have been curtains, or picking a tree, so I picked a really huge tree, closed my eyes and I finished up on the ground about quarter of an hour later in the fuselage, no wings, nothing else but me. I got out, I was a bit bloody but nothing much, and a pack of dogs belonging to shepherds, about twenty of them, cruel, beastly looking things, came along, and luckily a shepherd appeared and called the dogs off. He offered me some soup, so I went to his tent and had this soup – which nearly killed me! He put me on this mule with my little suitcase, but after about a mile I couldn't stick it, so I put him on the mule and I walked! I was patched up and stayed there for three weeks until my father sent me enough money to come home by train.

Tom also later noted that his nose was 'modified in crash'.

Back home, between February and May 1934, Flight Lieutenant Gleave, as he was by then, attended a flying instructor's course at the Central Flying School, passing out Category B2, and also qualified as an instrument-flying instructor on the Link ground trainer. Afterwards, Tom returned to Sealand, teaching elementary flying and as a 'Fighter Flying Instructor', joining the aerobatic team there and participating in British Empire Air Day displays. By this time, however, Hitler having come to power in Germany the previous year, it was becoming increasingly clear that another war with Germany was likely. Consequently, it was necessary to start expanding the RAF, and one means of doing so was changing over those officers with Short Service Commissions (which lasted for four years of active service before going onto the reserve) to medium-length commissions of up to ten years. For this reason, Tom was able to remain in the air force that year and continue flying. Another initiative aimed at expanding the reserve of trained pilots who could be called-up in the event of war was the University Air Squadrons, and between 19 June – 3 August 1934, Flight Lieutenant Gleave instructed at the Oxford UAS. Interestingly, the unit was commanded by Wing Commander Keith Park – who would go on to high command and great things.

On 16 March 1935, Flight Lieutenant Tom Gleave married Miss Beryl Pitts, whom he had met while with No 1 Squadron at Tangmere, in Chichester. Ominously, on that day Nazi Germany introduced conscription.

The following year would see the RAF beginning to significantly expand under Expansion Scheme 'F', as Britain reluctantly prepared for another war with a belligerent Germany; Tom described his service between 1936 and the eventual outbreak of the Second World War:

> Posted in December 1936 to 502 (Ulster) Special Reserve Squadron as Squadron Flying Instructor. Converted the squadron to Auxiliary status, becoming 502 (Ulster) Bomber Squadron, Auxiliary Air Force. Was reposted as Adjutant and Chief Flying Instructor. Raised to Category A1 as a Flying Instructor on 17 July 1937.

There was also a significant personal event that year: Tom and Beryl's son, John, was born.

Tom continues:

> Promoted to Squadron Leader and posted to HQ Bomber Command as a Staff Officer in connection with Bomber Liaison duties at Fighter Command HQ Operations Room, December 1938. During time at Bomber Command was also employed on writing Pilots' Notes and Maintenance Schedules for bomber aircraft, and drafting Air Sea Rescue plans.

Tom's flying began during the biplane era, Hawker Harts of 1 Squadron seen here over the South coast (TPG Estate).

On 16 March 1935, Flight Lieutenant Gleave married Miss Beryl Pitts in Chichester, the couple having met whilst Tom was stationed at Tangmere (TPG Estate).

On that fateful Sunday, 3 September 1939, when Britain and France declared war on Nazi Germany, Squadron Leader Gleave was 'Posted to Fighter Command for full duties in the Operations Room as Bomber Liaison Officer (one of three). Main duty was identification of returning friendly bombers, until managing to get a squadron on 2 June 1940.'

That day (on which the Dunkirk evacuation concluded), Squadron Leader Gleave arrived at Kirton-in-Lindsay to serve as a 'supernumerary' officer and pilot on 253 Squadron, to gain experience of both the Hurricane and current operational conditions and procedures. At the time, there were many Squadron Leaders serving in non-operational roles, all keen to command a fighter squadron in war. The majority had no operational experience on the new modern fighters, however, and hence the practice of such 'supernumerary' postings. Once familiar with the set-up, these officers would then be posted to their first command. In Tom's case, a week after he arrived at Kirton, the CO of 253 Squadron, Squadron Leader (later Air Marshal Sir) D.F.W. 'Batchy' Atcherley, was promoted to command RAF Castletown – and orders were received that Squadron Leader Gleave was to succeed him in command of 253 Squadron. Consequently, Tom remained with 253 Squadron.

253 had been re-formed at Manston on 30 October 1939, as a fighter squadron, initially operating twin-engine Bristol Blenheims. The following month, however, the squadron re-equipped with Fairey Battle light-bombers. Then, on 15 January 1940, news was received that the squadron was to convert to Hawker Hurricanes; 253's pilots then all spent time in the new type's cockpit, familiarising themselves with the controls and instruments, rehearsed Fighter Command Attacks with model aircraft, and attended daily lectures concerning 'matters relating to Hurricane squadrons'. On 14 February 1940, 253 moved from Manston to Northolt, and on the 22nd, twelve pilots attended a course of Fighter Command Area Attacks and radio procedure at

RAF Uxbridge. By 24 February 1940, sixteen Hurricanes were on charge, enabling 253 to begin an intensive period of flying training. On 27 April 1940, 253 Squadron was declared operational by day and night. In fact, at that time, 253 was the only completely operational fighter squadron at Northolt, and was based in a large 'C' Type Hangar with full office facilities. When Hitler infamously attacked the West on 10 May 1940, 253 Squadron moved to Kenley. Three days later, Green Section of 'B' Flight, comprising three pilots, flew to Merville in France, to reinforce 3 Squadron, followed by the whole of 'B' Flight, on 16 May 1940. Based at Lille-Marcq, two days later Pilot Officer David Owen Nicholas Jenkins (known by his family as 'Nick'), of Green Section, attacked a Do 17 but was hit by return fire and forced to crash-land at Amiens-Glissy – fortunately the young pilot was unhurt. His friend, Sergeant-Pilot Gilbert 'Mac' MacKenzie, however, was not so lucky…

By 19 May 1940, 'B' Flight was operating from Norrent-Fontes, and on that morning one of Green Section's groundcrew, AC1 Fred 'Taff' Powell, inquired of Sergeant MacKenzie how things were going. The 23-year-old pilot's response was discouraging: 'Not good at all.' Before midday, both "Mac" and "B" Flight's commander, Flight Lieutenant H.T.J. Anderson, were shot down and killed by German fighters. On 24 March 1946, an eye-witness to Sergeant MacKenzie's loss, a Mr D.A. Lonie, wrote to the Air Ministry:

> I have been reading of the great RAF hunt for graves of unknown airmen.
>
> I was Signalling Sergeant in the King's Own Royal Regiment's 6th Battalion, in May 1940. We were in a village in northern France named Cysoing when one of our planes engaged the enemy. After bringing one or two of the enemy planes down his own plane got into difficulties and he baled out. The enemy followed and machine-gunned him, and when he landed he was dead. Our men buried him and took particulars. His name was MacKenzie and he was a native of Glasgow. That is all I know, as his papers were put with Battalion HQ. I believe our papers were lost in France and do not think this was reported when we reorganised in England.

Sergeant MacKenzie was indeed buried at Cysoing, and 'Taff' Powell never forget their brief conversation on the morning of the gallant pilot's death – or another image of the unsavoury side of war, when 'Taff' watched several Me 109s hack down a Lysander communications aircraft over France, as if just for the fun of it.

Pilots of 253 Squadron's 'B' Flight at RAF Northolt on 8 May 1940; from left: Pilot Officers Dawbarn, Jeffries, Murch and Clifton; Pilot Officer Corkett is on the shoulders of Jeffries and Clifton, whilst Pilot Officer Jenkins is astride the Hurricane; Flight Lieutenant Anderson, unknown, Sergeants MacKenzie and Marsh, remaining pair unknown (via Lynn Reglar).

On 23 May 1940, Green Section's Pilot Officer Murch was shot-up by Me 109s over Bethune, but managed to limp home across the Channel to crash-land at Hawkinge. Murch was unhurt, but Pilot Officer Ford, shot down in the same engagement, was captured. The following day, 253 Squadron was pulled out of the carnage in France, returning to Kenley. During the Fall of France, the squadron had lost nine Hurricanes, with others damaged, four pilots killed and another captured in a battle already lost. It was a traumatic introduction to air-fighting – but as a consequence, the survivors had accumulated a degree of combat experience, setting them aside from those yet to see action.

At Kirton, Squadron Leader Gleave lost no time in getting to grips with the Hurricane – a very different and more advanced machine than the biplanes he had previously flown. By this time, Tom had 2,302.55 hrs flying time recorded in his log book, the vast majority on biplanes but some hours stooging around in the monoplane Miles Master and Magister communications aircraft. Neither were as powerful as the Hurricane though, and upon arrival at Kirton on 2 June 1940, Tom almost immediately flew Hurricane Mk I N2436 for an hour and five minutes, practising circuits and landings, and L1663 for another hour of 'local' flying. From then on, he flew relentlessly, practising aerobatics, formation-flying and dogfighting in particular. Although on one occasion he practised 'air-to-ground' firing at Sutton Bridge, there was no opportunity for aerial gunnery training – though in 1936, Tom had shown a great aptitude for aerial marksmanship:

At a demonstration at North Coates on 8 June 1936, flying Hawker Fury K3733, I scored 71 per cent hits on a ground target ... At a demonstration at Catfoss on 22 September 1936, flying Audax K5241 solo scored 94 per cent on a towed flag. Believed a record which still stands.

At Kirton, Tom soon concluded that the Hurricane 'was the grandest thing I had ever flown: treated right and properly handled it was a "Pilot's Delight".'

In 1941, as we will see, Tom published a memoir, *I Had A Row With A German*, the original title of which was *Eagles of Nemesis*, under the pseudonym 'RAF Casualty'. In the book, Tom describes his pilots, not just using nicknames as per the published version, but identifies all by name:

Of the two flight commanders, Bill Cambridge [Flight Lieutenant W.P. Cambridge, commander of 'B' Flight] was the tough, rugged, type who went flat-out at work and play and was a magnificent leader; Bruno Brown [Flight Lieutenant G.A. Brown, commander of 'A' Flight] was the quieter of the two, but just as keen and capable and produced an excellent flight. They were from different moulds and had different methods, but hit it off well and got the same results – I was lucky to have them.

Bill's flight included the following:

Flying Officer Wedgewood: He was deputy flight commander. I had known him as a pupil at Sealand and he still retained a great sense of humour. Because of his namesake who had been in the House of Commons, he was known as 'The Colonel'.

Pilot Officer Watts: A newcomer who arrived shortly after I took over, originally with the Fleet Air Arm but converting to fighters. Recently wed, he was nicknamed 'Newly Married'.

Pilot Officer Jenkins: Hailed from St Andrews and had put up a good show in France. Not surprisingly he was known as 'Jenks'.

Pilot Officer Bell-Salter: Escaped from France after destroying his aircraft – for want of petrol. He, too, had put up a good show there. He owned a very much open Austin Seven, and held occasional 'Gladiatorial' ramming contests with another identical 'buzz box' owned by another member of the squadron. The safest grand-stand seat was in one of the aircraft.

Pilot Officers Francis and Carthew: They arrived from a training unit shortly after I took over and quickly nicknamed 'Dopey' and 'Dimmy', which was no reflection on their mental ability – they were just young and inseparable.

Pilot Officer Trueman: A Canadian who was one of the later arrivals. He had been on bombers and was now converting to fighters. He was nicknamed 'Air Commodore Handlebars' because he sported a moustache – a real 'roadster' model – which he constantly twirled at the ends.

Pilot Officers Samolinski and Nowak: Two Polish pilots known as 'Sammy' and 'Knowhow', who arrived shortly after I took over and were great assets to the squadron.

Sergeant Clenshaw: Newly arrived but as keen as the rest.

Sergeant Innes: Had done more flying than the others and was a capable fellow.

Sergeant Dredge: A tall, strapping, fellow with quite a lot of flying to his credit, and a very pleasant type.

Another pilot, Pilot Officer Hemmingway, was posted away shortly after I took over and I was very sorry to lose him.

Bruno's Flight was made up of:

Flying Officer Strang: He was deputy flight commander, a New Zealander, Jack met the Hun in France and he too had put up a good show. He was also good at a party.

Pilot Officer Clifton: With a mop of black curly hair he could not escape the tab of 'Curly'. A tough, vivacious fellow, he owned the other Austin Seven. He too was counted among the 'veterans'.

Pilot Officer Murch: An ultra-efficient young man who had done well in France and in the UK. A great fellow, he was always very correct in all he did, which earned for himself the austere title of 'Group Captain'.

Pilot Officer Greenwood: Another 'veteran' from France. Nothing disturbed him. He should have been tabbed 'Smiler'.

Pilot Officer Corkett: Another survivor from France. Renowned for his ready wit and artistic talents, he had a wonderful philosophy.

In the published version, identities were concealed by just the use of nicknames, and the language used was much more bloodthirsty (and clearly not written by Tom himself). For example, in *I Had A Row With A German* we are told that Flight Lieutenant Bill Cambridge was 'dying to pump lead into the Hun', and that Flying Officer Jack Strang 'had already met the Hun in France and knew what to do with him'. This was an early memoir, published in 1941, and such books were intended to be morale-boosting, and clearly this kind of language is that of propagandists, not fighter pilots – renowned for modesty and under-statement for fear of – God forbid – being accused of 'shooting a line', which is to say boasting.

Interestingly, in his original manuscript Tom refers in personal terms to certain sergeant-pilots, very little mention is made of them in the edited and published version, although whereas brother officers are afforded the intimacy of nicknames, the lowly sergeants are referred to only by surname.

A 253 Squadron Hurricane Mk I at Northolt in May 1940 (via Lynn Reglar).

British society at this time was, of course, hierarchical, and the services reflected this, with officers, NCOs and Other Ranks segregated on the ground, each to their own mess. As Wing Commander George Unwin, a flight sergeant flying Spitfires on 19 Squadron during the Battle of Britain commented, 'Brian Lane, first our flight and then squadron commander, and I were at one in the air, and we flew together most of the time. Although we were friends, because he was an officer and me an NCO, on the ground we never socialised.'

Moving on, while 253 Squadron continued training hard at Kirton, on 10 July 1940 the Battle of Britain began. That was, of course, the date later decided by the Air Ministry, but in truth the fighting over Channel-bound convoys had actually begun on 2 July 1940. This early action involved fighter squadrons from 10 and 11 Groups, while those in 12 Group, further north, remained largely unaffected. On 31 July 1940, 253 Squadron left Kirton, not for southern England but to Turnhouse, near Edinburgh, in 13 Group. At that time, the squadron comprised twenty officers, 199 NCOs and airmen, and had on charge twenty-three Hurricanes and two Battles (the latter used for training). In Scotland, Squadron Leader Gleave and pilots also operated from the satellite airfield at Drem, continuing to train while providing some protection for nearby naval installations. There was, needless to say, little action. Indeed, as Tom later wrote, he only encountered an enemy aircraft 'up North' on one occasion, 3 August 1940. Early that morning, Tom, flying his usual Hurricane, P2960, SW-A, scrambled in company with Pilot Officer Nick Jenkins, soon climbing to 'Angels 20'. 'Ops' then notified the pair of an enemy aircraft approaching from the East. The Hurricane pilots could see nothing, however, until the sun glinted on a tiny speck some 15,000ft above them – a German high-altitude reconnaissance machine. Unfortunately the Hurricane, unlike the Spitfire, was not a high-altitude fighter, frustrating the two RAF pilots. As Tom later commented, 'We returned, disappointed, to the aerodrome, feeling like people who had been cheated at cards. On paper it was a perfect interception as regards course and speed, but height had beaten us.'

By now, the Battle of Britain was increasing in ferocity over southern England, but a promotion rather than a battle, was in the air for Tom, who was notified that he was to become an acting Wing Commander at the HQ of a new Fighter Command Group, 14, which was assuming responsibility for defending northern Scotland and, in particular, the all-important naval base at Scapa Flow in the Orkneys. This was not considered good news by Tom; he knew that at his age, nearly 32, it was unlikely he would be given another operational command at squadron level, and was therefore denied the opportunity to see aerial combat – which, of course, is what Squadron

Above and below: Then & now: Green Section of 253 Squadron's 'B' Flight pictured at Northolt in May 1940. The pilot wearing forage cap, extreme left, is Pilot Officer Jeffries, on right and in tunic is Pilot Officer Murch, and seated at front is Pilot Officer Jenkins (via Lynn Reglar).

Leader Gleave had spent years of his life training and preparing for. There was also a personal reason: such a staff job meant that he would not fulfil a vow he had made to do his 'humble share to rid the earth of one German, even if it cost me my neck'. This was war, and Tom explained the context of this promise after being recalled from leave to Fighter Command HQ when war broke out:

> I drove back ... sad at heart. I felt sorry for those who would soon have to do the same, some for the second time in a lifetime. I thought of my parents; they had had their share of war and had known, what was worse, the aftermath. Now the few years that might still be theirs to spend in peace and security, a fitting end to lives honourably lived, were to be darkened, perhaps ended. I thought of millions like them. I thought of my wife and son going south.

The prospect of leaving 253 Squadron, however, was cushioned by the fact that Tom knew and approved of his successor: Squadron Leader Harold Morley Starr, whom he had previously known as a pupil pilot.

Born in Swindon, Wiltshire, on 8 September 1914, Starr was educated at Clarence Street School there, and later at Cotham Secondary Modern School in Bristol. In March 1934, he took a SSC in the RAF, learning to fly at Sealand before a posting to 13 Army Cooperation Squadron at Old Sarum. On 5 June 1936, however, the engine of his Audax aircraft failed and Starr was seriously injured in the resulting crash at South Marston. So serious were his injuries, in fact, that Flying Officer Starr was expected to die. He survived, but always walked with a slight limp thereafter. He eventually returned to flying on 28 June 1937, joining 59 Squadron, another reconnaissance squadron, flying Hawker Hectors, before a posting to 2 Squadron, operating the Armstrong Whitworth Atlas in the army cooperation role at Hawkinge. Promoted to flight lieutenant in October 1938, the following May he was posted to Uxbridge as a staff officer, returning to 2 Squadron as a flight commander in November 1939. Promoted to Squadron Leader on 1 June 1940, having volunteered for fighters, a month later, Squadron Leader Starr converted to Hurricanes with 6 OTU at Sutton Bridge. Afterwards, on 21 July 1940, he joined 245 Squadron at Aldergrove, flying Hurricanes in the defence of Northern Ireland, in a supernumerary posting. When Tom's number came up for promotion and another staff appointment, Starr was chosen as his replacement and took over 253 Squadron on 10 August 1940.

According to Tom, Squadron Leader Starr was 'a very charming fellow, efficient and full of the right ideas', and 'was overjoyed at receiving his

Amongst 253 Squadron's groundcrew during the Battle of France was Fred Powell, centre (via Lynn Reglar).

first squadron command'. A great consolation to Starr's predecessor was that 253 Squadron 'took to him immediately', reassuring Squadron Leader Gleave that the 'fine fellows' he had previously commanded were in good hands. Tom remained at Turnhouse, handing over to the new CO, where the pair were interviewed by 13 Group AOC, Air Vice-Marshal R.E. 'Birdy' Saul, who informed Squadron Leader Gleave that before taking up his new staff appointment with 14 Group, he would be spending the interim at 13 Group HQ, 'to learn something about operations'. Tom, however, seized the opportunity to argue the case that he 'had already acquired some knowledge of the subject' and 'pleaded with him' for permission to instead remain with 253 Squadron, as supernumerary, for that period of time. The impassioned Squadron Leader explained that he was desperate to meet 'a Hun at close quarters', and felt that, having impressed upon 253 Squadron what they were going to do to the enemy once met, he was otherwise 'slipping off without the opportunity of showing them I was willing to practise what I preached'. Saul agreed to put the matter before the AOC of the new 14 Group, Air Vice-Marshal Henderson, who in due course agreed. As Squadron Leader Starr had no objection, Squadron Leader Gleave remained with 253 Squadron as 'vice', and 'life once again took on a rosy hue'.

On 23 August 1940, Tom was on leave but was recalled: 'Come back immediately.' Upon return to Turnhouse, he discovered that 253 Squadron had been posted to Prestwick, on Scotland's west coast, and that the move had to be completed early the next day. This was no mean feat, and the station became a veritable hive of activity. At Prestwick, life continued much the same for 253 Squadron over the next week, until Tom, having just returned from leave depressed, knowing that his extension of service with 253 Squadron was likely to end any day now, still without having engaged the

Sergeant Gilbert 'Mac' MacKenzie, killed in action 19 May 1940 (Stuart MacKenzie).

enemy, took an unexpected telephone call: 253 Squadron was to fly south the following morning, 29 August 1940, to relieve 615 Squadron at Kenley in 11 Group. Tom could hardly believe his ears – but was told he was not to go but was required at 13 Group HQ. Bereft, Tom implored the Sector Controller 'do something about it', and nothing of 'it' was ever heard again: Squadron Leader Tom Gleave was going to war at last.

RAF Kenley was actually the home station of 615 'County of Surrey' Squadron, an AAF unit flying Hawker Hurricanes. Having been based there since 20 May 1940, after its participation in the Battle of France, 615 had fought hard, during the Channel clashes with which the Battle of Britain had started, the coastal combats of the second phase and – significantly – the opening rounds of the third, the hammering of Fighter Command's airfields in 11 Group. During that time, Kenley had been heavily attacked, especially on 18 August 1940, the so-called 'Hardest Day', when targeted by the low-flying Do 17s of 9/KG 76 in an audacious raid which caused much damage and loss of life. Between 10 July 1940 and when relieved by 253 Squadron on 29 August 1940, 615 Squadron had lost ten Hurricanes destroyed and four more damaged, while five pilots had been killed in action with another succumbing to wounds a day after being shot down, and five more were wounded. With the squadron's last engagement, on 26 August 1940, no less than four Hurricanes had been lost, two of their pilots baling out and being rescued from the sea, while the other pair crash-landed. Clearly, the tempo of combat over south-east England was entirely different to pootling about northern England and Scotland – which was largely 253 Squadron's experience after the Fall of France. The difference, which some squadrons found traumatic upon arrival in the combat zone, was the presence of the lethal Me 109.

On 253 Squadron's last night at Prestwick, there was an air of celebration, the officers inviting the NCOs to their mess for a 'scrum'. A cushion improvised as a rugby ball, and after several vigorous tussles the series was

Sergeant MacKenzie's grave at Cysoing
(via Lynn Reglar).

declared a draw, the party eventually breaking up after 'a final drink'. Considering subsequent events, and the carnage 253 Squadron was about to have visited upon it, one cannot help but be reminded of the Duchess of Richmond's ball in Brussels on the eve of Waterloo…

Tom's book provides us a rich first-hand account – but it must be remembered that it was written for publication in wartime and therefore any comments or observations within could only be buoyant. In it, Tom describes how 253 stopped to refuel at an RAF base en route to Kenley, where they met pilots from 615 Squadron doing likewise before pressing on to Scotland. Tom records that 'They had a lot to tell us, and their experiences did much to make our chaps all the more keen to get down into the battle zone.' Of 253 Squadron's arrival at Kenley, Tom talks of helpful briefings, meeting old friends, and, being 'full of enthusiasm'. At the earliest opportunity after their arrival on 29 August 1940, 253 Squadron 'volunteered to stand-by with a flight, and our offer was accepted, so we made up two sections and stood-by'. While there can be no doubt that the squadron's confidence and morale was high, no mention, for fear of negatively affecting morale, was made in Tom's book of the damage to this proud fighter station caused by the heavy German attacks on 11 Group airfields, which remained ongoing. Bob Morris, however, an 18-year-old Spitfire engine fitter on 66 'Clickety-Click' Squadron, which arrived at Kenley four days after 253, spoke openly in 1995, and described the scene:

> it was an absolute shambles, there was hardly a building left standing. As we drove around the aerodrome to our assembly point, I saw a car park full of vehicles – but there was not one which had not been riddled by gunfire or shrapnel. There were shelters destroyed, buildings flattened.

Kenley had certainly seen its fair share of action – and much more was to come.

Damage to hangars and vehicles at RAF Kenley on 18 August 1940.

At 1600 hrs that afternoon, Squadron Leader Gleave and his composite flight of seven other Hurricanes was scrambled to patrol base at 2,000ft, Tom leading in Hurricane P2361, SW-X. An hour later the Hurricanes returned to base, their patrol uneventful. Then, at 2220 hrs, Squadron Leaders Gleave and Starr flew a nocturnal patrol, in formation, of thirty minutes, 'To check on night-flying facilities.' Compared with previous days, it had been a long but quiet one from the perspective of enemy air activity: several German formations had crossed the Kentish coast that afternoon, penetrating as far as Westerham and Maidstone, but the operation was over in an hour; during the evening, enemy fighters swept around Dover, but again these were over quickly. Both sides had lost nine fighters. The pattern of German air activity, however, suggested that the following day was likely to be busier. Indeed, dawn on 30 August 1940, brought fine weather, and it was on that day that the Battle of Britain entered its most critical phase, with the enemy concentrating even heavier attacks on 11 Group's all-important airfields. 253 Squadron, although more than just keen and confident, was about to discover just how ferocious the fighting was over southern England – and meet the lethal Me 109.

253 Squadron's first full day at Kenley began with curious enemy activity, with formations of up to 'twenty plus' flying towards Dover,

shortly before 0800 hrs, but none actually crossed the coast. This effort was intended to lure the 11 Group Controller into scrambling his squadrons, which would then be back on the ground, refuelling and rearming, when the main raids came in later. Wise to such subterfuge, only one section of RAF fighters reacted, the remainder staying firmly on the ground. Between 0915 and 0930 hrs, three more enemy formations approached Dover, and this time two 11 Group fighters were sent up to patrol the coastal airfields at Hawkinge and Rochford respectively. At 1030 hrs, however, the situation had clearly changed: three enemy formations of around twenty 'bandits' each were up over Calais, another, numbering 'fifty plus', further south, above Tramecourt. This enemy air activity, then, was the real thing, representing a significant threat – to which the 11 Group Controller lost no time in responding.

At 1025 hrs, a flight of 501 Squadron's Hurricanes had been scrambled from Hawkinge to patrol base, before being vectored to Dover at 1050 hrs. At that time, the rest of 501 Squadron took off, to patrol base. 603 Squadron's Spitfires were off from Hornchurch at 1035 hrs, to patrol Canterbury, and a minute later the Hurricanes of 85 Squadron raced off from Croydon, Dover bound. At 1045 hrs, 610 Squadron's Spitfires went up from Biggin Hill, also ordered to Dover. At 1030 hrs and 1040 hrs respectively, 1 Squadron was sent off from Northolt, and 56 from North Weald, but their orders are unknown, and those two squadrons did not subsequently engage. At 1100 hrs, fifty more German aircraft were plotted over Cap Griz Nez, and those detected over Tramecourt headed towards Dungeness, prompting more RAF squadrons to be scrambled: 253 Squadron from Kenley at 1055 hrs, 151 Squadron from Stapleford five minutes later, and 234 Squadron's Spitfires were sent from Middle Wallop in 10 Group to protect Northolt. Thus, the scene was set for derring-do.

This was the opportunity 253 Squadron had been waiting for. At 1050 hrs, Squadron Leader Starr sped off from Kenley, leading five 'A' Flight Hurricanes. Pilot Officer (later Squadron Leader) Alan Corkett remembered that:

> We were well aware of the urgency … In the circumstances Squadron Leader Starr did not wait for the squadron to form up on the runway but took off immediately. Pilot Officer Jenkins was flying on his port side as his No 3, and I was flying in the second section of three aircraft as No 2 (starboard side) to the section leader. As the leading section became airborne the controller ordered 'Buster', which means we were to go flat-out, 'Raid near Redhill'. We were, of course, at full throttle

in the take-off climb. The leader ordered us to open out and individual aircraft flew wider on their leaders and my section moved well out to starboard of the leading section.

At 1055 hrs, Flight Lieutenant Cambridge followed with 'B' Flight, an attack on Biggin Hill, Croydon, Kenley appearing likely by that time, and Squadron Leader Starr's formation was recalled from Maidstone to patrol base. At 1130 hrs, Squadron Leader Gleave, leading 'A' Flight's 'Emergency Section', comprising Pilot Officer Colin 'Dopey' Francis and Flight Lieutenant George 'Bruno' Brown, were also scrambled. All of 253 Squadron's fighters then assembled over Kenley and were vectored south.

As Tom's Emergency Section scrambled, the first bombs fell, exploding in the areas of Chislehurst, Bromley and Orpington, most likely dropped by the enemy formation which had crossed the coast over Dungeness before being engaged by 85 Squadron, and was unable to locate its intended target. By then, the Germans engaged by 501, 610 and 603 Squadrons were fighting their way towards Biggin Hill. The 253 Squadron ORB takes up the story:

Above left: The grave of Pilot Officer D.N.O. 'Jenks' Jenkins at St Margareet's, Bagenden, Gloucestershire.

Above right: The grave of Sergeant J.H. Dickinson at Egton (St Mary) Churchyard, Lancashire (Glenn Gelder).

at 18,000ft, near Redhill, they saw three formations of bombers escorted by thirty fighters, Me 110s and Me 109s.

'B' Flight at once attacked the bombers, which included He 111s, Do 215s and possibly Ju 88s but observed no results, with the exception of Pilot Officer Nowak (Green 3) who probably destroyed a Do 215. 'A' Flight, which was behind and below, followed in the attack and Yellow 3 (Pilot Officer Greenwood) fired all his ammunition into a He 111 which forced-landed, four of the crew seen climbing out.

This was a landmark moment: 253 Squadron's first confirmed aerial victory since arriving at Kenley, an He 111H-2 of 5/KG 1, which had bombed Farnborough and forced-landed at Haxted Farm, Lingfield, at 1135 hrs. One of the crew was killed, the other four captured.

The 253 Squadron ORB continues:

A series of individual fights took place, chiefly with Me 110s and Me 109s which had come to the rescue of the bombers.

Blue 1 (Flight Lieutenant Cambridge) delivered a beam attack which developed into a quarter attack. Finally, when the Me 110 was in a gentle dive with port wing streaming smoke, he gave it a long burst from astern, causing the starboard engine to pour out black smoke and driving the aircraft into a steep dive. When Flight Lieutenant Cambridge pulled out of his dive, the E/A was still going straight down.

Blue 2 (Pilot Officer Samolinski) attacked an Me 110 from above and astern, silenced the rear-gunner and saw his bullets entering wings and fuselage, sending it down in a spiral dive. He made a similar attack on a second Me 110, silencing the rear-gunner.

Blue 3 (Sergeant Innes) made a head-on attack from 800 – 75 yards. As he broke away he saw parts breaking off the machine, which then rolled over and dived towards the ground.

Pilot Officer Corkett recalled how:

Suddenly, the raid was clearly seen, ahead and above us, flying left to right. Almost at once, two aircraft (Me 110s from the escort) broke away and dived (in echelon) towards the port side of our formation. 'Jenks' aircraft was hit and as it dived steeply to port I saw either smoke or glycol vapour streaming from the underside of the fuselage. I do not know whether 'Jenks' baled out.

It was now that Squadron Leader Gleave led his Emergency Section into attack the Me 109s at 1145 hrs, three to four miles west of Maidstone, Flight Lieutenant Brown on his right (No 2), Pilot Officer Francis to his left (No 3). The sky was full of Me 109s. Tom later reported engaging fifty:

> At 17,500ft, large formation of 109s sighted travelling SSE. Attacked from sun into E/As' flank. Attacked one Me 109 at angle of 20° to line of flight – 175 yards range – with four second burst. Shot appeared to enter fuselage near cockpit and engine cowling. Tracer appeared to spiral fuselage and come aft, believe this was shattered Perspex. E/A turned on back and dived vertically down.
>
> Tracer and cannon passed either side of me. And I dipped, turning right and left, and pulled up. No sign of No 2 or No 3. E/A crossed my sights at 120 yards range. Gave him four second burst. Column of black smoke burst from what appeared to be leading edge of starboard plane, about 3ft from wing root. E/A turned across my path and dropped into dive, leaving long column of black smoke in his wake. Pulled up to avoid collision with this E/A and nearly collided with another 109, which flew straight across my sight at 60–70 yards range. Gave him three second burst. E/A pulled the nose up, appeared to lose speed rapidly and fall out of sky as though stalling into a dive. Gave him another short two-second burst to help him on. Cockpit appeared empty but saw no body leave aircraft. Turned towards sun to evade tracer and cannon.
>
> An Me 109 passed just to the right and slightly ahead. Gave him all I had at seventy-five yards range. Shot appeared to go slap into underpart of cockpit and fuselage. E/A rolled on back, flew inverted for a few seconds and then went into a vertical dive, still going all out. Dived from scrap to throw off 109s on my tail. No sign of No 2 or No 3, both missing. Returned to aerodrome.

This was truly extraordinary shooting – especially considering it was Squadron Leader Gleave's first experience of a mass fighter combat. Back

Right: Squadron Leader Harold Starr, who succeeded Squadron Leader Gleave in command of 253 Squadron (TPG Estate).

Below: The wedding of Squadron Leader Starr – the other officer is his brother, Norman, reported missing in 1944 (TPG Estate).

at Kenley, he reported having 'accounted for four Me 109s', officially claiming all four 'Probably destroyed'. Not having 'seen them break up, catch fire, or crash' however, 'they could not be counted as destroyed', so the squadron Intelligence Officer credited Tom with 'two probables and two possibles'. In his log book, though, Tom wrote, in red ink: 'Later converted

Squadron Leader Starr's grave, which also commemorates his brother, Wing Commander Norman Starr, at Swindon Cemetery.

to four confirmed by 11 Group and confirmed by Fighter Command HQ.' Given that only two Me 109s actually crashed in south-east England that day, and considering the number of Fighter Command claims for 109s destroyed, it is difficult to understand, it must be said, on what evidence this conversion was based. Nonetheless, whether or not these four 109s were destroyed, probably destroyed or damaged, it was quite some feat and a spectacular entré into the cut and thrust of air fighting.

In total, after this engagement, according to the ORB, 253 Squadron claimed three Me 110s destroyed, two Me 109s probably destroyed, one Me 110 damaged, one He 111 destroyed, and a Do 215 probably destroyed. Sadly though, this was not without loss.

Back at Kenley, news was soon received that Flight Lieutenant Brown had been shot down by a 109 and had forced-landed near Maidstone, injuring his legs and a shoulder. Pilot Officer 'Dopey' Francis was missing, however, and according to Tom, a few days later he heard that 'he had been found; he had crashed and received fatal injuries … I like to think that "Dopey" got one as he was the youngest in the squadron and a likeable chap.' Certainly, at 19 Francis was very young, but in fact he was not found until 23 August 1981, when his Hurricane, L1965, was recovered by the Tangmere Aviation Museum from its crash site at Wrotham in Kent; Pilot Officer Colin Dunstone Francis was eventually laid to rest at Brookwood on 29 September 1981.

Pilot Officer 'Jenks' Jenkins, the 21-year-old who Pilot Officer Corkett had witnessed being hit, was also missing. News was soon received, however, that, according to 253 Squadron's official report on the casualty, that his Hurricane, P3921, 'Was seen to crash from a great height. The pilot must have been killed instantaneously.' The aircraft crashed at 1120 hrs, in Butlers Dene Road, Woldingham, on Surrey's North Downs, between Oxted and Warlingham; in his original manuscript, Tom wrote that:

'Jenks' was missing, and that overshadowed everything. Soon afterwards we heard that he had tried to bale-out, but something had gone wrong and he had plummeted to earth. When his bloodstained parachute was returned to the Station the next day, we found that he had made no attempt to pull the rip-cord. He must either have been badly wounded, or hit something getting out. 'Jenks' was one of our best pilots and his death was a bitter blow to the squadron, the kind that breeds hate.

On 3 September 1940, a year to the day after war had broken out, Pilot Officer Jenkins was laid to rest at St Margaret's Church, Bagenden, near Cirencester in Gloucestershire.

In this action, the Hurricanes of both Squadron Leader Starr and Pilot Officer Samolinski were both damaged, although fortunately the pilots were unhurt and returned safely to Kenley. In his original *Eagles of Nemesis*, Tom wrote that Starr's:

> engine had been hit by an armour-piercing shell – with curious results. A neat hole a little less than half-an-inch in diameter had been made in the front of the port rocker cover, and, when it was lifted off, a small, solid, bullet of much less calibre was found lying harmlessly inside!

Pilots of 253 Squadron at Kenley after the Battle of Britain, on 1 April 1942 (TPG Estate).

The day's action, though, was far from over…

By 1300 hrs, the south-east was free of enemy activity. There was then a lull of two hours before the Germans feinted an attack, to which the 11 Group Controller responded by scrambling six fighter squadrons between 1500 and 1530 hrs. The coastal airfield at Lympne, unconnected with Fighter Command, was lightly bombed, and two German fighter formations swept to Redhill and went out over Beachy Head. Shortly after 1540 hrs, three German formations came in over Dover, travelling north-west, but it was not until 1555 hrs that British fighters were scrambled, 603 patrolling Manston, 501 the Gravesend-Chatham line, while 151 Squadron headed out to sea, patrolling a convoy off North Foreland. At 1615 hrs, 616 Squadron's Spitfires left Kenley to intercept a raid on Eastchurch, while the main enemy formation headed North of the Thames, one formation attacking the Vauxhall motor works near Luton. At this time, 11 Group requested assistance from neighbouring 12 Group, and one of these squadrons, 242, commanded by Squadron Leader Douglas Bader, together with 11 Group squadrons engaged the Germans as they withdrew.

Between 1645 hrs, a section of 253 Squadron Hurricanes comprising Pilot Officers Samolinski and Bell-Slater, and Sergeant Dredge, scrambled from Kenley, followed five minutes later by Squadron Leader Gleave, leading 'B' Flight's Blue and Green Sections, comprising three and four Hurricanes respectively. Tom later reported that:

> At approx. 1700 hrs we were ordered to patrol base at 1,500ft. Order received just after take-off to proceed SE and climb to 15,000ft. A few miles SE of Tunbridge Wells, Green Section turned east, the leader rocking aircraft and informing me of E/A to the east of us. They proved to be Hurricanes and Green Section turned south. I also turned and opened up to regain position, and shortly afterwards tracer and cannon tracer appeared over Green Section. I turned Blue Section and sighted seven Me 109s coming down from the sun with six more a short distance behind, all in line astern. Scrap developed into fast, circling, melee, all firing ahead. Saw Me 109 on tail of Hurricane, blowing off fabric and wood. Fastened onto E/A and gave him long twelve second burst from 180–200 yards range to less than 70 yards. E/A continued to turn behind Hurricane for a few seconds, then rolled onto back, flew inverted for a while. I kept firing and saw patches of black material coming away from the starboard wing, near the wing root, and from fuselage. A piece of wire or metal dropped away

as the E/A turned, still inverted and dropped into dive. Forced to leave E/A as three 109s were fastened on my tail. Dived all out, turning and threw them off and climbed again to scene of fight. No aircraft to be seen, nor sign of damaged Hurricane. Returned to base. Damaged Hurricane safe on tarmac. E/A's destruction confirmed after landing.

On this occasion, 253 Squadron had engaged the Me 109s of JG 26, flying a fighter sweep in support of a raid on Detling. In addition to Tom's claim for an Me 109 destroyed, Sergeant Dredge claimed a probable. Three JG 26 pilots ditched in the Channel after the combat, their machines damaged, and without doubt one of these would have been that claimed by Tom Gleave. As the four 'probables' claimed by Tom from the morning's engagement were apparently later confirmed by 11 Group and Fighter Command HQs, which overrode the Intelligence Officer's on the spot assessment, this further confirmed destroyed enemy fighter made Squadron Leader Gleave a rare 'ace in one day', an 'ace' being a term given to a pilot upon confirmation of five aerial victories.

Again, though, after this action, 253 Squadron had two more pilots missing: Sergeant Cooper had been shot down and crashed near Biddenden and was safe, but Sergeant John Holt 'Dicky' Dickinson, a 21-year-old from Lancashire, was dead – it being widely believed at the time that he had baled out, only to be machine-gunned by an Me 109 pilot while descending by parachute. As Tom wrote, 'It may be permissible in war to shoot someone descending by parachute … but only those devoid of all sense of fair fight and chivalry could do it.'

Today, the former RAF Kenley is a common and well-used leisure facility – this is the memorial commemorating all who served there and lost their lives.

It had been a full first day for 253 Squadron, and despite the losses, Tom wrote that 'Starr was very bucked, and I was feeling like someone in another world: I had kept my vow.'

The squadron was released that evening, and, ever-keen, Tom was at dispersal before breakfast the following day, Saturday 31 August 1940. He and Squadron Leader Starr had agreed to lead the squadron in the air alternately, so that the latter could stay on top of his paperwork. That morning, Starr had chosen to be at readiness, while Tom 'spent some time in the portable office clearing those old bits of paperwork – the necessary evils – that plague commanders at all levels'. The day was fine and cloudless, and the enemy was active over the Pas-de-Calais and Channel shortly after 0600 hrs. By 0730 hrs there was every indication that an attack was incoming, and so 253 Squadron, along with 1 and 501 Squadrons, was scrambled five minutes later, with orders to patrol the Kent and Essex coast. By 0750 hrs, sixty enemy aircraft, divided into four formations, two of them of 'twenty plus', were on the move. 1 Squadron was the first into battle, reporting that the raid, which was headed for Debden airfield, was bigger than indicated by radar and actually numbered some 100 bombers and Me 110 escorts.

Squadron Leader Starr and two sections of 253 Squadron Hurricanes were up over Kent at 0825 hrs – when Squadron Leader Starr was shot down. By what, or in what circumstances, exactly, it cannot be said, because no such detail appears recorded in squadron or casualty records – except a note in his casualty file, dated 17 March 1941: 'Deal area. Shot at and killed when descending by parachute.' The same file note also makes an identical reference to Sergeant Dickinson's fate, with a rider explaining that 'No witnesses can now be traced but it was generally believed on 253 Squadron that both bodies were riddled with bullets due to attacks by Me 109s while

The Queen Victoria Hospital, East Grinstead (The Guinea Pig Club).

descending by parachute.' In 2019, however, the *Daily Mail* reported on the sale of Squadron Leader Starr's medals, and quoted an eyewitness, a Mr H.G. Bennet, a gardener at Eastry House, near to where the pilot's body fell:

> It was as I returned to work that morning that I saw a parachute coming down over the Hammill Brickworks. As most of the dog-fights took place at some altitude, I didn't hear or see the aircraft, but as the parachute came drifting down, I saw quite a number of enemy aircraft circling. Suddenly, one of the Messerschmitts dived towards the pilot on the parachute, and then the rest also piled in – I could hear the sound of machine-gunning.

In his original *Eagles of Nemises*, Tom wrote:

> The Station Commander arrived and told me that Starr had been shot dead coming down by parachute. Months later I learned that one solitary bullet had shot him through the heart, and kind hands had carried his body into a nearby church. I found it hard to believe that this should be the end of someone like Starr, of a fellow of his charm and ability; of someone who had the right ideas about everything, carried his rank with grace, treated all and sundry with respect, and had one ambition – to do his duty well.

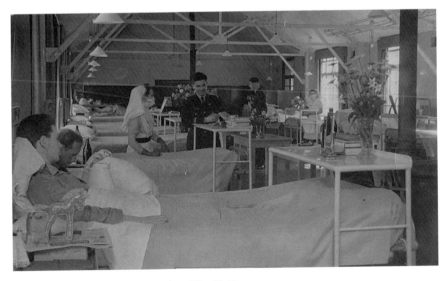

The interior of Ward 3 (The Guinea Pig Club).

This, however, is at odds with the long-held belief that Squadron Leader Starr's body was found 'riddled with bullets'. A single fatal shot is also contrary to the dramatic eyewitness evidence claiming that German fighters 'piled in', all firing at the defenceless pilot. For many years, it was claimed by at least one eyewitness on the ground that the youngest of the Few, Pilot Officer Martyn Aurel King of 249 Squadron, was machine-gunned over Southampton in similar circumstances – but now that his casualty file is available, we know his parachute collapsed that fateful day not because of enemy fire during the descent – but owing to damage sustained to the life-saving silk umbrella when his Hurricane was hit. Considering the amount of lead bisecting the sky during an aerial combat, it is not beyond the realms of possibility that a parachuting pilot could be hit by an indiscriminate round, and if Squadron Leader Starr was killed by a *single* round, as Tom Gleave states, one has to wonder whether this could have been what happened – and that eye-witnesses on the ground were mistaken. Nonetheless, whatever happened in the sky that day, a gallant officer was dead. They took the 24-year-old Squadron Leader Starr home, and buried him at Radnor Street Cemetery, Swindon. His widow, Bette, was too overcome with grief to attend her husband's funeral, and the tragedy of it all was that their only child, Carolyn, was born two months later (that, sadly, was not the family's only wartime loss: Harold's brother, Wing Commander Norman Starr, was reported missing when returning home from Belgium to be married in 1944 – the Anson aircraft he was piloting was hit by flak off Dunkirk, and crashed into the sea).

Understandably, at the time 'tempers' on 253 Squadron were 'raised to a white heat' regarding the perceived manner of Squadron Leader Starr's death, and Squadron Leader Gleave found himself once more in command. It would prove to be a day he would never forget – for all the wrong reasons.

At lunchtime, it became clear that another threat was developing. At 1234 and 1238 hrs respectively, German formations crossed the Kentish coast near Folkestone, and headed towards Biggin Hill and Kenley. By this time, these airfields had taken a real battering, and the situation for the defenders was becoming critical. Before the Germans crossed the coast, 79 Squadron had been scrambled from Croydon to patrol base. Then, at 1238 hrs, Squadron Leader Gleave was scrambled from Kenley, leading a section of three other Hurricanes, Pilot Officer Murch's section of three following minutes later. While 253 Squadron's 'Viceroy Leader' was vectored south, to join with another squadron to intercept 'Raid 20', further Hurricane and Spitfires were scrambled from Kenley, Debden and Hornchurch. Already that morning, North Weald and Debden had been badly hit, and the Duxford Sector had also been attacked, so the defenders were fully

Some of the Guinea Pig Club's founder members; from left: Squadron Leader Tom Gleave ('Squad'); Pilot Officer Geoffrey Page; 'Russell' (Anaesthetist or 'Knocker-out'); unknown; Flying Officer William Towers-Perkins; Sergeant Leonard Coote and 'The Maestro', Archibald McIndoe.

aware of how critical was the hour, and what was at stake. While the RAF fighters rushed into the air, however, two more large German formations approached Dover. The two raids which had crossed over Folkestone, forty Ju 88s escorted by Me 109s, headed for Croydon, and were intercepted by 79 Squadron's Hurricanes before hitting the target – though the airfield was then bombed, along with the Rollason aircraft factory, which was badly damaged. As the raiders withdrew, 253 Squadron entered the fray, at 1245 hrs over Orpington, as Tom Gleave reported:

> Formation turned over base and at a height of 12–15,000ft I glanced up and sighted an extensive formation of Ju 88s, flying in several parallel lines of aircraft in line astern. They were 1,000ft above and closing distance rapidly. When within machine-gun range own formation still forged ahead and I decided to attack before E/A opened fire. Pulled up and fired raking burst at No 5 in line of Ju 88s immediately above. Faked stall-turn at top of climb and dived, repeating process on No 3 of E/A. As I turned over at top of climb, I saw clouds of greyish white smoke pouring from port engine of the No 3 E/A.

Tom was credited with a Ju 88 damaged – but then, as Tom wrote in *Eagles of Nemesis*:

> at that point something happened which was to cause me inconvenience for many a long day. There was a metallic click above the roar of the Merlin; it seemed to come from the starboard wing and I glanced in that direction, but a sudden burst of heat struck me in the face, and from that moment I started to qualify for what Geoffrey Page, whom I came to know later at the hospital in East Grinstead, rightly described as the 'fried eggs and bacon course'.
>
> I had seen neither tracer nor cannon tracks near my aircraft and I assumed that I had picked up a stray incendiary – and that was the last fully rational thought I was to be capable of while I sat in the centre of that gigantic blow-lamp. Looking down into the cockpit I saw a long spout of flame issuing from the hollow starboard wing-root and curling up along the port side of the cockpit and then across my right shoulder. I had some crazy notion that if I rocked the aircraft and skidded, meantime losing speed, the fire might go out – but it didn't. The blaze became an inferno in a fraction of time and I concluded that baling out was the only solution; a forced-landing was out of the question as I reckoned I was still 7,000–8,000ft up.
>
> I reached down to pull out the R/T jack but the heat was too great. The skin was already rising off my right wrist and hand, and my left hand was starting to blister. My thin gloves were being progressively burnt away, but though finally they more or less disappeared and my hands caught the full blast of the flames, I now know that they saved my fingers from the far worse deformities that others have suffered. My shoes and slacks must have been burning all this time but I cannot remember any great pain – that was to come later. Shock is nature's anaesthetic – and if she can be very cruel, she can also be unspeakably kind.
>
> I undid my harness and tried to raise myself but found I had not the strength. I was comforted by another crazy notion – I still had my Colt ready loaded if things came to the worst. With the R/T jack still firmly held in its socket I decided to pull off my helmet, open the cockpit cover, and roll on my back, so that with a sharp dig forward on the control column I would be ejected from the blazing Hurricane. My helmet came off with a

 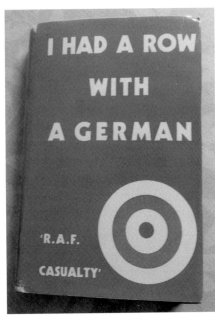

Above left: Squadron Leader Tom Gleave after reconstructive plastic surgery at East Grinstead (TPG Estate).

Above right: Tom's book, published in 1941 to raise money for the RAF Benevolent Fund.

determined tug. I pulled hard to get the cockpit cover open and finally succeeded, after using up a lot of my remaining strength. That there was a quick release for the hood passed me by in that strange, drowsy, mood. As the cockpit cover flew back there was a blinding flash. I seemed to be travelling upwards between walls of flame. Then I suddenly found myself turning over and over in the clear air with no sensation of falling – the flames mercifully were no more. Soon I ceased to travel forwards, or so it seemed, and began to fall earthwards, still turning head over heels. My hand instinctively passed over the Sutton Harness release grip and on to the rip-cord handle of my parachute – and I can be thankful that in my semi-coma my hand did not loiter on the way. I pulled hard and felt the Bowden wire being drawn through the strongly woven fabric tubing. Then came a gentle jerk as I was pulled into a vertical position, swinging comfortably and secure in my harness. I looked down at the rip-cord handle buried in the swollen mess that had been my right hand, and then disdainfully threw it as far away from me as I could. It was a gesture of temper at having been shot down. I did not remind myself of earlier days when the punishment for failing to bring back the rip-cord handle after baling out was a fine of half-a-crown, or so ran the story!

An interminable length of time seemed to have elapsed while struggling to escape from that inferno. From the time the incendiary struck to the time my parachute opened was, in fact, less than a minute. Like most pilots, I had always wanted to make a parachute descent, but now I could raise no enthusiasm for it as I floated down. I was feeling distinctly browned off.

That Tom's Hurricane, P3115, had exploded and thrown him clear in the process, was a blessing – but as the grievously burned pilot came closer to earth, the ground rushed up at him. In 1991, Tom described what happened next:

I stood in this field … thought I should see a doctor, so called out 'Anybody about?' Out of a cowshed nearby came a very stalwart man who insisted on putting me onto his back, and he carried me up to a house belonging to a Mrs Wilson. I regret, to my shame, that I kept saying 'How much longer?'

Mrs Wilson's son, Alec, recalled that 'Tom was in a terrible state, but all he was worried about was making a mess on Mum's nice clean bed, because of his injuries.'

Group Captain Gleave with Sir Archibald McIndoe in Paris after the war (TPG Estate).

Tom wrote that 'When I look back I feel ashamed of myself for all the trouble I must have given her. No one could have done more for me than she did, and I shall always be grateful to her.'

However, more help than that administered by the kindly Mrs Wilson was needed. In due course the local Air Raid Warden arrived with an airman on leave, and the pair managed to make the wounded Squadron Leader comfortable on the back seat before 'we pushed off for a nearby war hospital'. It was during that journey that Tom began feeling terrible pain, prompting the repeated question 'How much further?' Although the journey seemed like hours to the grievously wounded pilot, just fifteen minutes later the open-top car arrived at Orpington Hospital, and Tom was immediately treated 'for shock and secondary burns'. A shot of morphine sent merciful oblivion, and as Tom later wrote:

> From that moment I started accumulating a debt that mounted daily… Every time I see a nurse or doctor now I feel a hidden sense of humility, prompted not only by the ceaseless care and attention I received … but also what I saw them do for others far worse than myself, all but dead casualties who have become living miracles.

Tom's wife Beryl was officially informed, in error, on 3 September 1940 that he had been admitted to Orpington War Hospital but that her husband's 'condition was not serious'. Upon arrival there, Beryl actually found Tom encased in dried Tannafax – better-known as tannic acid – and on the 'dangerously ill list'. Struggling to find words, Beryl laconically inquired 'What on earth have you been doing with yourself, darling?' The only answer Tom could think of was simply, 'Had a row with a German' – which became the published title of his memoir.

Tom required specialist treatment, and on 29 October 1940, the 32-year-old pilot was transferred to the now world-famous Burns Unit, otherwise known as 'Ward 3', at the Queen Victoria Cottage Hospital, East Grinstead, suffering from burns to face, arms, hands and legs – or 'standard Hurricane burns', as Tom called his injuries. And so began a whole new and painful chapter in Tom Gleave's life, one which, perhaps more than anything else, defined him.

This was just two days, in fact, before the official end of the Battle of Britain – and 253 Squadron remained in the front line, at Kenley. Having lost two COs in one day, Flight Lieutenant Bill Cambridge then took over the squadron – but was killed in action on 6 September 1940. Then, 605 Squadron's Flight Lieutenant Gerry Edge was promoted to command

Above left: Tom Gleave's Guinea Pig Club crest.

Above right: Tom Gleave's Battle of Britain Fighter Association crest.

253 Squadron, but he too was shot down, baling out wounded, three weeks later and admitted to Willsborough Hospital, leading to Flight Lieutenant R.M.B.D. Duke-Woolley assuming command. During the Battle of Britain, 253 Squadron had lost eleven pilots killed, all flying from Kenley. Arguably Tom was one of the lucky ones, although as he began a process of eight operations at East Grinstead, he may well have questioned that.

The Queen Victoria Hospital had been chosen as one of four Emergency Medical Service units to specialise in treating burns victims, as the British government prepared for war during the late 1930s. Ward 3, on which Tom now found himself, was where officers and the most severely burned patients were treated. On 4 September 1939, Mr Archibald McIndoe, a surgeon specialising in facial reconstruction, arrived at the 'QVH' to run what was a new Centre for Plastic and Jaw Surgery. McIndoe was a 39-year-old New Zealander appointed as the RAF's Consultant in Plastic Surgery in 1938. At East Grinstead, McIndoe pioneered reconstruction techniques which became standard worldwide. One of the things he was to become lauded for in due course was banning the traditional use of Tannafax in treating burns, because although this hard protective coating prevented fluid loss and infection, the skin beneath contracted, causing problems when later reconstructing eyelids and fingers. Before such surgery, the acid had to be removed – which was excruciatingly painful. Instead, McIndoe – known by his patients as 'The Maestro' – pioneered the use of saline baths,

Above left and above right: Items from the Hurricane in which Tom Gleave was shot down in, presented to him over the years.

keeping wounds open and washing them frequently. Instead of the hard Tannafax, patients' dressings were loose, moist, bandages. He also refined the 'tube pedicle' technique of skin grafting for reconstructing hands and faces, and, most importantly, recognised the importance of emotional rehabilitation. Consequently, the interior of Ward 3, a wooden former army hut behind the main hospital building, was brightly painted and became a 'spirited environment', encouraged by McIndoe who provided a piano as a central point for socialising, and even a barrel of beer. The surgeon understood that the morale and masculinity of these young men equally needed reconstruction, to which end he not only selected attractive nurses but positively encouraged his patients flirting. As Tom himself said:

> Archie generated a bond of fellowship in which rank was forgotten. He believed that nothing should stand in the way of making terribly mutilated human beings whole again, and so we had much more freedom than was traditional in military or medical circles.
>
> Local people had to get used to the sight of us walking out to the pubs in the evenings, those who were lame or in wheelchairs assisted by those whose worst problem might be a considerably rearranged face. Archie wanted to boost our confidence and help us achieve our common ambition to get back into the war. He invited us into the operating theatre to watch him at work and it was there that we began to mutter 'guinea pig'.

To the great credit of the townsfolk there, East Grinstead became fondly known as 'The town that didn't stare.'

On the afternoon of Sunday 20 July 1941, after a Ward 3 Saturday night 'thrash', a group of recovering airmen patients decided to form a drinking club, '"The Maxillonian Club", whose members call themselves guinea pigs.' The minutes of that inaugural meeting were recorded by Pilot Officer Geoffrey Page, who had also been shot down in the Battle of Britain, suffering 'standard Hurricane burns'. Page's notes document that the club's purpose was to 'promote good fellowship among, and to maintain contact with, approved frequenters of Queen Victoria Cottage Hospital'. All members enjoyed equal rights, and were of three categories: patients, being Allied aircrew having undergone at least two operations at East Grinstead for burns or other injuries arising from a crash; 'The scientists', being the medical staff, and friends and benefactors. A sign of the times is that females were not eligible for membership, although, graciously, the committee could authorise ladies' evenings. 'The Maestro' was elected as President, Squadron Leader Gleave – known on Ward 3 simply as 'Squad' – Vice-President, and Flying Officer William Towers-Perkins, another of the Few, became Honorary Secretary. Other founder members among the Few were Squadron Leader Zdzislaw Krasnodebski (Polish, 'Poley Boy' in Tom's book), Flight Lieutenant Arthur Banham, Flying Officers John Fleming (a New Zealander) and George Bennions, Pilot Officers Eric Lock, Richard Hillary, Brian Noble and Josef Koukal (Czech), along with Sergeants Leonard Coote and Jack Mann. The 'good fellowship' that all involved achieved exceeded all expectations – and as 'Chief Guinea Pig', Tom Gleave would go on to devote much of his life to the welfare of members.

During his time at East Grinstead, Tom was officially posted as 'Non-effective, Station HQ, Kenley.' On 14 August 1941, by which time he had been promoted to Wing Commander, Tom was considered 'effective' and returned to duty at Kenley. On 19 August 1941, Wing Commander Gleave made his first flight since being shot down, a local sortie of forty-five minutes in a Magister, with Sergeant John Anderson – a fellow Guinea Pig – who had also flown with 253 Squadron until being shot down and badly burnt on 14 September 1940. The pair would make many such flights together over the next few days, and on 28 August 1941, Tom flew a Hurricane, on an air test, for the first time since 31 August 1940. On 9 September 1941, Tom flew a Spitfire for the first time, and four days later took temporary command of RAF Northolt until 29 September 1941. The following day, Tom reported to the Operations Room at RAF Tangmere, but was only there until 5 October 1941. On that day, he took over Manston as Station

Commander, where he continued to do a lot of non-operational flying, in various aircraft, especially his personal Hurricane, Z3439, TP-G.

It was during 1941 that *I Had A Row With A German* was published by Macmillan, and was well-received. It was, in fact, an early pilot's war memoir, preceding the substantial crop of 1942 publications, which included *The Last Enemy*, by founding Guinea Pig Richard Hillary. Upon publication of the book, Tom sent a copy to Mrs Constance Wilson, to whose farm he had been taken when shot down:

> Many thanks indeed for your great kindness in sending me a copy of your very interesting book. I feel very honoured to have come into it and really did so very little for you after all you and many others have done for us.
>
> Without you and your wonderful colleagues this little island of ours would have been a sad place today … Had I known then you could have got into a car, I could have taken you straightaway to Orpington, but probably the rest did help a little.

A letter was also received by Macmillan from Mrs Horatia Jenkins, mother of 'Jenks', who was living in St Andrew's, Fife, to whom Tom then wrote; her response makes sad reading:

> Thank you very much for so kindly writing to me about your book, and the mention of my son, Nicholas, in it. One clings to the smallest item of any record of those who are gone, and whose going has left life so empty for us here. I had a nice letter from Flying Officer Pring, who was Adjutant to 253 then, but that was all, as of course the Battle of Britain was in full progress and the squadron was suffering such heavy losses. I feel happy to think that you thought well of Nicholas (as he certainly appreciated you) and that he seemed to have been good and competent at his job. After his death, I received more than thirty letters about him, some from complete strangers to me – mentioning qualities in him which we had never appreciated. At home he was just loved. He was always 'fey' about flying and I think had some special instinct for it, as he seems to have done very well. I am glad to think that his courage did not fail 'even unto death'. He is buried in the Cotswolds, in a tiny village where he was born, and next to his father, who died when Nick was only nine weeks old.

We also knew some of the other people mentioned by you. Nowak, the Pole, Roy Watts, the 'Walrus' flyer, and one or two others, 'Curly' Clifton, who was a friend of Nick's; some of them he brought over when they were at Turnhouse.

He was absolutely miserable when they were moved to Prestwick on 21 August 1940, as he felt it was a backwater, and that they would be left out of the fighting. Actually, he was allowed a Magister on the 27th, and came home for two days' leave, so was here when the order came at 2 am on 29th, to go back to Prestwick at dawn. He flew over this house at about 8.30 am, from Leuchars. That was the last we saw of him, though he rang up my daughter from Prestwick to tell us he was going south 'to where his car was'. Flying Officer Pring then rang up on the Friday night (30 August 1940) to say he was gone. So it all seemed terribly sudden to us.

I am perfectly certain looking back that he knew he would never come home again. The only comfort left is the equal certainty that he is still helping in this awful war [presumably by being mentioned in the morale-boosting book].

May I thank you for your delightful book, beautifully written and full of interest, quite apart from our personal one. It is odd that I first heard of it from a stepdaughter of mine out in South Arica! The whole subject is tremendously interesting, and the progress and patience of your restoration a wonderful record.

The Rolls-Royce Merlin engine of Squadron Leader Gleave's Hurricane, now displayed at the IWM Duxford (Paul Heys).

114

I am glad that Nick was killed instantly, and not shot while coming down in his parachute like Squadron Leader Starr. His watch (broken) pointed to 12 o'clock and his ring, which I have on, was broken in half.

Thank you again for your letter. Nick was lucky to be commanded by you.

Tom Gleave's wartime flying log book and his silver cigarette case, which survived the flames on 31 August 1940.

The damaged cigarette case.

On 5 January 1942, *I Had A Row With A German* was reviewed in *The Times Literary Supplement*, which in part read that:

> The book is well worth reading if only because it shows the qualities of modesty and courage which seem to be inherent in RAF men … Instead of feeling that fate was unkind to single him out for such disfigurement his thoughts are all for those not so fortunate as himself, those who are maimed and crippled for life. He makes a touching appeal that they should not be victims of 'life's most vicious crime – man's ingratitude to man', and, practising what he preaches, is devoting the royalties from his book to the RAF Benevolent Fund.

For the survivors of the Battle of Britain, however, the war went on, and Wing Commander Gleave found RAF Manston heavily involved in operations over the Channel:

> in the midst of a snowstorm, came a squadron of the Fleet Air Arm, No 825, led by Lieutenant Commander Eugene Esmonde of *Bismarck* fame, to join us in the 'Channel Stop'. It was equipped with Fairey Swordfish aircraft, biplanes affectionately known as 'Stringbags' and manned by a crew of three apiece. I had met Esmonde previously, when he was in the RAF, a small, dapper little fellow who after serving in the RAF for a number of years took up civil flying. Alert and intelligent, he was a pleasant conversationalist with a touch of individualism. It was easy to like Esmonde.
>
> With the arrival of 825 Squadron we had more frequent visits from 'Bobbie' Constable-Roberts. He was the Wing Commander Air Liaison Officer to Admiral Ramsey at Dover, and a more suitable man to tie the RAF and RN together in that corner of the United Kingdom could not have been found. There were lots of plans agreed to help Esmonde make his Squadron a real 'killer' outfit in the dark hours over the Channel, and not the least was the production of modified flare installations for Hurricanes which were to cause quite a bit of amusement – but that was much later. Alas, Esmonde was not to be with us long enough to put any but the immediate arrangements into force.
>
> On 11 February 1942, Esmonde went to Buckingham Palace to receive the DSO for his gallantry in the *Bismarck* action. That evening two of his Swordfish set out to look for

ships along the Dunkirk-Ostend stretch of the Channel. While the Swordfish were away, two Manchesters came floating in to refuel and await daylight. It was also that day we heard the ominous news that women and children were being evacuated from Singapore, and with it came details of a gallant action by the Dutch Navy off the coast of Borneo in which three Japanese cruisers, a destroyer and a submarine were believed to have been sunk. There was a lull in the news from the Russian Front and a hush had fallen on the desert, broken only by the ceaseless air reconnaissance and fighter patrols of both sides – and that was no longer news. It left the ether clear for commentary on the sad events on the other side of the globe – and merely added to their poignancy. Within a matter of hours, all ears and eyes and tempers were to be suddenly switched to an area under our very noses – the English Channel.

The Joint Chiefs of Staff were aware that the Germans intended for their cruisers *Scharnhorst*, *Gneisenau* and *Prinz Eugen* to break-out from their base at Brest and relocate to a less vulnerable port. It was agreed that when this attempt was made, the RAF and Royal Navy would mount immediate counter-action. The codeword initiating this response was 'Fuller'. On the

morning of 12 February 1942, Squadron Leader Bob Oxspring, commanding 91 Squadron at Hawkinge, was informed by Squadron Leader Bill Igoe, the Biggin Hill Controller, of unusual enemy aerial activity over the Somme. Suspecting that the Germans were protecting some kind of shipping, Igoe ordered Oxspring to take a look, which he did, in company with Sergeant Beaumont. Subsequently following the French coast from

Group Captain Tom Gleave about to be surprised by presenter Michael Aspel before his appearance on *This Is Your Life* [TPG Estate].

Le Touquet towards the mouth of the Somme, the two Spitfires were suddenly assailed by a heavy flak barrage. Breaking, the pilots saw a large gathering of 'E' boats and destroyers escorting three much larger ships, all travelling at full-steam. They then observed two Spitfires far below, attacking the 'E' boats, and being unaware of 'Fuller', Oxspring broke radio silence and reported what he had seen to Igoe, who telephoned this news to the incredulous 11 Group Controller at Uxbridge.

Unfortunately, the 11 Group AOC, Air Vice-Marshal Leigh-Mallory, was at a conference at Northolt, and no one else appeared to grasp the enormity of Oxspring's report. Thirty minutes later, the two Spitfires he had seen engaging the German escorts landed at Kenley, these being flown by Group Captain Victor Beamish and Wing Commander Finlay Boyd. These pilots had maintained radio silence, but now their reports corroborated Oxspring's – while their more senior rank added gravitas. By the time a response had been decided, which was to launch the counter-attack air operation codenamed 'Fuller', the German ships were already steaming through the Dover Strait, towards the North Sea. Inclement weather had already rendered the Navy's proposed counter-attack impotent, and in any case there were no sizeable warships based in the Channel capable of decisively engaging the German force. Also due to the weather, Bomber Command was unable to attack as planned, because armour-piercing bombs had to be dropped from a minimum of 7,000ft, and the target was obscured by cloud. From the German side, Operation *Donnerkeil* had been masterminded by the General der Jadgflieger, Adolf Galland, following Hitler himself ordering the three battleships to move. Continuous escort was to be provided by four sections of fighters, two at high altitude, two lower-down, while the main German fighter force was not to be scrambled until the codeword 'Open Visor' was given. When Beamish and Boyd attacked the 'E' boats, Galland rightly guessed that the British would first send a reconnaissance before reacting in strength – and so the scene was set for what became known as the 'Channel Dash'.

Wing Commander Gleave's memories of 'Fuller' provides a vivid insight into both the background to a gallant Victoria Cross action and the heightened activity at Manston:

> 12 February 1942 dawned as cloud floated in over Manston. By the time it was quite light there were occasional slight falls of snow until about 10 am. Then the clouds thinned out and there were gaps of blue sky to be seen, and visibility spread in all directions to four or five miles. No operations had been laid on other than an early shipping reconnaissance by two

Hurricanes of 607 Squadron between Cap Griz Nez and the Somme estuary – they saw nothing unusual.

After breakfast at Westgate I went to my office in Streete Court and tore through the 'bumph'. Then I drove down to the airfield for my daily check on how the 'reconstruction' was getting along. Shortly after 1100 hrs I was called over to Flying Control. Esmonde was there and had been in touch with Dover. Something was astir! Could it be the 'Ugly Sisters'? I rushed back to Westgate to be 'on tap' and get things moving but within a few minutes of my arrival the phone rang: 'Fuller: get cracking, Tom, lad!' came a voice I knew well – it was Victor Beamish ringing up from Kenley where he was Station Commander. It was he, with Wing Commander Boyd covering his tail, who had first spotted the German Fleet making a mess on our own doorstep. I opened the safe and took out the envelope marked 'Most Secret – Fuller', and ripped it open. The contents were nothing unexpected and I stuffed them into my pocket, pressed the battery of six bell-pushes on my desk and lifted the telephone receiver off its double-yoke. By the time I had spoken to Flying Control and told them to brief all concerned, the sound of running feet echoed throughout the erstwhile former preparatory school. I would have dearly loved the excitement on any other occasion – but not this one. Though it was something to get your teeth into, the whole build-up was ominous – Brest was so far away yet only Victor Beamish seemed to know that the 'Ugly Sisters and their niece' had travelled so far from home. Alas, the day was to prove a sad and regrettable one.

As half a dozen officers and men burst into my room, heralded by the shortest and sharpish of courtesy knocks, I knew something I had not realised before – a broadside of six bells is worth six runners, is equal to any fire alarm and saves twenty minutes. I told them: 'The *Scharnhorst* and *Gneisenau* are in the Channel. Warn everybody. Our own squadrons will want bombs armed and ammunition belts made up. There will be a host of visiting squadrons for refuelling and rearming, and we shall need a 'running buffet' on the airfield for them all. There will probably be quite a few casualties to look after and no doubt the usual crashes, so warn the Station Medical Officer.'

Padre Church immediately set about organizing the refreshments – that was his specialty on 'flap' days – in his own inimitable way. The others got on to warning all and sundry and seeing to it that every officer, airman and airwoman on the Station was dragooned into some essential task to meet the need of the moment – from collecting bombs and ammunition from the bomb-dump to handling incoming and outgoing aircraft. I spoke to Hornchurch, took a call from 11 Group and then grabbed my cap and headed down to the airfield in my Stationmaster's wagon.

Esmonde was there with some of his crews in their briefing room – the original Duty-Pilot's Hut before Airfield Control superseded its antiquated purposes. It lay in the dip made by the Ramsgate Road, which cut across the eastern half of the airfield, and on the far side. When I arrived there, a few minutes after noon, the remainder of the Swordfish crews were just emerging from the hut and I was in time to see Esmonde, the last man, come out. He looked grim and was understandably in a great hurry – he'd had little warning to prepare his flight plans and get his aircraft, and not least his 'tin fish', on the top line. 'Good luck, Esmonde', I called to him. He waved back and forced a smile. My last close-up of that gallant fellow, who had aged in a trice, was the small figure of a man dressed in dark blue naval uniform, wearing an orange-coloured 'Mae West', and an unstrapped flying helmet on his head with the R/T leads dangling around his knees, and carrying a folded chart under his left arm as he strode at a tangent up the slope of the airfield to his Swordfish – parked near the Ramsgate Road.

At about 1215 hrs the six Swordfish, dressed in their light sea-camouflage, taxied down to near the dip. Then they turned uphill towards the west and took off singly, all of them to disappear over the brow as they became silhouetted against a bright horizon. Within a few minutes they returned, flying in two vics, the rear flight tucked in tight behind and below the leading formation. I was still standing well out into the airfield as they sped by, this time in the opposite direction, and I felt a sense of guilt that things like Swordfish, far easier meat than even Lysanders, Henschel 126s and Stukas, should go out in broad daylight in skies where Me 109s and Fw 190s roamed.

Cloud was broken with large gaps of hazy blue sky in between, and over the northern side of the airfield hung a large cumulous cloud like a giant chandelier. Against its dark base the shoal of Swordfish, as they had passed beneath, looked as black as the night-flying Albacores which were quickly to replace them. Now, they flew into a brighter patch of sky, their struts glinting as they sped eastwards towards the coast – all of them on their last flight, as it was to be for thirteen of the gallant company of eighteen who manned them, including the magnificent Esmonde himself. A wing of fighters was supposed to appear to escort the Swordfish and although, in the event, a squadron did meet up with them off the coast, the absence of any fighters within sight of Manston made the departure of Esmonde and his Squadron more akin to a sentence of death.

Close on the heels of 825 Squadron, Noel Mowat took 607 Squadron up to search the Cap Griz Nez – Calais area. All they found was four trawlers and they set one of them on fire – the German warships were already through the Channel. Unfortunately, though some Fw 190s in the area did not interfere, one Hurricane was hit by flak and dived into the sea. All was quiet until they returned – as some of the four-cannon Hurricanes of 32 Squadron took-off on a fruitless mission. Then silence reigned again, except around the perimeter where a host of people and vehicles flitted to and fro like the many hands of a giant circus about to erect the 'big top'. Soon after 1400 hrs, Noel led some of his Squadron out onto the grass again, bombed up once more, and some of the four-cannon Hurricanes of 32 Squadron moved down onto the airfield behind them. 607 were away first, 32 following to form up on each side as they headed out to seek the German battle-cruisers. A squadron of Spitfires joined them as top cover. They all had a hectic trip. About fifty miles out they were attacked by a large force of Me 109s and the Spitfires waded into them. Noel turned his Squadron to meet them too, and formed it into a defensive circle, becoming separated from 32 Squadron, which picked up a straggler from 607 and shepherded him home.

When the German fighters finally sheered off, Noel found himself within a few miles of a light-cruiser, which was obviously the *Prinz Eugen*. There was much flak from heavy and light guns stretching towards the North, where he sighted the *Scharnhorst* and *Gneisenau* surrounded by a fleet of escort vessels of all shapes and sizes, and overhead many fighters cross-crossed the area beneath cloud. Noel picked out two armed escorts, one behind and the other to starboard of the main group. He led four Hurricanes against the first, of about 600 tons, attacking at mast-height – it broke into two halves from the explosion of two or more 250lb bombs in its guts and quickly sank. One of the three remaining Hurricanes had been hit by the intense flak and the other two attacked the second vessel, one of about 400 tons. Flight-Sergeant Gill scored a direct hit and clouds of black, belching, smoke and flame completely enveloped it, hiding its fate – Gill had already sent an Me 109 heading for base with smoke pouring from its belly. By now, the Hurricanes were scattered and only four of them reached Manston, landing at about 1530 hrs. Allowing for the straggler which had arrived earlier, three were unaccounted for – including Warrant Officer Ommaney, a veteran by the standards of those times.

In the meantime aircraft had been pouring into Manston to refuel and rearm, and many were congregating in the circuit, waiting to be called down by Flying Control. A squadron of visiting Hurricanes touched down as several Hudsons joined the circuit and began to orbit, while beneath them two Beauforts, the first batch from 217 Squadron, followed the Hurricanes in. The Beaufort pilots hadn't a clue what all the fuss was about, and when told 'The *Scharnhorst* and *Gneisenau*' they raced back to their aircraft and were soon on their way to drop their visiting cards on them. All the while the Hudsons continued their merry-go-round and a few Beauforts joined them for a circuit or two before pushing off to sea on their own. Then a flock of Spitfires came pouring in – some in normal camouflage and others painted black. One squadron was led by Squadron Leader John Peel, and in charge of another came 'Dutch' Hugo – he and one of his compatriots had each bagged a 109. There were other claims too and Squadron Leader Smith, the Station Intelligence Officer, sifted the information brought back. Some of the Spitfire pilots remained in their cockpits for a quick get-away – either seaward or homeward. One of them was a Frenchman, a little older than the normal run of ages, and he wore an old type RAF flying helmet, or it could have been French. He sat peacefully in his winged chariot surveying the hectic scene around him. No one seemed to have attended to his needs and so I grabbed some sandwiches and a drink and took them to him. He was profusely grateful for his alfresco meal.

Noel Mowat led his survivors into the dispersal area just
as the last of the Spitfires had landed. Two Beauforts came
in with them to refuel and we learned that they had been on a
fruitless search for the German ships. We gave them the latest
known positions and one of the pilots went off again in a few
minutes. The other had some trouble or other and left very
late – I doubt he could have reached the area before dark.

Not from Noel's pilots nor from those of the Spitfires or
Beauforts could I get any coherent story of what had happened
to Esmonde and his squadron – only the grim comment from
one Spitfire pilot, which I already knew to my chagrin, that
'No Swordfish could live long out there.' I feared the worst,
inevitable as it had seemed.

Overhead the Hudsons still circled – they began to get
on my nerves. They had been doing it for an hour and
Flying Control could not contact them – nor had we any
idea where they were from. And if I am not mistaken some
of them, if not all, bore no squadron markings. On a quieter
day it might have been possible to put out white strips –
had we any – to form the letters 'B' and 'G' with an arrow
pointing north-eastwards, but the taxying and slipstreams
of a multitude of aircraft would quickly have mutilated
them and swept them away. Why group could not find out
to whom they belonged, or why one of them did not land to
ask what the form was, I shall never know. Albeit, at about
1600 hrs they suddenly sheered off northwards and I was
glad to see them go.

On the ground below came a lull in the landings until about
1630 hrs when a Beaufort landed and taxied up to the refuelling
and rearming point; it bore a few small bullet or shrapnel holes
but was otherwise undamaged. Its crew had attacked one of
the battle-cruisers and dropped their torpedo without seeing
any result – for it had been set upon by a bunch of Me 109s
and the air gunner had shot one down into the sea. There came
another, but shorter, lull and then in came our first casualties,
also in a Beaufort, which crash-landed itself to a standstill.
The crew were only slightly injured despite the fact that many
dents and holes the size of pudding basins pock-marked the
wings and fuselage – which now swelled the growing signs of
carnage around the airfield. They had had a warm reception
both from Me 109s and flak going in and emerging from their

attack, and that nothing vital to the aircraft being kept airborne had been hit was indeed 'a bit of jam'.

Within a few minutes another Beaufort came in. It, too, bore evidence of having been hit several times but with less effect, and all the members of its crew also had slight wounds – in their case all from flak. That aircraft proved to be the last that was to land from that now famous incident. The feverish activity of the early afternoon had by then petered out, and soon the undamaged aircraft still remaining began to depart for their home bases. There was still no definite account of the six Swordfish and the four Hurricanes – the fourth was by then known to have crashed into the sea with no hope of survival for the pilot.

I had given my Hurricane to 607 because of the shortage of IIBs, and now Noel lent me one to get away for a short while from the aftermath of the day's events. Everybody on the Station had worked magnificently but I was angry and grief-stricken at what had happened in the sky that day, over Manston and above the Channel. We could have done no more than we did to sift sanity out of chaos over the airfield – but that it had happened at all, while three major units of the German Fleet passed within spitting distance of us, rankled in my mind. More wounding by far, however, was the loss of Esmonde and most of the fine types he took with him, and of four fine fellows from 607 Squadron, and of Finch, a flight lieutenant in 217 Squadron, who had spent so much time with us to be near the best torpedo-bomber hunting ground. That it looked as if they had all died in vain was a stab to the heart. I found solace in the lonely cockpit of a Hurricane as I flew north-eastwards, out to sea. It was not long before I found myself flying in a well with tall sides of darkening, towering mist standing on the empty waters, and I turned south, skimming the gentle swell which was tremendously difficult to see. Somewhere beneath lay many new victims the sea had claimed that day, including Esmonde and many of his squadron, but how many we were not yet sure. I turned north-westwards, flying straight until the dark strip of the Deal coastline took shape just above the cowling, and then cut north over Pegwell Bay, to land up the dark slope beyond the dip. All was now quiet. The airfield was in murky shadow, deserted.

From Smith, in his wooden Intelligence hut, from others in the airfield mess and from Lee, who had been Rose's observer and was the only uninjured survivor from 825 Squadron, I pieced together a report on the Swordfish attack – Lee had just arrived back from Dover. The German ships had been sighted about fifteen miles beyond Calais. Esmonde led his flight, Sub-Lieutenants Rose and Kingsmill being the formating pilots, in over the destroyer screen to aim and release their torpedoes. The flak was intense and a shell ricocheted off the water and struck Esmonde's aircraft as he hugged the water. At the same time about fifteen Me 109s and Fw 190s dived down in an attempt to get at the Swordfish and the Spitfires intervened. But they could not prevent a FW 190 from attacking Esmonde's aircraft at point-blank range. The Swordfish shed its top plane and crashed into the sea. Meanwhile, Kingsmill and Rose were doing their best to dodge the German fighters and managed to get their torpedoes away, but both aircraft were already badly damaged. Rose, with his air gunner dead and himself wounded, made for some MTBs but was forced to ditch, and he and Lee were eventually rescued after being in their dinghy for an hour or more. One wing of Kingsmill's aircraft, however, was already on fire when he too went into attack and he and his crew were all wounded. With torpedo

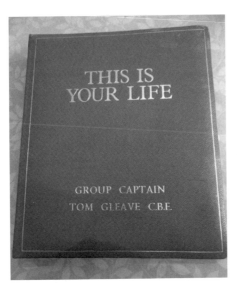 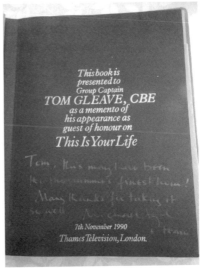

Above left: Group Captain Gleave's commemorative 'Red Book'.

Above right: The inscription within.

gone he made for base but his engine cut out and he, too, had to ditch. Fortunately it was near some British MTBs which quickly picked him and his crew up – their dinghy had been destroyed in the burning wing. Nothing was ever heard again of the other three aircraft, flown by Lieutenant Thompson, the leader of the Flight, and Sub-Lieutenants Wood and Bligh. They were last seen passing over the destroyer screen to drop their torpedoes.

That evening I sat in my office at Westgate writing a report for group on how those at Manston had acquitted themselves. Huddled over the fire behind us was a very attractive little WAAF officer, and the glare from the flames lit up the tears as they streamed down her face. She waited for news of one of those who didn't come back. As the moments fled by, they whittled away what was left of her hopes of seeing her man again – it was a kinder process than telling her the blunt truth. Once before she had waited for someone, who had been her first betrothed – and she had waited in vain. It was to be no different this time, and several hours later, when she could weep no more, she slipped quietly away into the night. But she was young, and that new wound would heal as quickly as the first. It was different for the parents of those gallant seventeen RAF and FAA men whose company we had shared until half

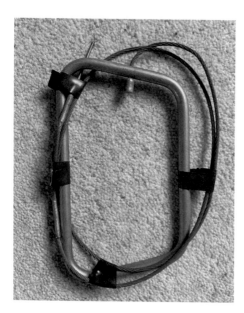

The parachute release handle, or ripcord, discarded by Tom on 31 August 1940 and presented to him on the programme.

that fateful day had been spent – and it was they who haunted my mind as I put pen to paper.

On the morrow, representatives of the press arrived to hear the story from Lee's own lips and he had to face several cameras ... A day or two later I said farewell to Lee and his men on Westgate railway station. They had cause to hold their heads high, and soon they were to know that their superb leader was to be posthumously awarded the Victoria Cross – the first ever won by a member of the FAA. They could then hold their heads even higher. Lee and his surviving brother officers received DSOs, and the only rating to return alive, the gallant Leading Airman Bunce, was awarded the Conspicuous Gallantry Medal.

It was actually Tom Gleave who made the initial recommendation for Esmonde to receive the VC for his 'signal act of courage'.

Operation Fuller, however, had failed; forty-two British aircraft being lost in 675 sorties, and an RN destroyer. Although damaged by a mine, *Scharnhorst* arrived at Wilhelmshaven on 13 February 1942, and on the same day, *Gniesenau*, also mine-damaged, and *Prinz Eugen*, both safely reached Brunsbüttel on the Elbe. From the enemy's perspective, in spite of the countless deeds of gallantry performed that day, the audacious *Donnerkeil* was a complete success – one which damaged the prestige of Britannia, which, reputedly, 'ruled the waves'.

Wing Commander Gleave was still commanding Manston on 19 August 1942, the day of the ill-fated combined operation and landing of Canadian troops at Dieppe. Manston again became a hive of activity, as numerous

Group Captain Tom and Beryl Gleave, who did so much for the Guinea Pig Club (TPG Estate).

Spitfire wings came and went throughout what was the day of heaviest air fighting since the Battle of Britain. Tom recalled that:

> One of the most outstanding features of that day which lingers in my memory was the enthusiasm of the Norwegians, groundcrews and pilots alike. As soon as their Spitfires were within fifty yards of the perimeter they were met by the groundcrews who leapt onto the wings while the aircraft were still moving and began to unbutton the rearming doors. The crews' attire consisted of plimsoles and a pair of shorts, and with their bodies tanned brown they gave the appearance of the legendary 'gremlins' – even if their motives could not have been more dynamically opposed! And one instance might serve to show the fanatical zeal of the pilots. One member of a crew was seen to be standing with his backside pressed hard against the fuselage of one of the Norwegian Spitfires. Eventually, curiosity on the part of an Engineering Officer resulted in the Norwegian airman being 'levered' away from the Spitfire, and the removal of his backside revealed a hole in the fuselage the size of a breadboard! I had no doubt that the pilot had ordered the airman to keep his aircraft 'serviceable'!

On 5 September 1942, Tom was promoted to Group Captain, and the following day became 'Group Captain Air Plans' on the Special Planning Staff at Norfolk House, Portsmouth, working on Operation ROUND-UP – later to become OVERLORD. By November 1943, he was Air Chief Marshal Sir Trafford Leigh-Mallory's 'Head of Air Plans', still at Norfolk

Group Captain Gleave in later life with a painting of the action after which he claimed four Me 109s destroyed (TPG Estate).

House, on the Allied Expeditionary Air Force, working on what was now officially OVERLORD. Tom and the American Colonel Phillips Melville were responsible, as the former explained, 'for the production of the overall OVERLORD Air Plan'. TPG wrote it and Phillips Melville criticized. For this, TPG was made a Commander of the British Empire (CBE) and awarded the Legion of Merit of the USA, later changed to a Bronze Star; he was also mentioned in despatches twice, and received both the French Legion d'Honneur and Croix de Guerre.

After the successful Allied landings and campaign in Normandy, on 1 October 1944, Group Captain Gleave, still 'Head of Air Plans', moved to Supreme Headquarters Allied Expeditionary Force (SHAEF), working under General 'Ike' Eisenhower, remaining there until 15 July 1945. By then, the war in Europe was over, the Germans having unconditionally surrendered on 8 May 1945. That July, though, Tom had to return to East Grinstead 'for further plastic surgery', returning to the Continent a month later as SASO to the RAF Delegation to France. Then, between 15 December 1947 and 27 January 1952, he served as a staff officer at RAF Reserve (or Home) Command, before becoming first a member of the Directing Staff, then as Group Director, at the RAF Staff College, Bracknell (7 February 1952 – October 1953). After more corrective plastic surgery at East Grinstead, however, Tom was invalided out of the service in October 1953, as a direct result of his Battle of Britain injuries.

Thereafter, Group Captain Gleave became a Cabinet Office historian, working in the team writing-up the history of the Second World War in the Mediterranean and Middle Eastern theatres, a project he would work on for over thirty-five years. It was for that work, in fact, that Tom was later made a Fellow of the Royal Historical Society and in 1974 became a consultant to the Cabinet Office's Mediterranean and Middle East official history.

While Tom was at the Cabinet Office, in 1958 the Few came together and formed the exulted Battle of Britain Fighter Association – membership of which was, and is, exclusive to the Few themselves (although at the time of writing, 2021, the Association's membership numbers solely Group Captain 'Paddy' Hemmingway, all other members now being deceased). Essentially, the Association's objective, looking ahead, was the welfare of members, and, with that in mind, maintaining the Few's public profile while commemorating the Battle of Britain. Tom Gleave was a committee member, later serving as Deputy Chairman and Historian. Indeed, it was through his good offices and access to official documents not yet in the public domain, that much early research was carried out into the identities of the Few and their units. Tom's own Battle of Britain history reached out when he attended the recovery of the Hurricane in which he had been shot down. The battered Rolls-Royce Merlin engine and other surface items had been discovered lying in Hazel Wood, on Mace Farm at Cudham, by Biggin Hill's Flairavia Flying Club, and on 26 February 1967, Tom, then aged 58, personally attended the recovery, pointing out to journalists present: 'That's my plane', adding, 'Emotion is hardly the right word about what I feel, but it has been an interesting day.' That engine, a direct and tangible link to Tom being virtually incinerated that fateful day high over Kent, is now preserved and can be seen at the IWM Duxford.

In 1968, Group Captain Gleave was an obvious choice to become an historical advisor on the film *Battle of Britain*, alongside the likes of Group Captain Peter Townsend, and Squadron Leaders 'Gandy' Drobinski and 'Ginger' Lacey, and from the German side none other than General Adolf Galland. Released at an impressive gala premier in September 1969, the Battle of Britain Fighter Association, and most importantly its President, none other than Lord Dowding himself, was delighted with the outcome. On 15 February 1970, however, Dowding died, Air Commodore Don MacDonnell, Laird of Glengarry and Chairman of the Battle of Britain Fighter Association, and Group Captain Tom Gleave, Vice-Chairman, attended the great man's simple cremation service three days later. On 12 March 1970, a memorial service was held for Lord Dowding in Westminster Abbey, and Tom was chosen to carry his former Commander-in-Chief's ashes, which were interred in the RAF Memorial Chapel there. It was a very great honour and an indication of the high esteem in which Tom was held by his peers.

As a historian, Tom Gleave lectured extensively and wrote countless articles. On 25 June 1990, however, at a symposium on the Battle of Britain held by the RAF Historical Society at the RAF Museum, Hendon, he became embroiled in a 'verbal dogfight' over Squadron Leader Douglas Bader's controversial 12 Group 'Big Wing' with Air Marshal Sir Denis Crowley-Milling, who, as an impressionable 20-year-old, had flown as Bader's No 2 in 242 Squadron. Tom was right when pointing out that of thirty-two scrambles the wing only engaged the enemy seven times, but wrong regarding the reasons for that, which, he charged, was owing to it taking too long for three or more squadrons to form up. 'Crow' steadfastly refuted this, pointing out that there was no time wasted assembling the formation, as Bader simply took off and everyone just followed him. Sir Denis, however, was a close personal friend of the, by then late, Group Captain Sir Douglas Bader and would hear no criticism of either his hero or the tactics involved, challenging 'Group Captain Gleave and his supporters uncompromisingly'. The fact is, however, that the evidence clearly confirms that the Big Wing was wrong, but not necessarily for the reasons its detractors argued at the symposium.

On 7 November 1990, the fiftieth anniversary year of the Battle of Britain, Group Captain Gleave was 'ambushed' at Duxford by TV presenter Michael Aspel, who whisked the bemused Tom back to London to film an episode of the popular Thames TV biographical programme, *This Is Your Life* (see bibliography). The studio was well-attended by family, including Tom's wife, Beryl; daughter, Angela and husband, Tim, himself a navigator on RAF fast jets; and grandchildren. Sadly, there was one close family member missing: Tom and Beryl's son, John, who had been killed in a canoeing accident in Canada. The programme was, however, a joyous occasion, a celebration of this great man's life, who comes across on screen as a kindly, amusing and popular man, a raconteur. In the audience were various of the Few, including Air Marshal Crowley-Milling, and fellow founding Guinea Pig, Wing Commander Geoffrey Page. Indeed, numerous members of the Guinea Pig Club were present to show their appreciation of their extraordinary 'Chief Guinea Pig', who inherited the role after Sir Archbald McIndoe's premature death in 1960. The Club had really been, along with the Battle of Britain Fighter Association, central to the Gleaves' lives, Tom and Beryl supporting the Club in numerous ways, Tom looking after members' welfare via his position as an RAF Benevolent Fund committee member. Indeed, the youngest Guinea Pig, Jack Perry, summed Tom up as 'a most generous and warm-hearted Guinea Pig ... and we all love you dearly'. Former RAF pilot and aviation archaeology enthusiast David Porter, however, had a surprise for Tom: in a hedgerow close to where his Hurricane crashed, the handle of Tom's ripcord had been found, which was presented to him. At the time, Falklands War burns' victim Simon Weston had a particularly high profile and was the show's final guest, paying his own tribute by describing Tom as 'A pig of a man.' It was a great episode, tribute and record of this wonderful man's life.

Group Captain Tom Gleave departed this world on 12 June 1993, aged 84, having led, by any standards, an extraordinary and full life, during which he became a quiet and compelling inspiration – and did nothing but good. As Tom said, 'I wouldn't have missed it for all the tea in China, to have taken part in the Battle of Britain and to have known Archibald McIndoe is more than many can achieve in one lifetime.'

Chapter Three

Wing Commander Ronald Gustave Kellett DSO DFC VM AE

Ronald Gustave Kellett was born on 13 September 1909, at Eldon in County Durham, the son of Matthew Henry Kellett and his wife, Louise Jeanne Antoinette Kellett. Ronald was actually the fifth of their seven sons, whose entry into this world was apparently unimpressive: according to the midwife, he was so small and weak, as to be 'not worth bothering with'. Subsequent, august, events would prove this a somewhat flawed assessment…

Ronald's mother's family, the Montchals, were Swiss Huguenots; his maternal grandfather, Charles Montchal, was descended from an ancient and noble French family and taught modern languages at his finishing school in Geneva. The Montchals owned a chalet at Chamonix, a world-class skiing resort at the base of Mont Blanc, the highest peak in the Alps and situated near France's borders with Switzerland and Italy. Known by her middle name, Jeanne Montchal was 19 when she married Matthew Kellett, who was then 33 and from an entirely different background.

The Kelletts had lived in County Durham for decades, starting out as lead miners and Weslyan preachers in the Weardale area before transferring their business interests to coal-mining and preaching Methodism. Ambitious, the Kelletts were hard-working, motivated and well educated. Matthew's father, Thomas Walton Kellett, was a colliery manager, and it was to that profession Matthew was apprenticed at the age of 16, achieving first class certificates at the Shildon Mechanics' Institute in Theoretical and Applied Mechanics, Mathematics, the Principles of Mining, and Building Construction. By 1897, Thomas Kellett had become ill, so the burden of supporting the family was shouldered by Matthew, the Kelletts then living at the Manor House, Auckland St Helens. Matthew, then managing Messrs Peases' St Helen's Colliery, and Jeanne married on 23 April 1902, at the Temple des Maccabees in Geneva's St Pierre Cathedral, before spending their honeymoon at the Italian lakes. It was a good match, combining two well-to-do families.

Afterwards, Matthew continued to manage St Helen's Colliery while being most active in local affairs as a member of various local government

The infant Ronald Gustave Kellett, pictured with two of his brothers (unless otherwise indicated, all photographs in this chapter courtesy Kellett family).

boards and committees. When the First World War broke out in 1914, Matthew Kellett was agent to Pease and Partners for three collieries, namely Eldon, Eldon John Henry and St Helen's, Auckland, later that year adding Windlestone to his portfolio. In 1915, however, Matthew so badly injured a hand in a shooting accident that it was amputated. Nonetheless, he remained industrious and involved in local politics, his positions including a seat on the Durham District Miners' Welfare Committee from its inception in 1922, until he died in 1940. His father's example undoubtedly influenced Ronald to follow in his footsteps, in various ways, in due course, and this atmosphere of hard work, community spirit and philanthropy would very much underpin his life.

Ronald developed an early interest in money. While shopping with his mother as a child, he was used to sampling foods like cheeses – but on one occasion requested a sample of money; the bemused shopkeeper retorted that he must be 'Lloyd George', who was Prime Minister at the time, and the nickname stuck in the family. The family sometimes visited Scarborough, and Ronald remembered hearing the rolling thunder drifting across the North Sea from the Battle of Jutland on 31 May 1916, when he was 6. The Kellett children enjoyed a privileged upbringing and lifestyle, and at home all had a retired pit pony to ride. Annually, the family spent their summers at Jeanne's Chamonix chalet, where once Ronald, fascinated by flying from an early age, jumped from the building's balcony using an umbrella as a parachute – inevitably the brolly failed to arrest his descent, but fortunately only minor bruising to both body and ego resulted. It was there, in the Alps, that Ronald learned to ski, and would enjoy many skiing holidays to the region.

Having initially been tutored at home by a governess, from 1917–1922 young Ronald attended Bow Preparatory School in Durham, then moved up to Rossall School at Fleetwood, north of Blackpool, following his four older brothers into Stag's Head House as a boarder. He would leave the school, owing to a point of principle, just before his sixteenth birthday. After Rossall, Ronald first worked with his father, learning about the coal industry, but his fascination with money soon led him to become a post boy, delivering the mail in Liverpool's stock exchange, where he subsequently gained his stockbroking qualifications. In 1929, Matthew Kellett took over the lease on Biddick Hall, owned by the Earl of Durham, who had mined coal in Durham since the Middle Ages. It was an impressive residence, at Bournmoor, near Sunderland and Chester-le-Street, but the political landscape of the time was far less appealing than this idyllic setting.

Coal mining was a troubled industry during the 1920s, further damaged in 1925 by the reduction of subsidies and return to the gold standard, which substantially contributed to British coal exports being uncompetitively priced. By 1926, for example, there had been prolonged industrial unrest in the coal industry, especially following the Samuel Commission's report which rejected nationalisation and recommended both wage cuts and longer working days. On 1 May 1926, mine owners staged a lock-out, which incensed workers and the trade unions; the trouble erupted into the General Strike two days later, in which transport workers, dockers, builders, printers and engineers all came out in support of the miners. Twelve days later the strike was called off, after the government recruited civilian volunteers and special constables to break the strikers, while the army maintained the supply of coal and essential supplies. Although returned to work, the miners remained frustrated and angry. Then, in 1929, the Wall Street Stock Exchange collapsed, heralding the Great Depression – generating in its wake exactly the socio-economic conditions in which extreme politics – not least fascism and nationalism – thrive.

Between the wars, Britain was a divided society, the noted social historian Charles Lock Mowat concluding that throughout this time there were 'several Englands ... their differences ... never so sharply drawn', while the celebrated novelist and broadcaster J.B. Priestly noted in his *English Journey* that there were 'four Englands': that of the southern counties and guide books, the industrial north with many silent furnaces, the prosperous Home Counties and the 'England of the dole'. These divisions in society were not just regional, they were also economic, but the two were inexorably connected. By 1929, the socialist Labour Party had taken the vote in many industrial and urban areas, and that year, for the second time, Labour formed a minority government. Many Labour MPs, however, became increasingly critical of the decision by their Prime Minister, Ramsay MacDonald, to reduce unemployment benefit, and when invited by King George V to form a National Government, the House of Commons comprised mostly Conservative MPs. MacDonald, therefore, sought to

Biddick Hall, near Bournmoor, the lease to which Matthew Kellett took over in 1929.

consolidate power and achieve a mandate via a general election, which was held on 27 October 1931. Contesting the strongly Labour Chester-le-Street seat on behalf of the Conservatives was a certain 22-year-old stock broker: Ronald Gustave Kellett.

Ten days before the election, Ronald addressed a well-attended meeting at Burnmoor Parish Hall in which he argued that tariffs were required to protect British industries. On other occasions he promoted his belief that low bank rates could only improve trade, and made clear the strongly held view that the north-east possessed all the skills and resources to prosper, providing local people invested in locally produced goods and services, instead of that wealth leaving the region and being spent elsewhere. It is clear from his speeches and writings at the time that the north-east, its people and economy, were genuinely dear to his heart – even though, for the past four years, he had worked in London as a stockbroker with Laurence, Keen and Gardener. Of this period, Ronald himself later wrote that:

> Britain was still the leading power in the world. In spite of our difficulties we still maintained a navy, army and air force while the Canadians had largely disbanded their armed forces as a result of the world slump; the United States had opted out of world affairs and was recovering from the Wall Street Crash. Britain had three million unemployed and most heavy

industries had languished since the end of the Great War. The new National Government was faced with a vast task of industrial reconstruction. Somewhat typically, the election was being fought to save the pound. We were still on the gold standard, though only foreigners could exchange our £1 notes for gold. The first measure to go off the gold standard, the second to make money cheap; at the time, you could, if you had credit, borrow money from the banks at 2½ per cent and buy government securities to yield 5½ per cent – the result was the patriotic measure to pay off the old 5 per cent war loans and replace with the present issue 3½ per cent War Loan. The credit and money made available in this way enabled the new steel works to be built and the new industrial recovery that continued until the outbreak of war. As a prospective candidate for Parliament, I had the opportunity to meet, mainly socially, many ministers of the Crown, and even in the quiet of London's Reform Club, membership meant that economic and foreign affairs were a fairly normal subject of discussion.

In 1931, the Liberals allied themselves with the Conservatives at the general election, which saw Labour lose eight of eleven seats in County Durham. One of the three seats Labour retained, however, was Chester-le-Street,

Ronald Kellett's mother's chalet in Chamonix, pictured in 1964.

considered the safest Labour seat in the country, the successful candidate, J.J. Lawson, taking 60.6 per cent of the vote against the Conservative Kellett's 39.38 per cent. So it was that Ronald returned to London and the stock exchange, and Labour governed until the next general election, in 1935 – but by then, the young stock broker had left his political ambitions behind.

On 25 July 1931, shortly before the general election, Ronald and his brother Herbert had climbed Mont Blanc (15,774ft), receiving a certificate confirming the achievement – which was no mean feat. On another climb there, Ronald and his guide made their ascent amid a fierce electrical storm, making the whole enterprise highly dangerous given that the rock is ferrous. Remaining put during the worst of the storm, Ronald and his guide had no option but to distance themselves from their metal mountaineering equipment by dangling it beneath them on a rope. Fortunately both survived the frightening experience, Ronald later admitting that it was one of two occasions in his action-packed life when he had felt 'lonely'. It would not be long, however, before the intrepid adventurer would be hundreds of feet above sea-level again – this time achieving his life-long passion for aviation and ambition to become a pilot. Of this development, he wrote that:

> In the autumn of 1933, I obtained an introduction to the 600 'City of London' Squadron of the Auxiliary Air Force through George Kerr, a friend of my eldest brother who he had been at Sidney Sussex College with. George was, I think, an unlikely aviator, but was a good scholar, making his living as a journalist and proud of being a clergyman's son.
>
> The choice of 600 Squadron was somewhat obvious as I was working with the stockbroking firm of Lawrence, Keen and Gardener, members of the Stock Exchange London, and the squadron's pilots and ground personnel were largely recruited from City institutions such as the Bank of England, Stock Exchange and Lloyds.

The origins and elite socio-economic status of the AAF has been described in previous chapters, but suffice it here to say that 600 was among the first four raised, forming at RAF Northolt as a bomber squadron on 14 October 1925. Initially equipped with Avro 504 trainers and Avro D.9A biplane bombers, the squadron moved to RAF Hendon in 1926, re-equipping with Westland Wapitis. The squadron's second CO, Squadron Leader the Rt Hon. Freddie Guest, a veteran of the First World War, took over on 19 November 1926, having previously been Sir Winston Churchill's Private Secretary, the great man having been Secretary of State for Air from 1921–22. Guest was, therefore, an experienced and well-connected officer who would do much to shape 600 Squadron.

Ronald Kellett later explained that his decision to join the AAF had been very much influenced by concern at the growing unrest in Europe following Hitler's rise to power:

> Stanley Baldwin, in many ways the national leader, had already stated publicly that the RAF must at least be as powerful as that of Germany, and when I suggested to him in 1931 that I would be more valuable as a pilot than as prospective Conservative candidate for the very socialist constituency of Chester-le-Street, he did agree, although he hoped, and indeed would work, to prevent war – the waste of life and effort involved with which he thought would be catastrophic, and so it proved to be. Little did we know at the time that the Russians were secretly training German pilots inside Russia in contradiction to the Versailles Peace Treaty and their international obligations, and Hitler was already banging the drum.

Ronald's first flight was made in an Avro Tutor (J8698) on 12 January 1934, with his instructor, Flight Lieutenant John Wallis. The following month, on 16 February 1934, Ronald made his first solo flight, after which it was a matter of completing the usual training flights at weekends while

remaining in his civilian occupation during the week. On 30 March 1934, he was commissioned into the General Duties Branch and became Pilot Officer Ronald Gustave Kellett, and, having successfully completed his elementary flying training, received the coveted pilot's brevet on 12 July 1934. Thereafter, Pilot Officer Kellett was able to make long-range flights across the country, to various airfields, including Usworth, near Sunderland,

Ronald Kellett pictured before the Second World War, whilst serving with 600 'City of London' Squadron of the Auxiliary Air Force.

often to visit family and friends, which 600 Squadron's pilots were encouraged to do for training purposes. As we have already seen in previous chapters, peacetime flying was not, however, without thrills, spills and tragedies, such as that which befell the squadron at the Hendon Air Pageant on 30 June 1934; on that day, 600's CO, Squadron Leader Stanley Collett, was killed in somewhat tragic and sensational circumstances. Son of Sir Charles Collett, the Lord Mayor of London, Squadron Leader Collet was escort to the Prince of Wales at the Pageant, and also participating in a 600 Squadron full-formation take-off and flying display. Occupying the observer's seat in Pilot Officer Lea's Wapiti, the pair took off but the crowd soon watched anxiously as the aircraft was clearly in trouble, veering towards the crowd before the pilot successfully regained sufficient control to return the machine to the airfield – where it stalled, crashed, and erupted into an inferno. Lea was thrown clear but Collett, believed to have been rendered unconscious by the impact, died, rather publicly, in the flames. The auxiliaries may have considered themselves an elite, impervious to, and dismissive of, the service's usual discipline and regulations, not least 601 Squadron among them, the fabled so-called 'Millionaire's Mob', but as we have seen countless times, death and tragedy are no respecters of social class. When all is said and done, flying in those days – even during peacetime and considering the comparatively primitive aircraft involved, and lack of electronic blind-flying aids – was a risky business.

Annually, the AAF squadrons attended a week-long camp at an RAF station, to practise operating together as a unit and preparing for the eventuality of being called to full-time service in the event of hostilities. In August 1934, for example, having been redesignated a fighter squadron the previous month, 600 Squadron's summer camp was held at Tangmere, the station's regular officers standing back and acting only in an advisory capacity while the auxiliaries took over all the necessary roles and tasks to see the squadron function efficiently. Both at the camp and beyond, like regular RAF squadrons, the AAF's units trained constantly for war. After re-equipping with the two-seater Hawker Hart, intended as a light-bomber but a variant of the single-seater Hart fighter, and Hawker Demon fighter, 600 Squadron's training expanded to include practising air-to-air firing with the Vickers machine-gun and Lewis camera gun, and dive-bombing, all of which became the primary focus of the 1935 summer camp, held at the Sutton Bridge ranges.

That camp began on 14 July 1935, Pilot Officers Kellett and Elworthy flying cross-country to Thornaby, south of Hartlepool, but were forced down by bad weather en route. As the senior man and pilot, Ronald sent his passenger, Pilot Officer Sam Elworthy to find a farmer and confirm

In August 1939, Ronald Kellett was posted as a flight commander to 616 'South Yorkshire' Squadron of the AAF, and is pictured here (seventh from left) with other officers of that unit at Leconfield. Also included are FO Jack Bell (KIA 30/08/40, extreme left); PO Hugh 'Cocky' Dundas (fifth left); PO Ken Holden (fourth left); PO George Moberley (KIA 26/08/40, sixth from right); PO John Brewster (killed in a flying accident, 06/04/41, fifth from right). At extreme left, kneeling, is PO Lionel 'Buck' Casson (PoW, 09/08/41), and FO Dick Hellyer (kneeling second from left).

their location, which was subsequently determined as being near Easby. Considering that Elworthy went on to become a MRAF and highly decorated baron, Ronald Kellett would later delight in recounting this story, given that Elworthy's hike across country to find some local knowledge was a somewhat unpleasant experience, given that the field was churned up by cattle and riven with their droppings! Another memory which caused wry amusement was the occasion on another cross-country flight when Ronald, short of fuel, landed on a road adjacent to a garage, filling up and telling the bemused owner to send the £80 bill to the Air Ministry; Pilot Officer Willy Rhodes-Moorhouse of 601 Squadron went one better though, and when the squadron was short of fuel he bought a garage and all its petrol for the unit's benefit! Such were the escapades and attitudes of the amateur auxiliary airmen, whose gleaming brass 'A' lapel badge, some opined, stood not for 'Auxiliary' but 'Argue and Answer Back'. Nonetheless, these men were totally committed to flying and serving their country in time of crisis – which they would do in due course.

Having been promoted on 20 September 1935, in February 1938, Flying Officer Ronald Kellett went on attachment to 46 Squadron at Digby, where he converted to what was the RAF's frontline fighter at that time: the Gloster Gauntlet, another biplane. Coincidentally, during that month-long deployment, Flying Officer Kellett was under the wing of none other than Pilot Officer H.F. 'Billy' Burton, who signed Ronald's log book on behalf of 'B' Flight's commander, confirming the 12.35 hours the auxiliary had flown on the new type. Then it was back to 600 Squadron and business as usual, flying the even more outdated Demon. On 1 July 1938, Ronald became a flight lieutenant, and early in 1939, 600 Squadron at last bade farewell to biplanes and re-equipped with the twin-engine Bristol Blenheim monoplane fighter. Flight Lieutenant Kellett first flew the new type (L1164) twice on 24 January 1939, when checked out by instructors. Thereafter he familiarised himself solo on the aircraft, flying the usual 'circuits and bumps', cross-countries and other typical training flights.

Again, as already explained in previous chapters, but a point worth reiterating, is that the RAF's biplanes were all obsolete from May 1935 onwards, when the Me 109 made its maiden flight – six months before Britain's Hawker Hurricane and nearly a year before the Supermarine Spitfire. By the time 600 Squadron converted to the Blenheim, the Hurricane had been in service for just over a year, the Spitfire for only five months. The Germans, on the other hand, had replaced biplanes with single and twin-engine fighters and bombers long ago, and had tempered these weapons during the Spanish Civil War of the mid-thirties. Forthcoming events would prove the Blenheim too slow and inadequate for daylight combat, but fortunately this would not affect Ronald Kellett; in March 1939, his five-year contract to serve as an AAF officer concluded and he was placed on the reserve list, a trained pilot available to be recalled in a crisis. By that time, his log book recorded a total of 536 flying hours, 11.35 of them at night, 11.25 on instruments, and 12.55 on the Blenheim. Purely civilian life was not to last long, however; on Tuesday 27 September 1938, Flight Lieutenant Kellett was recalled to 600 Squadron – for full-time service, which is significant. On 26 February 1935, Hitler had formally established the *Luftwaffe*, and a fortnight later further and openly defied Versailles by announcing German rearmament and conscription. With no reaction from Britain and France, thereafter Hitler had dismantled Versailles piecemeal. On 7 March 1936, for example, Germany remilitarised the Rhineland, and on 12 March 1938, German troops marched into Austria, once more uniting the two nations, all of which was forbidden by Versailles. It was, however, the Munich Crisis of September 1938, that led to the recall of certain experienced auxiliary officers, including Ronald Kellett.

Hitler had insisted that the Sudetenland, a border area between Czechoslovakia and Germany, largely populated by German-speakers and removed from Germany when Versailles redrew the map of Europe, be returned to Germany. The Czechoslovaks refused. The British Prime Minister, Neville Chamberlain, intervened but no agreement was reached during a series of meetings with Hitler between 15–22 September 1938. Three days later, RAF personnel were recalled from leave and all squadrons were placed on stand-by. With all eyes on the Sudetenland Crisis, on 26 September 1938, the officers of 600 Squadron were ordered to report to whatever was their nearest HQ. The squadron was told to stand-by at Hendon until 2300 hrs, but without further instruction or news, stood-down the airmen who were ordered to report back the following morning at 0800 hrs. At 0130 hrs that morning, the 'order to embody came through to Hendon'. All officers were notified of the requirement by telephone, the 'Embodiment', which is to say brought to full-time service, being complete by 1600 hrs. All peacetime equipment, such as camera guns, were removed from the aircraft and weapons were made ready. The squadron ORB noted that:

> The news, following the Prime Minister's broadcast the previous evening, was extremely bad and from all reports it seemed that nothing short of a miracle would stop a European war. In the evening tension was relieved somewhat by the news that the Prime Minister was going to fly out to Munich the following day and hold a four-day conference with Herr Hitler.

On 28 September 1938, the Munich Conference took place, involving Britain, France, Germany and Italy. The Czechs were not invited to this meeting determining their country's fate. The Conference agreed to cede the Sudetenland to Germany in return for Hitler's guarantee of peace. This bought vital time and was a victory for Chamberlain's controversial policy of Appeasement. While the RAF had started substantially expanding in 1936, as war appeared increasingly likely, the fact was, as the Under-Secretary of State for Air, Harold Balfour, later pointed out: 'In September 1938, the *Luftwaffe* could have shot the RAF out of the skies ... This, from a purely air defence of Britain view, is why I am a man of Munich', adding that thereafter there was an 'urgent drive over the next twelve months to prepare the RAF for war ... We did our best in the year left to us and for the air, I repeat, "Thank God for Munich".' By 10 October 1938, the situation had stabilised sufficiently for the panic to subside and auxiliary squadrons, including 600, to 'disembody'. There would be no war – yet – and auxiliary personnel trooped back to their civilian lives.

With RAF expansion came the formation of more auxiliary squadrons, among which was 616 'South Yorkshire' Squadron (substantially mentioned previously in this book), which formed at Doncaster airport on 1 November 1938. Preparations, however, had been ongoing for several weeks, 600 Squadron's regular adjutant, Flight Lieutenant D.S. Radford

Above left: Squadron Leader RG Kellett DFC drawn at Northolt by the war artist Cuthbert Orde on 17 September 1940.

Above right: Under the so-called 'double-banking' system, the new Polish and Czech squadrons had English-speaking squadron and flight commanders, who were shadowed by their foreign counterparts. At Northolt, Squadron Leader Kellett's Polish opposite number was initially Acting Squadron Leader Zdzislaw Krannodebski, pictured here, until the Pole was shot down and badly burned on 6 September 1940.

MC, being posted to be the new unit's first adjutant on 8 October 1938. With Squadron Leader The Earl of Lincoln in command, 616 was initially formed as a bomber squadron, but transferred to the strength of Fighter Command on 15 November 1938. On 20 March 1939, Flight Lieutenant Kellett's period of service with the AAF was extended by a year and he was posted to command 'A' Flight of 616 Squadron, the 'South Yorkshire' unit being equipped with the Gauntlet – by now dangerously obsolete – and a small number of Fairey Battle monoplane light-bombers, used for training. By 10 June 1939, 616 Squadron was able to field an operational 'Service Flight', comprising 'Squadron Leader The Earl of Lincoln, Flight Lieutenants R.G. Kellett and A.N. Nelson, Flying Officer R.O. Hellyer, and Pilot Officers E. St Aubyn and G. Moberley'. Frighteningly, the squadron's strength stood at just six Gauntlets and four Battles. Fortunately, change was very much in the air – as was war: on 3 September 1939, Britain and France declared war on Nazi Germany, following Hitler ignoring demands to withdraw his troops from Poland following the German invasion two days previously. The years of waiting were over and any temporary extensions of service were now irrelevant, as the country mobilised for war and both auxiliaries and reservists were mobilised on a war footing.

Among 616 Squadron's auxiliaries was Pilot Officer Hugh Dundas (whom we met in the chapter on Wing Commander Burton), who recalled that in September 1939:

> we were told that our Gauntlets were to be replaced by Hawker Hurricanes, and one day a single specimen of this famous breed was delivered to the squadron. We looked it over with awe and some apprehension. We climbed onto the wing and gazed with amazement at the mass of knobs, switches and instruments in the little cockpit. Eventually Ronald Kellett announced that he would fly it. We gave him plenty of good advice and assured him that we would be standing-by to watch the accident, which fortunately did not occur.

That flight took place on 9 September 1939, Flight Lieutenant Kellett flying 616 Squadron's sole new Hurricane, L2101, on a local flight of fifteen minutes. The following day, the squadron was ordered to re-equip with the superior Spitfire, a 'development' Dundas recalled that 'made us all very happy'. The dreaded 'knock-out blow' upon declaration of war had failed to materialise, by either side, and so, as Dundas also recalled, 'the first few

Brothers in arms: Squadron Leader Kellett (left) with Pilot Officer Jan Zumbach – who survived the war a highly decorated fighter ace and leader.

months of the war passed by in a happy blur of flying by day and parties by night.'

October 1939 was also a significant one in Ronald Kellett's personal life, because on the 15th, he married Miss Daphne Jane Sheaf at the Church of St Martha-on-the-Hill, just outside Guildford in Surrey.

Sadly, Daphne's mother had died in 1913, six days after her daughter's birth, from Addison's disease; her father, Eric Sheaf, later remarried, to Miss Jo Humphreys, when his daughter was 10. Having first studied at Cambridge University, Eric had graduated from Guy's Hospital around 1906, joining a Dr Mitchell at a Guildford practice before being appointed surgeon to the Royal County Hospital three years later – where he would serve for forty years, the only interruption being the First World War, when he served with the Royal Army Medical Corps in Salonika between 1914– 19. Daphne boarded at Queen Anne's Caversham, a highly recommended girls' school in Surrey, where she matriculated, achieving the equivalent of the School Certificate, and enjoyed sports, including playing Lacrosse for the school, which enjoyed an enviable reputation in the sport. In April 1930, Daphne holidayed in Austria with her father and stepmother, and the following year, aged 18, travelled to Paris to undertake a course in photography. Having received an inheritance from her late mother's side, in May 1934, the intrepid young traveller arrived by ship in New York, to stay with American friends for a few months. All of this experience encouraged a world-view.

In Daphne's mid-twenties, by which time she had treated herself to an SS Jaguar sports car, she attended a house party at the Lincolnshire home of her cousin, Neville Bavin, a keen huntsman. It was there that Daphne met Ronald Kellett, who was a member of the Cranwell Hunt and used to fly up to Cranwell to attend weekend hunts and was a guest that evening. A year later, Daphne and Ronald married, and after a short honeymoon set up home in a house-share with Squadron Leader John Grandy (later MRAF Sir), then a squadron commander in 13 Flying Training School, at 8 Newbegin Street, Beverley, Yorkshire.

After his nuptials, Flight Lieutenant Kellett resumed his service with 616 Squadron. On 30 October 1939, Ronald and two other 616 Squadron pilots travelled down to Duxford and collected three Spitfire Mk Is from 66 Squadron. Ronald ferried Spitfire K9804 back to Leconfield, where 616 Squadron was now based, but recorded no impression of the type in his log book. It must have been quite a contrast, though, to also fly an open-cockpit Gauntlet that same day, on a 'battle climb, 25,000ft', and on 'night landings'. Thereafter the usual training flights were ongoing, in addition to defensive patrols and investigating 'X-Raids'. This was, of course, the

'Phoney War', when the West sat back to await Hitler's next move – which was anticipated when the weather improved. This assumption proved correct on 10 May 1940, when Germany, achieving total surprise, invaded the Netherlands, Belgium, Luxembourg and France. With shocking force, the German advance was unstoppable. Preserved by their Commander-in-Chief, Air Chief Marshal Dowding, for home defence, little changed for Fighter Command's Spitfire squadrons however, which were sensibly not committed to a battle already lost in France. As seen in previous chapters, only Hurricanes went to the Continent, and so 616 Squadron's comparably monotonous daily routine, far away from the fighting at Leconfield, went on undisturbed. Five days later, however, a signal was received posting Flight Lieutenant Kellett; he was to join another new squadron, 249, at Church Fenton, in 13 Group.

Having been disbanded in 1919 after flying seaplanes during the First World War, on 16 May 1940, 249 re-formed as a single-engine fighter squadron at Church Fenton under the command of Squadron Leader John Grandy, a personal friend of Ronald and Daphne Kellett. The new unit's authorised establishment comprised sixteen aircraft, and in addition to the CO, two flight lieutenants, fourteen flying or pilot officers, twelve sergeant pilots, six flight sergeants, five sergeants and ninety-five 'Other Ranks'. On that day, Flight Lieutenant Kellett arrived to command 'A' Flight, and among the pilots was a certain Pilot Officer Tom Neil, who later described his new Flight Commander as being referred to by his nickname:

> 'Boozy' ... A rather stout little man with thinning fair hair, prominent pale blue eyes and some of the more obvious manifestations of shyness. 'Boozy', in contradiction of his nickname, always seemed to me the soul of sobriety. Though physically active, he gave the impression of being totally non-athletic and was in turn patient, irascible, charming, abominably rude, courteously understanding and disconcertingly dismissive. A wealthy man by any standards, 'Boozy' was also absurdly generous. A little short of transport in the squadron, he at once produced an ancient Rolls-Royce which he drove everywhere – including the rough grass of the airfield – with cheerful abandon, allowing any of us to do the same.

The following day, 249, a 'squadron in embryo', was ordered to Leconfield, and a day later Spitfires began arriving from 27 MU at Shawbury, in addition to two Miles Masters, so that pilots could be checked out under

Above left: After Squadron Leader Kranodebski was hospitalised, he was succeeded by Acting Squadron Leader Witold Urbanowicz, who had already seen combat over Poland and served with 145 Squadron at Tangmere. Urbanowicz, who survived the war, is pictured here at Northolt with Squadron Leader Kellett.

Above right: Squadron Leader Kellett at Northolt, high summer, 1940.

the watchful eye of an experienced pilot, usually the flight commander, before flying the precious Spitfire solo. On 20 May 1940, for example, Flight Lieutenant Kellett checked out Pilot Officer Neil in Master N7749, who then went on to experience the thrill of flying the Spitfire, which he described as 'Electrifying! Wonderful!'

Ronald Kellett later wrote of this time that 'the squadron mainly doing patrol work off the Yorkshire coast, occasionally chasing lone enemy aircraft out to sea as night fell, or on stormy, cloudy, days'. The main flying commitment, like 616 Squadron, with which 249 shared Leconfield, however, was training.

On 12 June 1940, Ronald was promoted to temporary Squadron Leader, although Squadron Leader Grandy remained in command, while the former continued leading 'A' Flight while recognised as Grandy's second-in-command. The two Squadron Leaders agreed a system where each worked one day, followed by the next off. Squadron Leader Kellett later recalled a particular incident from this time:

> It was a day in June 1940, and I, the second-in-command, was in command. The cloud base was a low 200ft and it was raining hard – a condition known as the 'Hitler Weather Year of 1940'. We assumed no action that morning, but the telephone rang with orders to patrol Hull at 20,000ft, to which the reply was 'Don't be silly, no squadron could fly through 20,000ft of cloud in formation, and where could they land?'
>
> Answer: 'Nowhere, you have parachutes!'
>
> Reply: 'If that is so, I volunteer to go with two of the best pilots, but the squadron – no!'
>
> Fifteen minutes later the telephone rang again, and the NCO says that the AOC accepts your offer – proceed. So, Flying Officer Nicolson and Flying Officer Smithson were detailed to fly with the second-in-command. We took off and were in cloud almost at once. At 12,000ft Control warned us of balloons over Hull … we came out of cloud at 20,000ft into bright sunshine and a white and level cloud base below. Sure enough there was the enemy about two miles to the south, and we went as fast as possible into the attack. The enemy dived into cloud, not to be seen again. We three returned north over Hull to continue the patrol over cloud – then a thermal tunnel appeared, the sun shone on Flamborough Head – too good to ignore! We went down the hole and broke up over the sea at about 100ft, doing about 400 mph. Slowing down a turn to the right, with Nicolson in the cloud, and me a few feet from the sea. We just managed to cross the cliffs south of Scarborough and land at Catfoss – a closed RAF station. We landed in a quagmire and taxied onto the tarmac. A good breakfast followed, we all having had a most exhilarating sortie.

On 8 July 1940, 249 Squadron moved back to Church Fenton, and it was there, on 19 July, that Squadron Leader Kellett was informed by the Orderly Room Clerk 'that I was posted to Northolt to form and train a Czech squadron. Typical banter at the time: "I hear you have a squadron of dud cheques!"' Squadron Leader Grandy signed-off Ronald's log book

'There I was, nothing on the clock but the maker's name': Flying Officer Jerzy Jankiewicz (MIA, 25 May 1942, extreme left) describes a recent aerial exploit to Squadron Leader Kellett (second left), Sergeant Stanislaw Karubin (killed in a flying accident, 12 August 1941, second right), who often flew as Kellett's wingman, and Pilot Officer Franciszek Korniki, who later commanded 308 'City of Krakow' Squadron (and survived the war).

with an 'above the average' assessment as a fighter pilot, and 'exceptional' as a 'pilot-navigator'; by this time, Ronald had accumulated 800.45 flying hours, including a substantial amount of time on both Hurricanes and Spitfires.

Squadron Leader Ronald Kellett: 'I arrived at Northolt, finding an Adjutant, Hadwen, but no Czechs or other personnel … A British warrant officer then arrived and we were told that the squadron would be Polish.'

And so began a new chapter in the life of Ronald Gustave Kellett.

On the night of 31 August 1939, Nazi Germany had invaded Poland in an undeclared act of war. Simultaneously, German troops crossed the frontier along its entire length, attacking guards and forward defensive positions. At dawn, the *Luftwaffe* bombed aerodromes and major strategic assets throughout Poland. In spite of all the diplomatic unrest that summer, the German attack achieved complete surprise.

31 August 1939 was also the first day of general mobilisation in Poland, reservists reporting to their units and operational Polish Air Force squadrons

dispersing to various airfields. Few, though, believed that war would actually break out, the reservists expecting little but an inconveniently long stay with the colours ahead of them. The Poles trusted that Britain and France would honour their pledge to support Poland in the event of Nazi aggression, and hoped that would be sufficient to deter Hitler. Many expected the Soviets to side with the Western Allies, unaware of the secret Non-Aggression Pact signed by the foreign ministers of Germany and Russia on 23 August 1939 – on which day Poland's fate was effectively sealed.

Sixty-three German divisions attacked Poland, facing fifty-six Polish. The German attack was spearheaded by fifteen mechanised *panzer* divisions, whereas the Poles only fielded two motorised formations. Indeed, the enemy's superiority of arms was considered 8:1. Moreover, the German *Wehrmacht* was a modern force, equipped and armed to current standards, whereas Poland went to war with the equipment of 1925. Importantly, Germany's diplomatic successes of 1938 and 1939 had secured strategic advantages in that Poland's northern frontier and most of the southern was controlled by Germany, and the attack was made simultaneously from north, south, east and west. Offensives on both flanks and steady pressure in the centre provided for envelopment. Nonetheless, by the campaign's ninth day, German losses were such that it was clear that the Poles' determined fighting spirit had been overlooked – a factor emphasised by the propaganda machine preparing German public opinion for news of heavy casualties. This fighting spirit, in fact, would define the Polish contribution to the Allied cause throughout the hard-fought Second World War.

In 1939, Poland, even more than Britain and France, was comparatively ill-prepared for a war in which air power played a crucial role. The immense capital investment required to create and maintain a modern air force was quite simply beyond the means of a newly independent country. The technical inferiority of its air force made Poland vulnerable – but the bravery of her aircrews was beyond doubt. The first German aircraft to be destroyed during the Second World War were two Do 17s shot down over Olkusz by Lieutenant W. Gnys, in total the Polish fighter pilots destroying 126 enemy aircraft during the campaign. The Polish fighter squadrons, including the Fighter Brigade and Army Cooperation units lost fifty pilots and 114 aircraft, while the bomber force suffered 90 per cent casualties in aircrew and aircraft. By 14 September 1939, though, losses were such that the Polish Air Force was unable to continue operations. Some squadrons lost their last aircraft on that day, others, threatened with being overrun, destroyed their remaining machines. Three days later, fittingly in a violent thunderstorm, the few remaining Polish aircraft crossed the Romanian border, ending the air fighting over Poland. On the same day, in another

In another posed shot, Squadron Leader Kellett, on the Hurricane's wing, along with, from left, Sergeant Karubin, Pilot Officer Kornicki and Flying Officer Jankiewicz, gaze wistfully skywards.

undeclared act of war and a real shock, Russia invaded eastern Poland. Polish Air Force flying schools, experimental and maintenance units evacuated their personnel to Romania and Hungary.

On 1 October 1939, German troops entered Warsaw. Six days later, Polish resistance finally ceased – although the Polish Home Army would continue fighting a partisan war until the Germans were finally defeated five years later. From a Polish viewpoint the short, tragic, campaign was a consequence of unpreparedness; the outcome, against ruthless and efficient aggression, inevitable. Nonetheless, Poland's defiant spirit, refusing to surrender without a fight, no matter what the odds, set a benchmark of courage that would resonate throughout the Second World War. It is important to understand the Polish character, fundamental to which is a powerful sense of duty and love of country. For 500 years, Poland had fought two or three defensive wars every generation. Poles know full-well, therefore, that material possessions, even the family home, can be lost – instantly. Polish soil, however, cannot be destroyed, and neither can national solidarity – an iron-will to endure whatever the odds. Consequently, the Polish nation has survived even when forced into exile. It is this long history of suffering and its profound effect on the Polish psyche that, more than anything, explains why, when Poland had fallen, the Polish armed forces trekked west, to continue the fight. It also explains why, when the call was made for the PAF to reassemble in France and later Britain, only the dead, those who were prisoners or ordered to remain in Poland, did not respond. For others, not continuing the fight and ultimately liberating Poland was unthinkable.

Organising the evacuation of the Polish Air Force was a huge task. First, crossing into such neighbouring states as Romania, Hungary, Latvia and Lithuania, the Poles were interned. In Romania, where the majority of air force personnel were interned, officers and 'other ranks' were immediately segregated. Unsurprisingly, Romania was unprepared for this influx of personnel, and things were chaotic. When the news was received that General Sikorski had re-formed the Polish government in France and was assembling the Polish armed forces there, this chaos worked to the Poles' advantage: many staged individual escapes, the majority travelling by boat via Constanza, Beirut, Malta and Marseilles. How these men must have felt, their homeland overrun, separated from their families, of which they had no news and vice-versa, can only be imagined.

On 25 October 1939, British, Polish and French delegates met at the French Air Ministry to decide the best way forward. The Poles argued that their air force should be re-formed in Britain, given their familiarity with British aero-engines but ignorance of French equipment. The French countered that the Poles should be equally divided between Britain and France, believing that Polish squadrons could be quickly formed and would be welcome reinforcements on both sides of the Channel. Finally, it was decided that 300 Polish aircrew and 2,000 ground staff would be stationed in Britain, the rest in France. Unfortunately, the West was unable to resist Hitler's assault, when it came, on 10 May 1940, and so with the Fall of France, the Poles were on the move again, travelling to Britain by various means and routes, to once more continue the fight. Blackpool became the central collecting point for the Polish airmen, who continued to arrive throughout the summer and until the autumn of 1940. As Churchill told the leader of the Polish government in exile, General Sikorski, on 19 June 1940, 'We are now united for better or for worse.' Sikorski had, in fact, already signed the Anglo-Polish Accord, which included the requirement that PAF now in England should, without delay, form an army cooperation squadron, four of bombers and two fighter units. Initially absorbed by the RAFVR, Polish personnel actually belonged to the technically autonomous PAF, while remaining either embedded in RAF units or simply continuing, at least administratively, to serve in their original PAF formations.

The main issue, however, was the language barrier, because although many Poles spoke French fluently, they had no English. There was, though, another problem: Air Chief Marshal Dowding, for some reason he never explained, initially mistrusted 'foreign pilots' – by which he specifically meant Poles and Czechs, but this negative perspective did not extend to French, Belgian, Dutch or Norwegian airmen. Nonetheless, in accordance with Churchill's undertaking to Sikorski, the first Polish fighter squadron, 302, was formed at Duxford on 13 July 1940, three days after 310, the first Czech squadron – and on 2 August 1940, Squadron Leader Ronald 'Boozy' Kellett found himself at Northolt, forming, and in command of, 303 (Polish) Squadron – which at first existed in name only. That Ronald spoke French fluently, had experience of forming new squadrons and converting pilots to the new monoplane fighters, doubtless explained why he was selected for this role.

Squadron Leader Kellett:

> The day in August arrived when a body of men wearing dark blue battledress and berets arrived, with strange words of command and an unusual facial appearance. They were soon sorted out into flights 'A' and 'B', and 'C' for maintenance, and bit by bit order appeared out of chaos. We officers met in the mess and we learnt something of the battle of and their escape from Poland to France, and arrival in England. They mostly spoke French, which enabled me to communicate reasonably freely with them.

To overcome the language difficulty and procedural differences, a system of 'double-banking' was adopted in these foreign squadrons, with RAF officers in charge but their roles duplicated by Polish officers, who shadowed their

303 Squadron groundcrew applying squadron markings during the Battle of Britain.

English-speaking counterparts. 303 Squadron – named after Kosciusko, a Polish national hero who had been General Washington's adjutant in the American War of Independence, and later a national leader – was formed from two Warsaw-based PAF squadrons, which were smaller than RAF squadrons. Consequently, the Polish 111 became 'A' Flight, and 112 'B'. The Polish officer duplicating Kellett's role was Squadron Leader Zdzislaw Krasnodebski, while the Canadian John Kent, commanding 'A' Flight, was shadowed first by Flight Lieutenant Henneberg, then Flight Lieutenant Urbanowicz, and in 'B' Flight, Flight Lieutenant Athol Forbes' Polish counterpart was Flight Lieutenant Lapkowski. Like Kellett, Forbes also had good French, while Kent's was poor, so the 'A' Flight commander took to learning Polish, which was much appreciated by his Polish subordinates.

On 3 August 1940, certain of 303 Squadron's pilots were sent to RAF Uxbridge on an R/T course, and for others English lessons began. Today, it is difficult to imagine how primitive some things were just over eighty years ago; Sergeant Reg Nutter, a Hurricane pilot of 257 Squadron, also attended that R/T course and recalled that:

> This proved to be quite interesting as it had a two-fold purpose – to train pilots in R/T procedures and to train the controllers who would later control us from Operations Rooms. Marked out on the playing fields was a large map of the British Isles and a part of Western Europe. We pilots were given tricycles, which had formerly been used to sell ice cream! In the box at the front was a TR9 radio, which, at the time, was standard aircraft equipment. We wore headphones and were surrounded by a set of blinker like boards, which restricted our vision. The driving chain and sprockets were arranged in such a way that when we pedalled twenty-five times the wheel moved round just once! Thus our speed across the maps matched the speed of fighter aircraft across the ground at normal throttle settings. Down in the stadium a complete Operations Room had been built. This was fully manned by trainee controllers, WAAF Plotters etc. On top of the stadium was a spotter who passed our position, and the position of the person designated as the 'enemy', down to the Operations Room. The 'controllers' could then vector us by radio to make interceptions. We both learned a lot from the course but found it somewhat difficult to sit down on our final return to the squadron. Pedalling around in the hot sun in a serge uniform made one quite sore in a certain part of one's anatomy!

At Northolt, work was ongoing to convert the Poles to the Hurricane. Many of the Poles were experienced pilots, and had even seen combat – but although some had flown obsolete French monoplanes, none had flown modern RAF fighters. That said, both of Squadron Leader Kellett's English-speaking flight commanders had only just converted themselves to the Spitfire and Hurricane, and, along with their CO, experienced a pilot though he was, neither had yet been in combat. So, as with many other squadrons at the time, everyone was learning. In addition to the language barrier, the Polish pilots faced another difficulty, in that the controls of British aircraft were contrary to Polish machines. For example, in Polish aircraft the throttle was pulled back to accelerate, whereas in British designs power was increased by pushing the throttle forward. All of this took time to overcome, but did nothing to mollify the Poles' frustration at being unable, as yet, to fight Germans. Nonetheless, after the Poles were first checked out in the Link Trainer simulator, training continued apace, on the ground and in the air.

Squadron Leader Kellett commented that 'Converting the Poles to Hurricanes was going well, apart from one or two landings with the undercarriage up.' This, however, was far from uncommon when pilots were changing over from flying biplanes with fixed undercarriage; the 303 Squadron CO continues:

> We had all learned certain Polish words: 'Klapy' = flaps [which biplanes did not have], and 'potwozie' = undercarriage, so in the air we could remind the pilots of these needs. The rumour circulated that the Poles were so keen to land that they failed to put the undercarriage down – typical schoolboy humour imparted to high places. I would have none of this, as they were very quickly being converted to Hurricanes and had retractable undercarriage for the first time.
>
> There was an incident that illustrated the problem of language and non-communication. A principle of the dispersal of aircraft was no aircraft should be nearer than, say, twenty yards from the next, and on seeing two aircraft wing tip to wing tip, I ordered a Polish airman to start one so that it could be taxied to another place. There was a certain amount of gesticulating which I ignored. I should have noticed that the air pressure for the brakes was nil, but once the aircraft was started I taxied onto the slope of the taxi-track. I tried the brakes to turn the aircraft but they didn't work – and within seconds the eight-ton aircraft had crashed into one of the dispersal huts,

destroying its propeller and not improving the hut either! As chance would have it, the Command Accident Officer was just walking to dispersal and witnessed the event. He told me not to report the accident, saying there were too many to deal with and that he quite understood the reason.

An awkward thing happened. The men and NCOs were paid but the officers, strangely, were not. Gieves, the outfitters, had come to fit their uniforms but the authorities had not decided as to their pay. Of this I was unaware, but assuming they would get RAF pay, I drew my own cheque at my private account, against which the Accounting Officer paid them the money. When the second month's pay was due, this process had to be repeated, but the accountant still held the cheques and said he could not continue the arrangement. I decided that if the third month was the same, I would draw my own cheque on the Bank of England and instruct my bank to collect. I hadn't spent eleven years in the City for nothing and knew that the Bank of England would accept some responsibility.

At this time we received visits from the Air Minister, Lord Sinclair, who discoursed in French with the Poles and showed himself to be the sincere, good and unselfish man he was. This visit was entirely informal. Indeed, a little later Churchill turned up as an area near Northolt had been bombed that night and he wanted first-hand knowledge of the damage. He was in great form and full of vigour. We expressed regret at the civilian damage and loss of life; 'In these times', he said, 'they must learn to put up with it.' I was able to mention the matter of officers' pay – it was not, after all, the Crimean War. 'They must be paid', he said. Furthermore, within six hours of the receipt of the money, all loans were repaid and my cheques torn up. He also said, 'I value the commander of a fighter squadron today as much as a Cabinet Minister, but don't tell them.' However, he was off to his work within minutes, but had done a great deal for morale and certainly showed none of the anxiety he must have felt.

During the training period I had, with the agreement of General Ujesjski, recruited more pilots from the Polish collecting depot at Blackpool and think we had about thirty-two operational pilots in the squadron. It was therefore possible for each pilot to be on duty twenty-four hours on and twenty-four off. We changed over at one o'clock. No pilot on duty was allowed to leave the Mess, early bed and early rising, the squadron being on readiness from half an hour before sunrise until half an hour after sunset. We suggested to the ground crews that they should do the same but British and Polish NCOs replied that while our pilots were in the air they wanted to remain on duty, and so it was. I don't believe any Squadron had better NCOs or aircraft maintenance than 303.

The Group Captain offered my Squadron an old lorry as a dispersal wagon – I said that would not do and that I should use my own Rolls-Royce, an old, open, four-seater. It would have been bad for morale to use an old lorry when other squadrons had cars, even though not Rolls-Royces. The car was looked after as well as the aircraft and proved to be an excellent morale factor, arriving at dispersal from the mess with as many as twelve pilots in it.

We soon started Squadron training in fighter tactics. It was soon clear, however, that the four or so attacks laid down by Fighter Command were unworkable, as the R/T orders could not be understood. Instead, we perfected one attack only and each battle was made to fit the attack, i.e. not the method of attack to suit the battle.

It is often said that Air Chief Marshal Dowding was remote and detached from his pilots, but Ronald Kellett writes that during the Battle of Britain, which was in full swing while the Poles trained, he was to 'receive many visits from him and Air Vice-Marshal Park'. The matter of fighter tactics, however, provoked a sharp reaction when discussed with the Commander-in-Chief:

These matters were discussed with Dowding on his various visits, but above all he asked 'Have you shown them the bloody wall where we shoot pilots who kill their own side?' I replied that certainly the Poles practised aircraft recognition and reminded him that these men had seen the real thing in Poland and France.

On 30 August 1940, 303 Squadron was up from Northolt on an affiliation exercise with Blenheim bombers when the raid came in against Hatfield, intercepted by Squadron Leader Douglas Bader's 12 Group-based 242 Squadron and certain 11 Group units. In the 1969 film *Battle of Britain*, the events of that day, as befalling 303 Squadron, were somewhat embellished. In the epic movie, *Blackhawk Leader* (Barry Foster playing 'Squadron Leader Edwards', the English-speaking cinematic CO of 303 Squadron) gives his pilots a course to steer, away from the trouble, but one, 'Ox' (Andrezej Scibor), sights the enemy, leading to excited Polish chatter over the ether. Unable to contain himself, 'Ox' responds 'Repeat please', feigning receipt – or ignorance – of the order, and peels off to engage the Germans, followed, one by one, by his comrades – while 'Squadron Leader Edwards' flies on, momentarily oblivious, until out of the corner of his eye he catches sight of what is going on and with a cry of 'Oh, Gawd, streuth!' and makes after his errant Poles – by now successfully in action. Squadron Leader Kellett recalled the truth of what happened:

> On the last training occasion we had twelve Blenheims as 'targets' when we were warned that enemy aircraft were in the vicinity. We were to guard the bombers. I ordered the squadron to assemble above and behind the bombers and cease 'attacking'. It was, however, too much for Paskiewicz, who, having seen an enemy aircraft, attacked and shot it down.

Some of 303 Squadron's Polish groundcrew, held in high esteem by Squadron Leader Kellett, pictured with Hurricane V6684, emblazoned with both the Squadron's badge and Battle of Britain victory score.

Fortunately, the Blenheims were not attacked, and I reported to Group Captain Vincent (Northolt's Station Commander) and Air Vice-Marshal Park that we were ready for combat.

Flying Officer Ludwik Paskiewicz (Green 1) reported that:

> We took off in two flights, (A and B) for exercises in attacking Blenheims, at 1615 hrs. After climbing to 10,000ft, we flew northward. After a while we noticed ahead a number of aircraft carrying out various evolutions. The centre of the commotion seemed to be about 1,000ft below us, to starboard. I reported it to the CO, Squadron Leader Kellett, by Radio Telephone, and, as he did not seem to reply, I opened up the throttle and went in the direction of the enemy. I saw the rest of the Flight some 300 yards behind me; behind me were the burning suburbs of some town and a Hurricane diving with smoke trailing behind it. Then I noticed, at my own altitude, a bomber with twin rudders – probably a Dornier – turning in my direction. When he noticed me, he dived sharply. I turned over and dived after him. When turning over I noticed the black crosses on the wings. Then I aimed at the fuselage and opened fire. When I drew very close, I pressed down for a new attack and then I saw another Hurricane attacking and a German baling out by parachute. The Dornier went into a steep turn, and then I gave him another burst. He dived and then hit the ground and burst into flames. I then approached the other Hurricane and saw its markings: VC I. I have been firing at an enemy aircraft for the first time in my life.

Paskiewicz was credited with a 'Do 17' destroyed near St Albans, shared with Pilot Officer J.B. Wicks of 56 Squadron. The enemy aircraft concerned was actually a Me 110 of 4/ZG 76, however, the starboard engine of which was disabled by Paskiewicz before being attacked by Wicks and exploding at Barley Beans Farm, Kimperton.

According to *Destiny Can Wait: The History of the Polish Air Force in Great Britain* (1949): 'Squadron Leader Kellett neither restrained Paskiewicz nor allowed the other pilots to follow him. He continued the exercise, which consisted then of protecting, instead of "attacking", the Blenheims.' In reality, therefore, all but one of Kellett's pilots had obeyed his order, and there was clearly sympathy for Paskiewicz's ill-discipline. Nonetheless, what could have happened to the Blenheims, had all the Poles followed Paskiewicz, as in the film, bears no thinking about.

The Canadian commander of 303 Squadron's 'A' Flight, Flight Lieutenant John Kent (second left) walking in for press photographers with, from left, Pilot Officer Miroslaw Feric (killed in a flying accident, 14/02/42), Flying Officer Bogdan Grzeszczak (killed in a flying accident, 28/08/41), Pilot Officer Jerzy Radomski (survived), Pilot Officers Jan Zumbach (survived), Witold Lokuciewski (survived), and Boguslaw Mierzwa (killed in action, 16/04/41); Flying Officer Zdizislaw Henneberg (MIA 12 April 1941); Sergeants Jan Rogowski (survived) and Eugeniusz Szaposznikow (survived and who also flew as one of Squadron Leader Kellett's wingmen).

It is not widely appreciated, in fact, that certain aircraft within a squadron at this time were fitted with a navigational device called 'Pip Squeak', which automatically blocked all transmissions for fourteen seconds of every minute while broadcasting a 'fix' on the aircraft's location. It is likely that a squadron commander's aircraft would be fitted with this device, which may explain Squadron Leader Kellett's lack of response to Paskiewicz. Either way, the actual circumstances involving 303 Squadron on 30 August 1940 were rather different to the exaggerated (but more entertaining) version in *Battle of Britain*.

Notwithstanding a certain amount of 'artistic licence' by post-war film-makers however, after Paskiewicz's victory Squadron Leader Kellett 'reported to Group Captain Vincent [Northolt's Station Commander] and Air Vice-Marshal Park that we were ready for combat'. And so it was that after less than a month, 303 Squadron became operational and entered the fray in earnest.

There was a time, not so very long ago but especially when Poland remained behind the post-war Soviet 'Iron Curtain', that the story of the PAF during the Second World War, including the Battle of Britain, was comparatively unknown. That, however, is not the case now, and the story of 303 Squadron in particular is a well-trodden path by historians today. Consequently, instead of reconstructing 303 Squadron's Battle of Britain, at the risk of unnecessary duplication, the following is that story in Wing Commander Kellett's own, and previously unpublished, words.

Group Captain Vincent and the controller were concerned to see that 303 had a good start in the battle. They sent 'A' Flight to do an interception, which from our point of view was brilliantly timed. The sun was in the west and the enemy were turning for home. We saw a flight of Messerschmitts and were able to dive on them out of the sun. My two 'equipiers' and I attacked and were soon firing at the enemy aircraft who started evasion. Flight Lieutenant Henneberg and his two equipiers saw another group of enemy aircraft about to support their comrades. At any rate we returned elated to base with four Messerschmitts accounted for and no losses.

There is a certain similarity about air battles and to detail them all would not only be boring but beyond my memory. However, the good and bad stand out.

The Germans had possibly recruited all their pilots from railway and tram drivers as they were, at this period, flying in very rigid formations. Teutonic like they all had their own Führers. The first squadron attack on a German formation showed me that the leaders of the close escort fighters were standing back and above the bombers so that they could see when our fighters were in contact with their bombers, but there was an area of 100 yards in front and 500 yards behind, below and on the flank where they could see nothing. The obvious tactic, therefore, was to dive in front of the fighters and make a feint on the bombers, pull up under the fighters and give the leaders of the close escort fighters a good burst of gunfire from underneath. This tactic was immediately adopted by 'A' Flight doing the feint, while 'B' Flight attacked the bombers. The result justified the tactic as almost immediately the close escort dived out of the battle – leaving time not only for 'B' Flight to attack the bombers but for 'A' to follow 'B' Flight on the tail of the enemy formation.

Northolt's Station Commander, Group Captain Stanley Vincent, looks on whilst Squadron Leader Kellett presents the pilots of 303 Squadron to King George VI, 26 September 1940.

Although our attacks were successful, and also proved to be sound from the point of view of our own casualties, we found that the enemy aircraft were slow to catch fire in spite of close-range firing. We had strict rules about scoring – the enemy aircraft had to either catch fire or hit the ground. There was little problem with knowing whether you were hitting the target, as you could see the incendiary bullets exploding on the enemy aircraft. About one in five of the bullets were De Wilde explosives, but because of self-sealing fuel tanks and armour plating protecting the pilots, our sighting pattern seemed inadequate, so in spite of orders we aligned all our eight guns to converge at a point 200 yards dead ahead. This seemed more effective.

The Squadron Leader's role was to bring his pilots into contact with the enemy in such a way that his formation maintained cohesion until the firing commenced – after which it was every man for himself. Thereafter it was virtually impossible to reform and make renewed concerted attacks – partly due to language problems but also because of the distance travelled in a few seconds and the large number of aircraft in the sky. The real battle was fought at 15,000ft and above while below it remained a beautiful, peaceful day over sunny Kent. Individuals or pairs were, of course, at liberty to finish off winged birds trying to escape, but very early in 303's fighting days, pilots were instructed to stay over land and not pursue enemy aircraft over the Channel. The C-in-C pointed out that there was ample sport over England. This adequately describes the first major battle against a big enemy formation; it was the tactic we tried to bring off in all our battles. The problem was, of course, to see the enemy formation in plenty of time and sum up the various components. Sometimes you could see the enemy over France from 10,000ft over London.

I will now describe a bad battle [6 September 1940]. It happened early in the morning when the sun was low in the east and there was a heat haze up at 15,000ft. We were told to steer an easterly course and climb to 15,0000ft. I searched the sky for the enemy but the first I saw was the bomber formation below me. Obviously, all surprise was gone and we were going headlong into the fighters. I decided to attack the centre of the bomber formation, which the squadron did. The Controller had made an error of judgment, as we should never have been placed on a collision course but bought round from a flank.

It is not possible for me to say how each pilot fared. I can only describe my own experience. I picked my bomber, a Heinkel [at the time, Squadron Leader Kellett claimed a Do 17 destroyed, which post-war researchers actually now believe was in reality a Me 110 of Erprobungsgruppe 210, which, having also been attacked by Hurricanes of 1 Squadron, exploded at Foyle Farm, Crowhurst], and opened fire at about 200 yards. I could see the gunner trying to get a bead on me, so I kicked the right rudder and his cupola and gun disappeared. I continued firing at the left engine, but no flames. I was being hit by the bomber behind me and finally the ammunition in each wing exploded and my guns stopped firing. At the same time, the Heinkel's left engine caught fire. I received a blow on my left knee and the cockpit was covered with smoke and a red liquid. I yelled 'I'm getting the hell out of here!', put the

Group Captain Vincent explains a point of detail to His Majesty, whilst Air Vice-Marshal Keith Park, AOC 11 Group, looks on with Squadron Leaders Urbanowicz, with PAF cap badge, and Squadron Leader Kellett.

Hurricane into a spin and thought I would get out at 8,000ft. I took it out of the spin and found I could control it, stick hard back and over to the left and a speed of 150 mph. I then found the canopy would not move, nor could I move the emergency jettison device.

Biggin Hill appeared just below me and I started a long approach, but the Heinkel I had just shot down came down with me and kept getting in the way. However, it crashed near Biggin Hill and I landed at 150 mph. It took the whole of the long runway. I did not use the flaps as the Hurricane was nose-heavy, one tyre was punctured and so the aircraft ran with the left wing low. However, the brakes were working so I swung it right before going through the boundary onto the road.

Airmen came out of the dugout and axed off the canopy, and I was bundled into said shelter as bombs were still exploding on the runway I had just used. I reported to the Operations Room, relocated above a small shop near the airfield, owing to bomb damage, and asked them to inform Northolt that I was safe. It had been a near thing. The aircraft had virtually no rudder or elevators left, a hole in each wing large enough for a man to jump through, but, even worse, the incendiary rounds used by the Germans had burnt holes in my parachute and ruined my helmet, goggles and uniform.

In his post-action personal combat report, Squadron Leader Kellett wrote that 'After diving I realised that it was very difficult to control the aircraft as there was a big hole in the starboard wing and the aircraft was very right wing low. There was no elevator control and not much rudder control.' Safely landing that Hurricane, therefore, represented an astonishing feat of airmanship, it must be said, especially as it was possibly the most badly damaged RAF fighter to do so during the Battle of Britain.

Squadron Leader Kellett continues:

The Station Medical Officer insisted that I go to Farnborough hospital, where I saw poor Krasnodebski. He had been shot down and landed in the hospital grounds by parachute, been operated on and was in bed [this Polish officer is 'Poley Boy' referred to by Tom Gleave at the Queen Victoria Hospital, East Grinstead, in the previous chapter]. I was X-rayed to see whether my leg needed treatment but was discharged. On the way back to the station the doctor showed me the crashed Heinkel, not a man alive, a sorry mess. He then arranged an ambulance to return me to Northolt. I told the Station Commander, Group Captain Vincent, what had happened and he assured me that it would not happen again, and indeed it did not. We lost five aircraft and had four pilots wounded in that engagement. The aircraft were all replaced during the day and I led the squadron that evening at full-strength. We soon regained our form but as a result of that bad episode the Group Captain suggested that as Flight Lieutenant Forbes had been wounded, it would be wiser if I led the squadron alternately with Flight Lieutenant Johnny Kent, as we had to have an English-speaking leader at all times to understand and comply with the Controller's instructions.

About this time we were ordered to fly in a wing, the usual order being No 1 (English), No 1 (Canadian), and 303 (Polish), the latter leading. No 1 (English) took off east to west first, the other two squadrons west to east after No 1 was airborne, the two No 1s forming up behind and below 303. I won't discuss wing tactics as we did not alter ours, but will mention one

303 Squadron, September 1940.

event which could have had a calamitous outcome. We were told No 1 (Canadian) and 303 take-off, 303 leading; there was no mention of No 1 (English). We taxied out and formed up on the west side of the airfield but due to a small rise in the centre of the field we could not see No 1 (English) Squadron. We came to the top and saw that they were taking-off too – a very nasty moment! A quick decision, I put the throttle through the 'gate', giving maximum boost, black smoke poured from the exhausts and by luck we were over the top of them and no collision. The Group Captain, poor man, standing on the tarmac, must have had a nasty shock, and as I looked down I saw with relief that there were no smoking wrecks on the airfield.

The record of 303 was by now well-known and often mentioned by the BBC on the morning news. We often received messages of congratulations from the War Office. In addition, one had almost daily conversations with Air Vice-Marshal Park, who was at all times polite and considerate, inviting criticism of his controllers and himself, and listened to any suggestion regarding tactics. Our greatest honour, though, was a visit by the King, George VI. I was only told on the morning of His Majesty's visit, and the squadron was

166

duly paraded by the aircraft, pilots and groundcrew ready for action. It seemed a somewhat strange task to present pilots and NCOs who knew no English to the monarch, but it went well. I remember introducing Sergeant Sobek to the king with the words 'A fine armourer, Sir.' The king shook his hand and replied that he was glad he was a good armourer.

After the inspection was finished, I particularly asked the adjutant to see that the king signed the squadron's history book, which had been kept up to date by the Poles. Just before he signed the squadron's book I was asked the date, and confessed I couldn't remember. I asked Upton, who said that it was 25 September 1940 [the king's visit actually took place on 26 September 1940]. So I said 'The twenty-fifth, Sir.' His Majesty replied 'Funny, when I got up this morning it was the twenty-sixth, but anything can happen in war!' I gave the signal for caps off and the cry for 'God save the King.' Certainly, a loyal shout resulted, but I never knew what it meant!

'Battle Alert' was sounded and we were off to fight a raid coming in over Portsmouth. I remember the course, 180°, at first being told 15,000ft, and then 10,000ft for altitude. I ignored the lower height but increased speed. It proved another classic battle. The enemy were executing a left-hand turn just over the target. The sun was high but perhaps slightly behind them. We jumped on the tail of the enemy bombers from the sun while they were concentrating on their turn. The tactic worked perfectly. I think that twelve of us shot down thirteen enemy aircraft for no loss at all, and we returned to Northolt delighted with ourselves and the good luck that the king had brought us.

By this time, the squadron was a thoroughly united team and was certainly enjoying off-duty time as well as presenting a disciplined and efficient Squadron in action.

The reader will have noticed my use of the word 'equipier' to describe pilots who flew either side of their leader. Their role was to attack with and protect him wherever possible from a surprise attack, so more or less stuck with him. I always flew with two or three pilots who had the somewhat strange names of Wunche, Karubin and Szaposznikow. I regarded them as somewhat akin to the 'Three Musketeers' and as the weeks went by I knew I could rely on their abilities and particularly their loyalty.

Göring's final fling was the two Sunday raids during which we received the order to 'Patrol Whitehall to the City' – I think we were kept as last reserve and as a result were too late to make our standard attacks. I made a head-on attack – it was like flying through a rainstorm of bullets, tracer showering us like rain. I attacked the leader but was set upon by three fighters and spent the rest of the attack looking after myself. Fighter Command's score was badly adrift that day and certainly 303 had a poor day. Nevertheless, an inquiry was made into the claims for enemy casualties and Group Captain H.A. Pearson of Fighter Command HQ arrived to investigate our scores. I am glad to say that we were completely exonerated but it was a slight on our honour, which I, for one, resented. It changed my attitude to claiming victories and I never claimed another. It did not, however, decrease our zest for shooting the enemy. One or two incidents in October 1940, after the main battle was won, illustrate this.

The Germans had resorted to fighter sweeps with few, if any, bombers. On one of these occasions there was a thin layer of cloud at about 17,000ft, which could be seen through from below, but not from above. We found a squadron of twin-engine Me 110s in a defensive circle above the cloud – an easy target. We attacked from below the cloud and saw the enemy tighten up his formation as we picked them off one by one. Alas, when there were about six left, the enemy turned for home.

On another occasion almost the whole of 11 Group was spread all over Kent when I spotted a lone Dornier, escorted by one Me 109, crossing the Group's front. It passed various squadrons unnoticed before 303 pounced on the luckless pair. The fighter was disposed of in seconds, and in line astern, one after the other, we filled the Dornier with lead until it crashed in Kent – we circled the oast house until we were certain that no one had got away, and then returned to base. The pilots were so keen that I found holes in my wings which had come from behind, so eager were they to attack and impatient for me to get out of the way.

The Poles, however, seemed to sense that the Battle was over and that the Germans would not return in such numbers, so I signalled the War Cabinet thanking them for their congratulations but saying a drink would be welcome. A number of cases of gin and whisky duly arrived and a party for the entire aquadron was given in the hangar, Group Captain Vincent being our guest of honour – he must have had a frightening experience as the Poles threw him up to the hangar roof three times; he was a heavy man but fortunately caught before he hit the concrete floor.

There were two visitors of note I have not mentioned. One was Balfour, the Under Secretary of State for Air, who turned up on the morning of 20 September 1940, one of two days when flying was impossible due to fog. He told me, somewhat rashly, that there would be no German attacks that day. 'Good', I said, 'I will go and see my daughter [Joanna Montchal Kellett] in Guildford, who is now several days old and I have yet to see her or my wife.' The other visitor was a beautiful and intelligent woman, no less than Madame Curie, who was Polish-born and therefore able to converse with our Polish personnel in their mother tongue.

About the middle of October 1940, we learned that the squadron was to be moved to Leconfield, near Hull, and that my two flight commanders were to be promoted and given their own squadrons. Around this time, Balfour decided to present the squadron with a fine radiogram which duly arrived at Northolt. The move was carried out by air but unfortunately the radiogram failed to reach Leconfield – leaving me the task of thanking the minister for the radiogram which never actually arrived. All our enquiries drew a blank!

We had a great reception at Leconfield. The Earl of Middleton entertained us, together with the Cameron Highlanders who were based at Beverley. Much to the indignation of the Poles, Pilot Officer Lillywhite, who was a Central Flying School instructor, arrived to approve individual flying standards and prepare the squadron for night flying. When I explained that he was a 'Professor' who trained future professors, they settled down and he became a most popular member of both the squadron and our social life.

It soon became obvious that Fighter Command could not produce flight lieutenants who, either by age or experience, could be expected to lead the Poles. I therefore told Air Vice-Marshal Leigh-Mallory, our AOC now we were in 12 Group, and Air Chief Marshal Sholto Douglas, the new C-in-C Fighter Command, that we should let the Poles take over and withdraw all British personnel.

There were four small incidents that occurred while 303 was at Leconfield that are worth mentioning. One was a raid by two Heinkel Bombers. We had a flight over the coast at 10,000ft, awaiting the arrival of enemy aircraft, and one flight in readiness by the hangars. Suddenly, I heard the roar of engines as the enemy bombers turned around the hangars at about 20ft, bomb doors open, machine-guns firing. It was too late for us to take off. Alas, one airman was killed by a splinter, and five of our aircraft damaged by falling tarmac, and the enemy got away.

On another occasion we had two aircraft on patrol over the sea off Scarborough. I had warned control about the dangers of a 'Haa' – a Yorkshire fog that comes in from the sea in certain weather conditions and soon covers the land. It is generally about 20ft up and happens in fine weather, and is due to high

Above left: The grave of Pilot Officer Paskiewicz at Northwood – who recorded 303 Squadron's first aerial victory on 30 August 1940, but was shot down and killed the following month (Author).

Above right: The Czech Sergeant Josef Frantisek, with seventeen victories, was one of the top-scoring pilots of the Battle of Britain – but was killed in a flying accident; this is his grave at Northwood (Author).

moisture content in the atmosphere. I had asked the controllers to keep an eye on a reserve landing field. The Haar appeared at the eastern end of the airfield and control was 'phoned – they had done nothing – so I took off and found that I could see the shapes of the hangars through the fog. The two Polish pilots were soon collected and we landed safely in formation. Alas, the Station Commander chose that moment to drive across the aerodrome and arrived at dispersal in a temper. 'You nearly killed me, Kellett!', he shouted, while I parried with, 'Is the airfield for aircraft or your car, Sir?' The Poles thanked me for helping their pilots land but otherwise my action had not been noted, except by the angry Group Captain.

During our stay at Leconfield we had a mess dinner attended by Air Vice-Marshal Leigh-Mallory and local guests. After dinner I told him that he would be honoured by the Poles but should give anything loose, watch, money etc, to his Aide de Camp. He had no other warning, but when we entered the ante room he was duly picked up and thrown to the ceiling three times – he went up like a ramrod and even if surprised, appeared to enjoy it.

After a few more fruitless efforts to find British flight lieutenants, my advice to let the Poles take over the command of the squadron was accepted. I was then posted to form 96 Squadron, and had to say a hurried goodbye to 303 Squadron.

The Battle of Britain was certainly seen by Churchill to have been vital in the nation's survival, and it certainly was a turning point in the British contribution to victory. The record of 303 (Polish) Squadron was outstanding if measured only by the score of enemy aircraft shot down, easily exceeding any other squadron in the Battle.

We had the aircraft, and far better ones than could be purchased from the USA or elsewhere, at that time. We also had a unique, sophisticated and highly efficient air defence organisation. We lacked trained pilots; 303 had some thirty pilots, whereas most British squadrons were down to fourteen or sixteen. In addition, the PAF brought to Britain trained pilots of whom about eighty participated in the Battle of Britain. In this context it should not be forgotten that only about 400 pilots were in action in 11 Group at any one time, and 20 per cent of these were Polish airmen – which may well have been the crucial factor.

Suffice it to say that by this time, members of the Polish forces were, everywhere, regarded as first-class allies and they have, and I believe will continue to have, a special place in the affections of my countrymen and women.

During the Battle of Britain, Squadron Leader Kellett personally claimed the destruction of five enemy aircraft, in addition to two probables and another damaged. By his own admission, however, owing to the query regarding 303 Squadron's high number of such claims, he stopped submitting combat claims. Overall, between 30 August and 31 October 1940, 303 Squadron lost nine pilots killed in action, and claimed the destruction of 128.5 enemy aircraft, making it the highest claiming squadron of the Battle. According to the British historian Richard King (see bibliography), seventy-five casualties attributable to 303 Squadron can be identified in German quartermasters' loss records. The American researcher John Alcorn (see bibliography), however, suggested that only forty-four such German losses could be identified, putting 303 Squadron fifth in the overall list. The very nature of aerial combat, though, especially when many aircraft are engaged, naturally leads to over-claiming, as the speed and confusion of combat

On 16 January 1941, General Sikorski invested (from left) Squadron Leader Kellett, and Flight Lieutenants Kent and Forbes, with Poland's Virtuti Militari, Vth Class.

deceives the human eye, a single casualty being therefore inadvertently multiplied several-fold on the balance sheet. Indeed, following vigorous post-war analysis we now know all fighter squadrons overclaimed to some extent. Nonetheless, and be all of that as it may, the Poles' stellar performance was enough to make even Dowding change his view, paying tribute after the Battle to the 'unsurpassed gallantry' of Polish and Czech pilots, and admitting, 'I hesitate to say that the outcome of the Battle would not have been the same', if not for the brave contribution of these men, numbering 145 Poles and 88 Czechs – trained pilots all and some with combat experience. That said, and this is often overlooked in the reckoning, RAF aircrew had fought in the Fall of France and over Dunkirk, so Fighter Command was not entirely without such experience.

Of this, though, there can be no doubt: the contribution made by the Poles during the summer of 1940, 303 Squadron foremost among them, was as inspirational as it was essential – creating a legend in the process – and the leadership and personal example of Squadron Leader Ronald Kellett went far in effecting 303 Squadron's achievement. This was a man with a world-view, well-travelled, with great experience of a diverse range of peacetime man-management situations, from collieries and regional politics to the financial industry. For all of those reasons, in addition to being an experienced auxiliary pilot and officer with monoplane experience, had marked him out as potentially the perfect English-speaking CO of 303 Squadron. Without doubt, Ronald Kellett had showed his Poles respect and helped them feel both at home and a welcome part of what was happening; most importantly he had led by personal example, which was recognised by an early 'double', being first the award of the DFC, then appointment to the DSO – well-deserved decorations indeed.

On 1 October 1940, Squadron Leader Kellett's DFC was gazetted:

> By his excellent example and personality this officer has been largely responsible for the success of his squadron which in one week destroyed thirty-three enemy aircraft, of which Squadron Leader Kellett has destroyed three. His leadership and determination in attacking superior numbers of enemy aircraft have instilled the greatest confidence in the other pilots of his squadron.

On 25 October 1940, the DSO followed:

> Squadron Leader Kellett as commander of his squadron has built up and trained his personnel to such a fine fighting pitch that no

fewer than 113 enemy aircraft have been destroyed in the space of one month, with very few casualties sustained by his squadron. He has frequently led the wing formation with judgment and success. The gallantry and fine leadership displayed by Squadron Leader Kellett have proved an inspiring example.

Having bidden farewell to the Poles and 303 Squadron, Squadron Leader R.G. Kellett DSO DFC VM took command of the new 96 Squadron at Cranage, on 18 December 1940.

By this time, the night Blitz on British cities was in full swing, the enemy having been forced to crossover to nocturnal raids owing to such heavy losses by daylight, which were unsustainable. Although safer for the German aircrews, due to Britain's still inadequate night defences, the trade-off was less accurate bombing. While the purpose-built Bristol Beaufighter, with Airborne Interception radar, had reached 604 Squadron, based in the West Country, the urgency of the hour dictated that single-engine day-fighters were pressed into the night-time role. Consequently, 96 Squadron was initially equipped with black-painted Hurricanes, then a number of Boulton-Paul Defiant two-man turret fighters arrived. The weather that winter was bad, however, limiting flying, although Pilot Officer Rabone destroyed a raider on the night of 22 December 1940. With 'A' Flight detached to Squires Gate, and 'B' Flight remaining at Cranage, Squadron Leader Kellett flew numerous nocturnal patrols in Hurricanes, before flying a Defiant, N3433, for the first time on 22 February 1941. Over the next few days he would fly a mixture of both types on largely uneventful patrols. Possibly the most exciting occurrence was on 16 January 1941, when General Sikorski invested Ronald with the Polish Virtuti Militari, in recognition of his magnificent leadership of and commitment to 303 Squadron the previous summer.

Squadron Leader Kellett recalled his time in command of 96 Squadron:

> The instruction to operate at night arose from local unrest at having no air defence at a time when the Liverpool Docks were so crucial in the matter of supplies from America. To some extent we had to train by day in order to operate at night – that is to fly the flag by day and make a noise at night.
>
> The pilots were posted in from other fighter squadrons, often without regard to their night flying experience or suitability. The squadron was based at Cranage, home of the Central Navigation School. We were most unwelcome, and although given a hangar, two dispersal huts and a squadron

office, there was no room in the mess. We had to find digs outside, and such food as we needed during the night was provided from a field kitchen. The station at Cranage was in many other ways unsuitable as our base. The weather tended to be thick with industrial haze, and we were shut in by Welsh hills on the west, the Pennines to our east, and the Wrekin to our south.

The location of the airfield at night was marked by a red flashing beacon. This was normally moved around to avoid the enemy locating the airfield. Glim Lamps showed the landing area but as far as I remember these were invisible above 2,000ft. We had a great deal of trouble with the flashing beacon. Farmers did not like it and nor did the local population and we had to deploy an armed guard to protect it from damage. The local army unit undertook to have it for a short period, but even they had to ask for its removal.

The C-in-C, Air Marshal Sholto Douglas, who had replaced Dowding, called on the squadron. He was amused that I wore a gas mask. He agreed that the facilities were deplorable and said that a new station near Wrexham was being built, but that to get greater speed was like pounding a cushion, it got you nowhere. The Hurricane, he admitted was a very poor night fighter as exhaust flames were blinding if you looked forward and below – it was essential to fly on instruments alone to a height of over 1,000ft before looking round at all. He thought that we could be re-equipped with Defiants before long but it would be some time before the Beaufighter and the necessary radar equipment would be available.

I asked him whether I could have the ground NCO from 303 Squadron, and he agreed I could have any named NCO from the RAF. He also agreed that unsuitable pilots could be returned without the necessity of adverse reports. Referred to the problems of the flashing beacon and was informed that we had complete powers in the matter of its protection. The solution to most of these difficulties lay with the luckless adjutant, a man called McIvor of about 33 and fresh from the City. It was bad enough to have to deal with problems and in accordance with regulations, but to deal with the exceptions as well must have been a nightmare. I went with the C-in-C to make my only visit to the Group Operation Room in Liverpool – a cold night with the Blitz around at its height.

Back at the airfield we were busy testing out pilots for night-flying. We had a dual Battle bomber especially converted for this purpose. The instructor got a seat near the tail, some 30ft from the engine but it felt more like thirty yards, and the visibility from the back was strictly limited. It was a forgiving aircraft, however, and did the job. Later, we got a Master, which was an easier aircraft for this sort of instruction. I had two good flight commanders, one of whom was a Czech. He struck me as a very accurate and competent pilot, so I asked him whether he could persuade his authorities to build up a Czech flight, and this was put in train.

In view of the wealth of hazards we decided to have a section based at Squires Gate, Blackpool, and this was a help. However, what with day flying and endless interference by group, I had to instruct the Group Captain not to return to the airfield. This action produced the AOC, Air Vice-Marshal McLauchler, who, though somewhat displeased, understood it was impossible to operate efficiently if one was kept up all day and all night. He suggested that I did not need to fly with the squadron, but I told him that I did not accept that view.

Above left and above right: In 1946, Ronald Kellett resumed his auxiliary service, reverting to the rank of squadron leader, commanding 615 'County of Surrey' Squadron at Biggin Hill. He is seen here with the unit's honorary commodore – none other than Sir Winston Churchill.

I firmly believe no one should give an order to another which he would not carry out himself and only I could decide whether the weather conditions were too dangerous. In fact, the Group Meteorological Officers were magnificent and although we had weather forecasts half hourly when necessary, I never found them at fault.

The whole period of some four months was singularly unsuccessful from the point of view of shooting down enemy aircraft. The only enemy I saw from a Hurricane was two exhaust flames going over me, very close at 90°. I turned immediately to follow but saw nothing more. At night during a Blitz the sky was full of exploding anti-aircraft shells, and without airborne radar aids success was a virtually impossible task. During the period with Defiants my air gunner saw an enemy and fired a few rounds at it, but that was the sum total of real action.

I did pay a visit to the C-in-C at Bentley Priory, where to my amusement, but not his, a staff officer had planned a gas attack on the HQ – and both of us were left choking in his office.

While at Cranage I received the sad news of my father's death and the AOC agreed that I could fly across to Usworth to attend the funeral, which I did, but had to report for duty by nightfall. It was only a thirty-minute flight each way, and a family car picked me up for the fifteen minute drive to the nearby church.

At this time, eating carrots and taking pills to improve night vision were the rule but had little effect, although teams of doctors started a series of tests on night vision. I don't know how effective they were but they were adopted before posting pilots to the night flying units.

Just as the nights were getting shorter and the days longer I was promoted to Wing Commander and posted to the lead North Weald Wing of five squadrons to start offensive operations over France. By this time I was very tired, however, and suffering from rheumatic nodules around my neck, making looking around very painful. I was given a fortnight's leave and sent to the RAF Hospital at Torquay where I was given the attention of a famous doctor. I was given massage and radiant heat and every comfort. In addition, the local AOC in charge of RAF recruits, Brigadier Critchley, lent me his car, allowing

Squadron Leader Kellett pictured in 1947 with the Walrus seaplane he purchased for 615 Squadron.

me to see something of Dartmoor while the nurses looked after my baby daughter, Jan, so I could be with my wife.

Before leaving the subject of 96 Squadron, I can say that an operational Squadron had been built up and the moment airborne interception radar equipment became available, they became a worthy member of that somewhat elite group of operators.

The credit for the defence of Liverpool and Manchester in the winter of 1940/41, in many ways, should go to Colonel Deft, who had built dummy airfields and harbours away from the centres of population. Other geniuses, who bent the Knickebein radio beam, which the Germans used to aid their navigation and identify the bomb dropping area, also made an important contribution. Additionally, the Almighty created a pretty miserable pattern of weather!

With the spring of 1941, along with Fighter Command's new 'Non-Stop Offensive' policy came creation of the new appointment of 'Wing Commander (Flying)' (as explained in previous chapters), to lead the new wings, usually of three squadrons, now based at all Sector Stations. It is an indication of how highly respected the newly promoted Wing Commander Kellett was that he was chosen among the first Wing Leaders – who included such leading lights as Wing Commanders Douglas Bader and the South African 'Sailor' Malan.

WING COMMANDER RONALD GUSTAVE KELLETT

Ronald Kellett left 96 Squadron on 8 March 1941, and was promoted to Wing Commander on 14 March 1941. His arrival at North Weald was delayed, however, owing to his period of hospitalisation, as a result of which he did not fly again until 1 May 1941, when he made a local recce in a Hurricane from North Weald. At this time, the Spitfire was in the process of replacing the Hurricane as Fighter Command's frontline day-fighter, but North Weald's squadrons remained Hurricane-equipped, 56 and 249 Squadrons being based at North Weald itself, while 17, 242 and 605 Squadrons operated from the nearby satellite of Martlesham Heath.

Wing Commander Kellett continues:

When I arrived at North Weald I was delighted to find that Group Captain Stanley Vincent, who had commanded Northolt during the Battle of Britain, had also been posted to command the Sector in which the wing would be based. The wing HQ was at Blake Hall, as was the Operations Room. The Senior Controller was Wing Commander John Cherry who had also been at Northolt during the Battle of Britain.

The four day-fighter squadrons were equipped with Hurricane IIs, which had twelve Browning guns, and two-stage superchargers for high altitude flying. The role of the wing was basically acting as close escort to our bombers, leaving the Spitfire wings the opportunity to attack enemy fighters drawn up by our bombers.

The Wing Leader was given operational command of all squadrons and the Operations Room. This, of course, could hardly be expected to suit the Group Captain, who was relegated to a greater extent of administration than hitherto. The control also covered the night-fighter squadron (coincidently 96 squadron), although in fact they were allowed to operate on their own.

Our first series of operations entailed sweeps over France at high altitude of about 40,000ft with oxygen but no pressurisation. This is probably the limit of human endurance, as one's patience at that altitude is easily exhausted, and if one becomes at all angry you are also exhausted. Another difficulty was on descent, unless done very gradually, pilots suffered from the 'Bends', which can be very painful and prolonged. However, the Germans ignored these sweeps and certainly did not come up and attack us. The distance to which we were effectively able to operate was Lille in the north and

Abbeville in the south. This was as far as our fuel would take us and leave a reasonable margin to get us back to our base at North Weald.

Our next duty entailed escorting bombers consisting of up to three squadrons of Blenheims from the day bomber group. I started by visiting the bomber station to let them know the sort of formation we should fly. At that time we knew where to expect the largest concentrations of enemy anti-aircraft guns, although from a fighter point of view no one seemed to care. Flak looked like harmless puffs of cotton wool by day, although one did not fly through it straight and level but turned, gained and lost height. To my surprise the Group Captain of the bombers was uninterested in flak positions as they had found enemy fighters never attacked while they were over the guns.

The day came and we made our contact with the bombers before crossing the English coast, our escorting squadrons flying with two behind and two above, one on each flank. They had orders to concentrate themselves wherever the attack from the enemy fighters seemed to develop – one would expect this up sun from the formation. The bombers held perfect formation through the flak as if on parade and the enemy were able to inflict considerable damage and casualties. When past the coast and through the mile or so of flak the enemy could be seen lining up above us and in the sun – strangely enough they concentrated their attack on the rear end of the bombers, so I called back the fighters protecting the flanks and from this there developed a tactic called 'The North Weald Beehive'.

The fighters, all forty-eight of them, would cover an area 500ft above and below the bombers and 200 to 400 yards behind them. The fighters would fly in a sort of figure of eight, which meant that at any time there would be a number of fighters pointing towards the enemy fighters. These were instructed to fire even if the sights weren't perfectly on the enemy. This tactic proved most effective. Not only did we lose few of our pilots but only on one occasion was one of our bombers lost to enemy attack – and that was a lucky shot from an enemy fighter at a range of 1,000 yards.

There were two unsatisfactory features to our escort duties, although we had been able to safeguard the bombers from enemy fighters. Firstly the loss and damage to our bombers due to enemy flak, and secondly the very poor results from the bombing – as it was rare to hit the target. On one occasion, in an attempt to get more enemy reaction, we were ordered to leave the bombers and do a low attack on an airfield, rejoining the bombers before they crossed the coast on their return. The close escort was taken over by a wing of Spitfires. It proved a dangerous and unrewarding operation. We dived on the airfield but no aircraft were visible on the ground, although, some 100 or so could be seen high up against the clouds. We had to fly north and gain height to rejoin the bombers and were hard pressed by the enemy all the way back to England.

The merit of the Hurricane was manoeuvrability, not speed. Without height we were very vulnerable and had to turn and fight every time an attack developed. Theoretically, the Spitfires should have pounced on the assembled fighters but I did not know whether they had seen them or not. At this time the Spitfire Vs were having their own difficulties as the new, improved, Me 109F and especially the FW190 were proving difficult, and were in many ways superior fighters. It was not until the Spitfire IX came on the scene that the air battle over France began to swing decisively in our favour.

We had a number of new developments in 1941 that reduced our casualties. First of all was the new VHF radio telegraphy, an amazing improvement on the HF radio telephone used in the Battle of Britain. We also had self-sealing petrol tanks, rubber dinghies fitted under our parachutes and an Air Sea Rescue Organization. The three latter developments were, to some extent, copied from the Germans but the new radio telephone was quite remarkable, clearer than a good landline, even when over France. Anyone losing their way had literally only to transmit 'Hello' twice to be given a bearing for base.

We learnt over time that the 'Beehive' was the safest place to be when attacked. If, for any reason, a pilot lost the formation his best way home was to fly as low as possible over France, not forgetting to give the anti-aircraft a taste of his twelve machine-guns as he flew over the coast. A low-flying aircraft was unable to make effective use of his R/T and would be told to take a course of 300° and climb when in sight of our coast, when he would be able to obtain a bearing for home.

By early 1941, we already had the beginnings of an international air force. In the North Weald Wing we had

Trafford Farm, Benenden, Kent, which Ronald and Daphne Kellett made their family home.

Whitney Straight, commanding a squadron composed of Norwegian, French and British pilots, while 88 Squadron comprised American pilots who had volunteered to fight with the RAF and were, in fact, the first Americans to join the fight. We also had a regular USAAC officer, but he was purely an observer who did not fly.

The first four-engine bombers, the Short Stirling, had appeared on the scene by midsummer. Although three of them carried as many bombs as three squadrons of Blenheims, they seemed no more able to compete with the German flak in spite of turning and weaving through the flak. From aerial observation their bombing was better than the Blenheim but still not good. They also seemed so big that they could have carried a full-sized billiard table in their fuselage. Our wing never lost one of them to the enemy fighters but casualties from anti-aircraft fire appeared an everyday occurrence. On one occasion the bombers had got through safely to their target over Lille when one was shot down by the enemy right over the target and I think hit the steelworks, doing more damage than the bombs. In all cases some of the crew escaped by parachute but these operations appeared to me to be at too high a cost in terms of casualties against worthwhile targets.

In addition to the wing operations we were doing nuisance raids over France at such targets as enemy headquarters and gun positions. They were carried out at low level and rarely encountered opposition, other than flak. It was always tempting to get the enemy generals out of bed at four or five o'clock, and the hotels in Ostend were usually well occupied by that species.

The targets for these raids were left to the Squadron Leaders and Wing Commanders to select, although we did understand that the Generals' HQs were not considered to be the most suitable targets.

We had a visit from the Inspector General. With another officer I stood in for Group Captain Vincent, as he was away on sick leave. I took the IG round the station and discussed the operations with him. I explained that as a close escort wing we were able to do this effectively with our equipment but the day bombing was on such a small scale that it had little or no effect on the enemy's war effort. Moreover, the Hurricane was too slow for fighter-to-fighter combat. The cost of the operation over France in 1941 struck me as excessive in terms of pilots and our best equipment lost without any real advantage, except proving that we could operate over enemy territory. I thought we should be in the Middle East, supporting our own troops, not a popular view but with my brother Laurence being with the 8th Army, I may have been a little biased.

The upshot was that the wing was re-equipping with Spitfires and Don Gillan, who did the record-breaking Hurricane flight from Edinburgh to London in 1938, at speeds in excess of 300 mph, was appointed Wing Leader, while I was posted to take over his job at the Air Ministry. I left him my wad of French francs and wished him good luck.

On 17 July 1941, having flown operationally for nearly two years, Wing Commander Kellett left the North Weald Wing and reported to the Directorate of Training Operations at the Air Ministry:

My deputy at the Air Ministry was Squadron leader Cridland, who was from Bristol and like myself, an auxiliary. Before the war he was a competent and well-to-do business man of about 28. I think he was keen to get a more exacting job and was duly posted to Norfolk House. With his help, however, I gained a

Daphne and Ronald Kellett with friends on a post-war skiing holiday.

fair idea of how the Air Ministry worked and in exchange Squadron Leader Cam Malfrey arrived, who, coincidentally, was also from the Bristol Squadron. When reporting to his Wing Leader, Bader, that he was to be moved, he was asked why? He supposed that he was too old, he was 35 at the time. 'Hmm!' said Bader, 'You must be as old as God!'

'Yes', he replied 'I knew his father!'

Cam was a New Zealander and was a well-known tennis player.

Perusing the many files that circulated it was interesting to observe that a politician succeeded in getting his son out of the firing line, and more than one senior officer tried but didn't succeed. I did note that Dowding, whose son Derek was flying, never tried. I don't know how I came across my own file but noted two points – one that I was considered night blind, (I didn't agree) and the other was that Group Captain Keynes had written that two years of operational flying was too much: there were, after all, Guardian Angels in human form. I never found out, but suspected it might have been the result of a talk with one of my City bosses, Billy Darwin, who was related to the Keynes family and was himself a Great War soldier.

While at the Air Ministry I used to lunch at the Saville Club and often met Compton Mackenzie and Richard Hillary, the badly burned author of *The Last Enemy*. One day, Compton took me aside and said he thought it a bad thing that Hillary was going back to flying – who was doing a good job at the Ministry of Information and he thought it was really a matter of bad nerves that made Hillary want to return to flying. I told him I would do what I could. I thought it wrong in principal that badly maimed people should go to our OTUs, as this could be bad for morale. I discussed this with my Director and his Deputy who agreed that I should speak to the Personnel Department – but I quickly found that this posting was at the C-in-C level, so I resorted to the medical authorities, who agreed to act. Sadly, they sent a letter-gram which would arrive the morning after Hillary had been killed night-flying.

At one period while I was at the Air Ministry, Wakefield, the MP, invited me to lunch, ostensibly to discuss politics. I told him that we pilots were disgusted at the treatment of Dowding after the Battle of Britain had been won, and personally I was not very happy about our losses over France – when our troops in the Middle East should be getting greater support.

A large part of my Ministry work entailed looking at files and writing minutes in which it seemed quite the fashion to blame all accidents on training, particularly as about 90 per cent of such accidents are due to pilot error. On one occasion I had a file enquiring why a pilot, who had served with his squadron in Russia, was taken off flying. I rang up his CO and learned that he had never flown in Russia but had been responsible for a number of taxying accidents and was therefore considered unsuitable for an operational fighter squadron. Thinking that this was another tiresome enquiry I wrote 'We naturally do the best we can with the material available to us. In this case we appear to have gone too far.' Back came the non-secret file by dispatch rider with a minute from the Under Secretary of State for Air: 'Yes, what has he done that shews we have gone too far?' I told him the facts. It was obvious that he should have been taken off flying long before he had reached a squadron! In fact, as the war continued the source of suitable pilots was drying up.

On New Year's Eve 1942, Wing Commander Kellett was posted to the 'Air Ministry Unit', with unknown staff duties, where he remained until 7 July 1943 when transferred to 'The Special Duties List' and posted to Uxbridge. From there, Ronald went on loan to Turkey, as an instructor at the Turkish

Ronald Kellett was also a keen sailor, this being a favourite yacht of his, the *Damien B.*

Air Academy, where he would remain for some time. *The Times* reported on the project after the war in Europe had ended (8 May 1945), on 21 July 1945:

> One of the strangest air forces in existence at the moment is that of Turkey. It is composed of British Spitfires, Hurricanes, Blenheims, Beauforts and Lysanders; of German Fw 190s, He 111s, an assortment of Junkers and training aircraft; and of American Kittyhawks and Liberator bombers.
>
> Judged by the standards of the great powers, the Turkish Air Force is neither large nor powerful, but seen against the background of Turkey's 'thin' national resources it is a remarkable achievement. The force has not only been supplied largely from Great Britain, but has been trained by the RAF. Several hundred Turkish pilots have received their wings in Great Britain; others have been trained by British instructors in Turkey; and still more have been trained in the Middle East.
>
> British equipment officers and men have also attempted to produce for the Turkish Air Force something equivalent to the RAF's equipment branch. Warrant officers and NCOs have instructed the Turks in radio, armament, direction-finding, electrical work, and airframe and electrical maintenance. The work of British instructors is much appreciated throughout the Turkish Air Force. The instructors, for their part, find the average Turkish pilot both apt and keen.
>
> A staff college is run by Group Captain W.R. Sadler of Newmarket, and Wing Commander R.G. Kellett DSO DFC,

of Oxshott, Surrey, a Battle of Britain veteran. The Turks are taught normal staff college subjects, including air strategy, employment of air forces, air tactics, staff duties, and organisation. Flying instruction is under the direction of Wing Commander E.H. Irving, an Australian.

If the RAF, after the war, is able to open its flying courses, technical and staff colleges to the young airmen of Turkey, as well as those of other small Asiatic and European countries, there will be an unmatched opportunity of forming friendships on which good international relations have their best basis.

More than 100 airfields have been built in Turkey by the British or with British supervision. Equipment sent to Turkey, as well as aircraft and spares, includes bombs, ammunition, pyrotechnics, hangars, parachutes, flying clothing, ambulances, trailers, tractors, lorries, petrol tankers, fire tenders, cranes, and general ground equipment, including radio and electrical stores.

The Turkish Air Force follows neither the British nor the German plan. It is totally subservient to the Army. Its bombers are all intended for close tactical work with the Army, and there is no strategic air force. The Army decides the type and duration of training needed for aircrews. An air force officer attends a military college for three years, during which he spends six months learning rifle drill, and he then attends the Harp Okulu in Ankara for two years, where he learns something of military science but nothing of flying.

It is only on completion of this course that he attends a primary air school, and the average age of the would-be pilot when he starts instruction at the elementary school is twenty-two. The result is that the average age of the qualified pilots in the Turkish Air Force is very much higher than in the RAF.

That month, Wing Commander Kellett returned home, reporting for duty at the Air Ministry on 1 August 1945. A fortnight later, following the dropping of two atomic bombs, Japan surrendered, bringing the Second World War to an end. On 7 September 1945, Ronald was released from service, his last day being 26 November 1945. It had, for sure, been a long and exciting road that led him back into stockbroking, becoming a partner at Laurence, Keen and Gardner in 1948. In August that year, Ronald and Daphne Kellett moved to Trafford Farm, at Benenden in Kent, where their two sons and three daughters were raised. The farm boasted pigs, for a time, chickens, and a herd of shorthorn

Ronald Kellett pictured at Larkshill in 1964.

cattle for milking. Ronald enjoyed sailing and hunting, and taking the family on exciting holidays in his open-top Rolls-Royce. Owing to the potential threat from the Soviet Union, however, the auxiliaries were reactivated very soon after the Second World War concluded, and so Wing Commander Kellett resumed his part-time service on 1 August 1946 – ironically commanding 615 'County of Surrey' Squadron, at Biggin Hill – the arch-rivals of 600 Squadron, in which he had originally served.

After the Second World War, the RAF had been downsized once more, and various squadrons disbanded. With the Axis powers defeated, a new world order had emerged, the United States leading the capitalist Western democracies, known as the 'Western Bloc', while Stalin's Soviet Russia formed the geopolitically converse and communist-controlled 'Eastern Bloc'. In Britain, Churchill had lost the general election of July 1945, but remained leader of both the Conservative Party and the Opposition, and in early 1946 spoke in America, warning of an 'Iron Curtain' having 'descended on the Continent', behind which was aligned the Soviet states. So began the 'Cold War', in which the opposing blocs vied for political influence. While there was no 'hot' war between the superpowers, which would instead support indirect, peripheral, 'proxy' wars in the years ahead, the threat was always there. Consequently, twenty pre-war auxiliary squadrons were re-formed and equipped with fighters, among them 615, which re-formed at Biggin Hill on 10 May 1946, equipped with Griffon-engine Spitfire F.14. It may be no coincidence that Wing Commander Kellett signed-on again in the same year as Churchill's famous speech, given that the pair knew each other and the great man happened to be Honorary Commodore of 615 Squadron.

While commanding 615 Squadron, Ronald Kellett remained in his civilian occupation, again flying at weekends and during annual camp. Between 2–16 August 1946, the squadron's camp that year was held at Horsham St Faiths, in Norfolk; the Kellett family shares with us a story from that time, illustrating Ronald's generous and philanthropic approach to life:

Wing Commander Kellett's medal group, from left: DSO and Bar, DFC, 1939-45 Star with Battle of Britain Clasp, Aircrew Europe Star, The Defence Medal, The War Medal, Air Efficiency Award with Bar, and the Polish Virtuti Militari – now preserved at the Battle of Britain Bunker, Uxbridge.

He was aware that the groundcrews could not experience flying in the squadron's single-seater Spitfires, which they had been able to do in the squadron's pre-war two-seater biplanes, such as the Hawker Hart, and so, with this in mind, he became aware of a Supermarine Walrus amphibian aircraft for sale in the Irish Republic – subsequently purchased the aircraft. He then arranged with Flight Lieutenant Freddie Sowrey (later to become Air Marshal Sir Freddie Sowrey) to fly over to Dublin, collect and fly the Walrus to Biggin Hill. After arriving at Dublin Airport they took the Walrus for a test flight. The aircraft, however, was in dire need of maintenance, and even a float was missing, so with the plane yawing to one side, Ronald reduced the speed to find how the aircraft handled at low airspeed – but as it reached the stall, the engine stopped. Freddie asked Ronald if he had flown one of these before – no he had not! Fortunately, they had enough height to restart it in a dive and so landed safely. Afterwards, while taking the bus into Dublin, Ronald discussed with Freddie the duty-free items he would like Freddie to purchase in Dublin; in the meantime, Ronald would be collecting a suit he had ordered.

The following day, back at Dublin Airport, Ronald and Freddie were going through Customs, in order to take the Walrus back to Biggin Hill, when the Customs Officer asked

Above left: Wing Commander Kellett's 'Armorial Bearings', approved by London's College of Arms.

Above right: Daphne Kellett passed away on 3 April 1994, and was joined by her husband in the churchyard of their local parish church, St George's, Benenden, after his passing on 12 November 1998 – the headstone recording, simply, that Wing Commander Ronald Gustave Kellett DSO DFC VM was 'One of the Few'.

Left: On 30 August 2014 – the 64th anniversary of 303 Squadron's first victory – a memorial plaque commemorating Wing Commander Kellett was unveiled at St George's. Designed and created by Geoffrey Aldred, the Nabresina stone is shaped to represent a Hurricane's wing, and shows such a fighter flying over the Fairlight Cliffs – a familiar sight to the aircrew of both sides during the Battle of Britain.

whether they had a successful shopping trip in Dublin. Taken aback, Ronald expressed admiration at their effective intelligence. Laughing, the Customs Officer explained that he was sitting on the seat behind them in the bus.

They arrived at Croydon Airport to go through customs there, but the airport was flooded and spray from the undercarriage had stopped the engine. Freddie, therefore, had to climb on top of the fuselage to hand-crank the inertia starter, so they could taxi to the customs clearance. At this point they sensibly left the engine running but the noise irritated the Customs Officer, who asked that it be switched off, to which Freddie and Ronald replied that they could not comply, because they probably would not get it started again. So, the Customs Officer told them to leave. And so the Walrus made it to Biggin Hill for the ground crew of 615 Squadron to enjoy.

615 Squadron's week-long annual camp that summer was in Norfolk, near the beach. They were spending a day on said beach, with the Walrus moored up, when it was time to fly back to the RAF base. With all aboard, they started to taxi, but instead of taking a direct path to take-off, the aircraft ended up going around in circles, much to their embarrassment. People ashore became concerned and called out the coastguard who came to the rescue! It was found that one of the floats had sprung a leak and was weighing the aircraft down to one side. As the aircraft was privately owned but sporting the RAF roundel, Ronald had to hurriedly make sure that the local press kept silent, thus ensuring that the RAF did not become aware of the incident. Subsequently, it was found that a licence had not been given for the aircraft to land at the Norfolk RAF base and so it had to fly back to Biggin Hill.

The Supermarine Walrus concerned, G-AIZG, ended up as scrap, which was discovered by Sir Freddie Sowrey in the 1960s. He then had the Walrus restored, which now resides at and can be seen at the Fleet Air Arm Museum in Yeovilton.

On 18 January 1949, Wing Commander Kellett once more left what was now the Royal Auxiliary Air Force. Continuing to work in the City, he also took a keen interest in the farm; again, the family tells us more:

The passion for flying remained, and in the Seventies a field at the farm was laid out as a landing strip while Father had a

Luton Major light aircraft built, which was similar to a Piper Cub, and then a prototype, the Kittiwake II; he had hoped to run a small production line. He also enjoyed sailing, and while living at Trafford Farm we initially sailed by a clinker-built large sailing boat *Moby Dick*, which I think was Mother's and prior to which it belonged to her father. He then bought a yacht around 25ft called *Kresta Freda*, then the apple of his eye was *Damian B*, a 35ft Jolina class ocean racer. He had a 'shoot' on the farm and either had made or improved a pond or two to entice mallard ducks, and kept pheasants. I think he also tried his hand at painting when he retired. He loved orchids and had a collection of cymbidiums in the lean-to greenhouse. He loved red wine and kept a cellar of wines at the house, and with his brother, Alfred, and nephew, Peter, they created a small vineyard and for a few years made white wine.

Aged around 62, Ronald Kellett retired, forecasting his death at age 75 and ensuring that his cellar was sufficiently stocked to last another ten years. As it happened, Daphne pre-deceased her husband, in 1994, and Ronald eventually passed away, aged 89, on 12 November 1998 – fourteen years longer than his prediction. He was, for sure, endearingly eccentric, a highly intelligent and motivated man possessed of a social conscience and world view, gregarious – and a natural leader. Air Vice-Marshal Johnnie Johnson, officially the top-scoring RAF fighter pilot of the Second World War, always said that the theory of leadership and man-management could be taught, 'but being a truly great leader is a gift, like that of a great writer or artist'. Clearly, Ronald Gustave Kellett had that gift in spades. Family members also recall Ronald as being:

> loyal, generous, fiery and fearless – but fearsome when in a rage … he had clear vision and a very quick mind, and could be very mischievous. He maintained a close allegiance to his Polish friends throughout his life – who nicknamed him 'Dysio', our closest equivalent being the Beano comic's 'Dennis the Menace'!

In closing his uncle's eulogy, John Kellet recalled that Ronald had 'retained his lively mind to the last … Not always an easy man, he was a stimulating companion with well-informed and provocative views on matters of current interest. I see him as the epitome of the courageous Englishman' – and with that, nobody could disagree.

Chapter Four

Pilot Officer Richard Alexander Howley & Sergeant Albert George Curley

The age of Imperialism and Empire, for sure, provided exciting opportunities for ambitious and adventurous Europeans, the first overseas British colony having been claimed as early as 1583, on the largest island in the world: Newfoundland, otherwise known as 'The Rock', off Canada's Atlantic coast. The 'New World' provided tremendous opportunities for both adventure and advancement, attracting intrepid Europeans from far and wide. In 1840, Richard Howley emigrated from Cashel, Tipperary, Ireland, marrying Eliza Burke and setting up home on 'The Rock' at Mount Cashel, St John's. Their son, James Patrick Howley, was born there in 1847, who become an eminent naturalist, geologist and historian of Newfoundland's indigenous peoples. Likewise James's son, Richard Alexander Howley, was also born in St John's – who would tread a more august path in the Royal Navy.

An engineering officer who had first served aboard both HMS *Jupiter* and *Victorious* in the Channel Squadron, when the First World War broke out on 28 July 1914, Lieutenant Howley was on HMS *Irresistible*, an ironclad battleship. On 27 September 1914, there was a happy occasion, however, when he married Norah Eileen Delamere in an impressive naval wedding in Weymouth, Dorset. On 18 March 1915 though, *Irresistible*, having been deployed with other ironclads to support the Dardanelles campaign, was pounding Turkish coastal forts when the ship was battered and sunk by the 'Hamidieh I' battery. Of the ship's company 150 were lost, and in far away Newfoundland James Howley would soon receive formal notification that his son had been 'admitted to Malta hospital suffering from a severe lacerated shell-wound of right ankle'. Ominously the official letter concluded that the young officer was 'making slow progress'. A more encouraging telegram arrived, however, indicating that this 'hero of a hundred wounds' was now convalescing in Plymouth, England. Eventually recovering sufficiently to return to duty, after this ordeal and given the extent of his injuries, Richard Howley's operational days were over and so he was posted, on loan, as an engineering instructor to the Royal Naval

Above left: Pilot Officer Richard 'Dick' Howley – born in Canada but listed as a Newfoundlander amongst the Few (Tina Howley Harney).

Above right: Like many other young people during the 1930s, Dick Howley's first experience of powered flight was with the pioneering aviator Sir Alan Cobham's 'Flying Circus'.

College of Canada, in Halifax, Nova Scotia, and also called upon to deliver morale-boosting and inspirational accounts of his experiences to encourage recruitment. His troubles, though, were not yet over.

On the morning of 6 December 1917, the SS *Mont Blanc*, a freighter heavily laden with explosives, collided with the Norwegian ship SS *Imo* in Halifax harbour – and spectacularly exploded. The Richmond area of Halifax was consequently devastated, the dockyard, where the College was located, virtually obliterated. 1,782 people were killed, and Engineer-Commander Howley was among the 9,000 injured. The College building having virtually collapsed around him, the instructor walked home – and promptly feinted through blood-loss. Nonetheless, once more he survived, and returning to duty continued teaching at the College which, in September 1918, was relocated to Esquimalt, British Columbia.

Norah Howley had joined her husband in Canada, a son being born to the couple on 16 April 1920, in Esquimalt, and, like his father, named Richard Alexander Howley. During a period of time spent in England, a

Dick Howley whilst learning to fly at Shoreham in 1938 – he always signed his correspondence off with 'Happy Landings' (Tina Howley Harney).

daughter, Emerald, was born, in Southsea, on 3 June 1922. In 1926, the Howleys returned to St John's and 'The Rock', where another daughter, Tina, arrived on 18 September 1932. Having retired though, Commander Howley was so troubled by his war wounds that in 1933 the family moved to England, where it was felt better medical treatment would be available and a naval pension would go further. The family settled in Bognor Regis, on the West Sussex coast, so it was that young Dick Howley moved schools from St Boniface College, St John's, to Colebrook School at 2 Colebrook Terrace, Bognor Regis. This small private boys' school, founded in 1886 by William Grice, Chairman of the local council, accommodated thirty boarders and the same number of day pupils, aimed to provide, according to the school's magazine of 1933, 'a sound commercial education'. Such a career, however, failed to inspire Dick: he had been bitten by the flying bug.

In 1937, aged 17, Dick Howley took flying lessons with Sir Alan Cobham at Shoreham airfield. A former RFC and RAF flying instructor, de Havilland test pilot, and pioneering aviator, Cobham had brought aviation to the masses during the 1930s, his enormously popular 'Flying Circus' touring the country and impressing crowds with daredevil aerobatic displays in addition to providing joy rides. Indeed, those 'jollies' were the first experience of powered flight for countless people – many being young men who were so inspired that they went on to join the RAF – including Dick Howley. Having already achieved his private pilot's licence, on that fateful day of 3 September 1939, having accepted a Short Service Commission of six years, Richard Alexander Howley junior was gazetted as a 'Pilot Officer on Probation' in the General Duties Branch of the RAF, and began his service flying training.

Of this period, Tina Howley Harney, recalls that:

> My brother, Dick, made many friends in training and was more often than not in the company of Pilot Officers Eric Baker, a New Zealander, and Jack Leeds, from Ontario; they were known as 'The Terrible Trio', and would often spend their leave at our family home. Only one would survive the war: Eric, although he became a prisoner of war, who visited us on his way home to New Zealand.

With service flying training successfully concluded, on 7 October 1939, Pilot Officer Howley reported to 141 Squadron, at Turnhouse in Scotland.

141 Squadron was yet another fighter squadron disbanded after the First World War now among those being re-formed, having done so, in fact, just three days before Pilot Officer Howley's arrival. The previous day, 36-year-old Squadron Leader William Arthur Richardson had been posted to command this new squadron. Having taken a SSC in 1930, Richardson had initially flown biplane fighters with 23 Squadron at Kenley, where he was a contemporary of Douglas Bader, and was granted a Permanent Commission in 1936. Thereafter he had served in Malta with an anti-aircraft cooperation unit before further home service, first as a flying instructor, then as a staff officer at HQ 13 Group. Richardson was an experienced officer and pilot, therefore, but with no experience – as yet – of the new monoplane fighters.

Initially, 141 Squadron had no aircraft until, on 10 October 1939, three Avro Tutors and a Tiger Moth, all of which were biplanes, were received from

603 Squadron, the auxiliary Spitfire squadron with which 141 shared Turnhouse. A Link ground trainer also arrived, and so began a period of flying training with somewhat obsolete and limited resources. Orders were soon received for 141 Squadron's move to Grangemouth, which had been completed by 20 October 1939. The following day, as would later prove significant, 'One fitter armourer', according to the squadron's Operations Record Book, 'was attached to Boulton and Paul, Wolverhampton for instruction course

Pilot Officer Howley with an Avro Anson aircraft at Sealand in 1939 (Tina Howley Harney).

on turrets' – much more of which in due course. The squadron still had no aircraft, however. On 24 October 1939, Fighter Command HQ gave permission for 141 Squadron's pilots to at least receive dual instruction on a twin-engine Avro Anson monoplane trainer belonging to the civil air navigation school also based at Grangemouth. Unfortunately, because the school was 'in arrears with their own flying time, no instructors were available', but at least a degree of solo flying took place in the machine.

On 26 October 1939, 141 Squadron again received the Tutor aircraft from 603 Squadron, which, being equipped for night-flying, provided Squadron Leader Richardson an opportunity to let his pilots train after dark. Indicative of the general state of affairs at the time, however, on the same day, 141 Squadron received 'eighteen tons of ammunition … for rearming of Spitfire aircraft'. The next day, Pilot Officer Williams had to travel to RAF Church Fenton by train, there being no aircraft available, 'to collect information re Blenheim aircraft'. That day, it was not twin-engine Blenheim monoplanes taken on charge by 141 Squadron, but six antiquated Gloster Gladiator biplane fighters. A day later, five Blenheims were received, the squadron now operating two very different types of aircraft, while Pilot Officer Howley proceeded 'to Fighter Command HQ, Stanmore, on special duty of collecting and carrying secret documents to Squadron'. More Blenheims arrived, and on 31 October 1939, Pilot Officer Howley undertook over an hour's dual flying practice on an Anson. On 10 November 1939, however, Pilot Officer Howley was ferrying a Blenheim from Hullavington but crashed at Sealand in challenging weather – the aircraft was badly damaged but fortunately the young pilot was unhurt. The flying at this time still revolved around both the Gladiator and Blenheim, with more of the latter type being ferried in daily. The pilots trained, and with their Gladiators, Blenheims and an Anson, would provide the fleet flypasts over the Firth of Forth – although given the obsolescent nature of these aircraft it can only be considered debatable as to how impressive the senior service found these sorties. On 30 November 1939, the weather still poor, Pilot Officer Howley 'returned to Station from Prestwick by rail, his machine being slightly damaged when landing there en route from Grangemouth'; again, Dick was unhurt. On 1 December 1939, Pilot Officer M.G. Yelland, flying a Blenheim with a crew of two on an 'RDF reconnaissance' was not so lucky; the aircraft was seen to dive out of low cloud, at 200ft, at high speed, crash and explode – killing all aboard. The inexplicable accident was a sobering incident.

By New Year's Eve 1939, all of 141 Squadron's pilots were qualified to fly the Blenheim by day and night, but while the winter weather and 'Phoney War' persisted, the pattern of monotonous flying remained

On 10 November 1939, whilst serving with 141 Squadron, Pilot Officer Howley crashed at Sealand whilst ferrying a Blenheim aircraft in bad weather – fortunately the pilot was unhurt (Tina Howley Harney).

constant. Interestingly, the ORB records that on 7 January 1940, 'Pilot Officer Howley returns to unit from parachute course at Locking.' This is contrary to the experience of another of the Few, Sergeant Peter Hutton Fox, who was a 19-year-old Hurricane pilot shot down over the Dorset coast on 30 September 1940: 'I had no parachute training beyond being told to pull the handle – and the first time I did was when I baled out!'

On 26 February 1940, Grangemouth was visited by Air Chief Marshal Dowding, Fighter Command's chief, and Air Vice-Marshal Saul, the 13 Group Air Officer Commanding. This is interesting, because there is an inaccurate perception that the apparently austere Dowding remained largely ensconced in his office at Bentley Priory, rarely engaging with his Command on a personal basis. The evidence, however, presents a different view, which is not uncommon, because 'Stuffy' Dowding often visited his stations and squadrons, even flying himself on occasion.

From an operational perspective though, the war had yet to touch 141 Squadron up in Scotland. German air activity had been limited so far to lone reconnaissance bombers prowling around, the first of which to be destroyed over Scotland had been claimed by Spitfire pilots of 602 and 603 Squadrons on 28 October 1939, and another, claimed by 602, on 9 February 1939, but so far these early interceptions had not involved 141. On 1 April 1940, 141 Squadron was signalled to the effect that it was to re-equip with the Boulton-Paul Defiant turret fighter. That this order was given on April Fool's Day has a degree of tragic irony about it, as things turned out...

The Defiant was a twin-crewed, single-engine fighter – with a difference: the pilot had no self-operated forward-firing armament, just an air gunner behind him in a turret with four machine-guns. As Dowding later wrote:

The 'Terrible Trio'
during training: from
left, Dick, Eric and Jack
(Tina Howley Harney).

> The Defiant ... had two serious disabilities; firstly, the brain flying the aeroplane was not the brain firing the guns: the guns could not fire within 16° of the line of flight of the aeroplane and the gunner was distracted from his task by having to direct the pilot through the communication set.

The aircraft, however, was developed before the war, when the RAF only expected to intercept unescorted German bombers approaching the east coast over the North Sea. The idea was that the Defiant pilot, not personally concerned with firing, could concentrate on positioning his fighter below and slightly in front of any target, providing his gunner an unmissable shot, and, moreover, operating in concert, a large formation of Defiants could bring multiple guns to bear. Consequently, in 1935, the Air Ministry's specification F.9/35 invited aircraft designers' tenders for a two-seater turreted fighter, suitable for day and nocturnal operations, with a top speed of at least 290 mph. The powered turret was to provide a 360° field of fire – but only in the upper hemisphere, the gunner unable to shoot forwards, straight and level, owing to the propeller arc. This meant that when firing forward, the angle was always elevated. Nonetheless, on 28 April 1937, the Air Ministry ordered eighty-seven Defiants straight off Boulton-Paul's drawing board even before the prototype had first flown.

In June 1938, the Assistant Chief of the Air Staff (ACAS), Air Vice-Marshal Sholto Douglas, informed Air Chief Marshal Dowding that he must form nine squadrons of Defiants, out of Fighter Command's strength of thirty-eight, for day fighting. Dowding, however, as Air Member for Research & Development prior to taking over Fighter Command, was technically minded and had previously been heavily involved with producing the specification resulting in the Spitfire and Hurricane – and

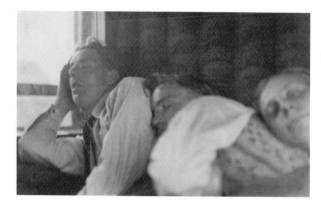

The 'Terrible Trio' on a long wartime train journey: from left, Eric, Dick and Jack (Tina Howley Harney).

knew that the Defiant was exactly what was *not* required in the day-fighter role: being half a ton heavier than even the Hurricane, it was too large, slow, and insufficiently manoeuvrable, notwithstanding the forward-firing issues.

During the First World War, Douglas had flown the two-seater Bristol fighter, a highly successful type, hence his support of the two-seater Defiant programme. The Bristol Fighter, though, had an advantage the Defiant lacked: forward-firing armament, a fact enjoyed by every successful fighter aircraft ever built. Some have argued that the Defiant's electrical-firing system permitted the pilot to personally fire the guns, facing forward, but as previously explained, although that is so, the shot had to be oblique, not direct, which greatly complicated things in what required split-second decisions and timing. Douglas also believed two-seaters to be best for offensive operations over enemy territory – Dowding's counter argument being that the forthcoming battle would be defensive, not offensive, and he did not want pilots risking their lives unnecessarily by fighting over the sea or the Continent, because if brought down chances of survival or a safe return to England were much lower. Again, Dowding was right.

Astonishingly, an Air Staff Note on the 'Employment of two-seater and single seater fighters in a Home Defence war' in June 1938, attracted an enthusiastic minute from Air Vice-Marshal Donald Stevenson, the Deputy Director of Home Operations, arguing in favour of more Defiant squadrons over those of Spitfire and Hurricanes. Dowding robustly countered and won the argument, thankfully, and he, undoubtedly, had a much better understanding of actual fighter combat than most at the Air Ministry.

By the outbreak of war, though, only three Defiants had reached the RAF, and those for trials only. Consequently, given later events, it has been argued that the Defiant's lengthy development and time taken to enter service contributed to making the type obsolete before ever firing a shot in anger. Why? Because although the Defiant's top speed was 304 mph, the enemy now had modern bombers not much slower (He 111, 273 mph, Ju 88, 292 mph), and the heavy Me 110 twin-engine heavy fighter flew at a maximum speed of 295 mph. Moreover, the more manoeuvrable Hurricane, which entered service in 1937, had a top speed of 335 mph, while the nimble Spitfire, following on a year later, hurtled along at 353 mph. The Hurricane and Spitfire, then, provided a much greater performance advantage, so Air Vice-Marshal Stevenson's enthusiasm for the Defiant, based upon that data alone, is difficult to fathom.

At that stage, the Me 109, even with a top speed of 354 mph, was not really a consideration, though, because no one anticipated Hitler's unprecedented advance to the Channel coast of May 1940 – which in the event, as explained in previous chapters, changed everything; the acquisition of French airfields put even London within the Me 109's limited range, meaning that German bombers would, in the event, be escorted by this excellent fighter.

Above left: In January 1940, Pilot Officer Howley attended a parachute course at RAF Locking – this is how baling out was described in the 1942, RAF-endorsed, boys' book *Britain's Wonderful Air Force*.

Above right: Pilot Officer Howley at home on his last ever leave, with younger sister, Tina (Tina Howley Harney).

Above left: Another poignant snapshot from that last leave: Pilot Officer Howley with his father, Engineer Commander RA Howley RN (Tina Howley Harney).

Above right: Last snap: Dick with girlfriend Mercy on his last leave (Tina Howley Harney).

Furthermore, the enemy were able to fly strong fighter sweeps from these locations, reaching out across the Channel to southern England and London. This made the Defiant, described by Group Captain John Wray as 'The Flying Brick Shit House', extremely vulnerable in daylight skies shared with the 109. It is perhaps easy to argue that hindsight is a wonderful thing, and indeed it is, but Dowding knew full-well that the Defiant was a disaster waiting to happen; the whole sorry tale is yet another example of what Air Vice-Marshal Johnnie Johnson, officially the RAF's top-scoring fighter pilot of the Second World War, described to me personally as 'the incompetence of the Air Staff.' Sadly, lives would be lost because of it.

On 8 April 1940, pilots of the already Defiant-equipped 264 Squadron delivered the first two of that type, fresh from 24 Maintenance Unit, to 141 Squadron at Grangemouth. 141 Squadron pilots were then conveyed to RAF Cosford, near the Boulton-Paul factory in Wolverhampton, returning with four more Defiants, and by 13 April 1940, most of 141's pilots had flown solo of the new type. Over the next few weeks, more aircraft – and air gunners – continued to arrive, while the squadron continued familiarisation with the Defiant and training.

Tina Howley Harney:

> Dick was a happy-go-lucky guy, thrilled to be flying what he told Dad was 'a secret new plane that could travel at 400 mph'.

202

A Boulton-Paul Defiant turret-fighter of 141 Squadron (via Andy Long).

> He always loved machinery and had an old Morgan sports car
> he tinkered with. He played the guitar and his favourite song
> at the time was 'Begin the Beguine'.

The other, and original, Defiant squadron, 264, had been equipped with the turreted fighter since December 1939, and was operational, based at Duxford in 12 Group, by 10 May 1940, when Hitler attacked the West. Typically, two days later, Air Vice-Marshal Leigh-Mallory, ever keen to get 12 Group into action, sent 'A' Flight of 264 Squadron on an offensive patrol across the North Sea, to the Hague, escorted by the Spitfires of 65 Squadron's 'B' Flight. That the Defiant required protection from Spitfires from the outset, even when untested in battle, speaks volumes. The Defiant crews returned elated, having shot down two unescorted German bombers, one being shared with a section of Spitfires.

The following day, however, came a reality check. This time, it was the turn of 264 Squadron's 'B' Flight and the Spitfires of 66 Squadron's 'A' Flight, the fighters taking off at 0430 hrs and heading over the North Sea to harass enemy transport aircraft ten miles north of The Hague. At 0515 hrs, the Dutch coast was crossed, the RAF formation proceeding inland on a northerly course when Dutch AA fire opened up, forcing the fighters to take evasive action. Then, a number of Ju 87s dive-bombing a railway line were spotted by the leading Spitfire pilots, who led the whole formation into attack. Four of the dive-bombers, from 12(St)/LG 1, were destroyed. Then … disaster. High above, keeping a watchful eye on the *Stukas*, lurked the Me 109s of 5/JG 26 – which lost no time in surprising the British fighters. Within a matter of seconds, five of the six Defiants were shot down – one spectacularly exploding in mid-air. Three 264 Squadron aircrew were killed; five wounded and/or captured; two crash-landed and evaded. Only

Above left and above right: The Defiant's hydraulic turret accommodated an air gunner and four electrically fired .303 Browning machine-guns.

one aircraft, flown by Pilot Officer H.S. Kay, survived the encounter. In response, 264 Squadron shot down just one of their assailants, *Leutnant* Karl Boris, who baled out west of Dordrecht. The Spitfires, unsurprisingly, fared somewhat better, with just one of their number being damaged.

Ironically, on the day 'B' Flight was massacred over the Dutch coast, the Defiant's manufacturer telegrammed 264 Squadron, referring to the previous day's success: 'Squadron Leader Hunter and Squadron. Congratulations on first blood.' Then, the following signal was received from Air Vice-Marshal Leigh-Mallory on 15 May 1940:

> I want to congratulate 264 Squadron most heartily on the success of their operations over Holland which have proved the success of the Defiant as a fighter. I much regret the loss that "B" Flight suffered in the second operation. The courage and determination displayed were of the highest order and create for 264 Squadron a tradition that any squadron might well be proud of.

And from the Chief of the Air Staff: 'You have done magnificent work during the last forty-eight hours in Holland and Belgium and fully justify the confidence placed in you. Keep it up.' While the bravery of the Defiant crews in their entirely inappropriate fighter aircraft are beyond reproach, and can only be admired, considering the balance sheet it is difficult to see anything 'magnificent' about it.

By that time, things were looking bleak in France, it becoming patently obvious that the *Blitzkrieg* was unstoppable – in no small part owing to the aerial supremacy achieved over the battlefield by the Me 109. On 23 May 1940, Squadron Leader Hunter and his operational crews flew over to operate from Manston, from where they patrolled over the French coast during the days ahead. On 26 May 1940, the situation had deteriorated to such a catastrophic extent that the decision was made for the British Expeditionary Force to retire upon and evacuate from Dunkirk – from which point the purpose of air operations was to provide cover for this desperate undertaking. On 27 May 1940, Squadron Leader Hunter himself came into contact with the Me 109 for the first time; espying eight German fighters, Hunter ordered his aircraft into line astern. The 109s, on this occasion, mistaking the British fighters for Hurricanes, attacked from the rear – and paid the price. Two 109s, of I/JG1, were shot down. The following day, 264 Squadron engaged twenty-seven 109s over the Channel, Hunter ordering his men to form a defensive circle. In the ensuing combat, the Defiants claimed six Me 109s destroyed – but lost three of their number of the process. On 29 May 1940, in addition to claiming two further 109s destroyed, 264 Squadron was attacked by twenty-one Me 110s – fifteen of which Hunter and his pilots claimed destroyed. That evening, Hunter's Defiants claimed eighteen Ju 87s and an 88 destroyed, generating a further congratulatory signal from Air Vice-Marshal Leigh-Mallory. Again, this great success was partially attributed to the enemy attacking from the rear, an error the Germans would not repeat.

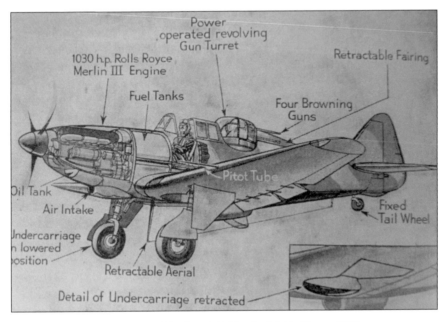

How the Defiant was presented in *Britain's Wonderful Air Force*, 1942.

The comparatively primitive training of RAF air gunners early in the war.

By 3 June 1940, the Dunkirk evacuation had concluded, by which time 264 Squadron had returned to Duxford. 141 Squadron, doubtless inspired by 264 Squadron's performance, were keen to enter the fray but the next move, on 29 June 1940, was not south, but back to Turnhouse. On 9 July 1940, however – the day before the Battle of Britain officially began – 141 Squadron was ordered to move to 11 Group, Squadron HQ to be at Biggin Hill in Kent, while its Defiants were to operate from West Malling, near Maidstone, which was an advance airfield for both Biggin Hill and Kenley. By 13 July 1940, the move was complete. The following day, Squadron Leader Richardson led a flight of six Defiants on their first operational sortie in 11 Group, a patrol of West Malling at 8,000ft. That this was uneventful was a good thing, because clearly the Controller had yet to learn that such a height was suicidal, given that the enemy fighters swept in at high-altitude, ready to pounce from the sun, enjoying the advantage of height and surprise. Further, similar, patrols were made over the next few days without meeting the enemy. At this time, the Battle of Britain was still being fought over Channel convoys and south coast, as the enemy probed defences and tested the RAF's reaction to these preliminary forays. On 18 July 1940, with this and a rapid response in mind, 141 Squadron flew further south, from West Malling to operate from Hawkinge, just inland of Folkestone, Fighter Command's closest airfield to the Germans, just twenty-two miles away across the Channel.

By this time, Dick Howley had teamed up with air gunner Sergeant Albert George Curley, of Bushey, Hertfordshire, who had been born in

County Cork, where his father, Major John Curley, a professional soldier, was stationed with the 6th Dragoons, on 30 September 1907, and was 32 years old in July 1940. A few months before the Second World War began, Curley had enlisted in the RAFVR as an airman, volunteering for aircrew. After being called to full-time service on 1 September 1939, he became an air gunner, joining 141 Squadron when the unit converted to the Defiant.

Pilot Officer Howley and Sergeant Curley flew their first operational patrol of the Battle of Britain between 2045 and 2145 hrs on 18 July 1940, in Defiant L6983, a patrol over Hawkinge during which no enemy aircraft were seen. The squadron landed at West Malling but would operate from Hawkinge again the following day – with Dick Howley and Albert Curley on the board to fly.

At 0845 hrs on 19 July 1940 – coincidentally Squadron Leader Richardson's 37th birthday, an old man by fighter pilot standards – 141 Squadron again left West Malling for Hawkinge. This time, Pilot Officer Howley and Sergeant Curley flew down to Hawkinge in Defiant L6995, there to await events.

Officially, the Battle of Britain was nine days old, although in truth the fighting over the Channel had actually begun on 2 July 1940. The fighting on 10 and 11 July 1940, however, had been the heaviest since the Fall of France, confirming what was the beginning of a German aerial assault on Britain. This confirmed Air Chief Marshal Dowding's very great concern that defending the Channel convoys would put an immense strain on his fighter squadrons along the south coast, not least because of the speed the enemy could reach these targets from his new French bases, and the frequency of attacks that provided for. The main danger, as Dowding knew full-well, was downed aircrew being lost to the Channel, British air sea rescue arrangements, unlike the Germans, being in its infancy. Nonetheless, the course of battle is always dictated by the enemy, who has the advantage of deciding strategy, selecting targets, and choosing the time and place to attack. Consequently, Fighter Command had no option but to react accordingly to incoming threats, wherever these developed.

After the Fall of France, the English Channel was deserted – all except for the black, dust-encrusted, colliers known as the 'Coal Scuttle Brigade'. To industrial Britain, coal was essential, firing as it did the power stations, furnaces and railways. According to some estimates, the weekly requirement was for a staggering 40,000 tons. This, however, Britain did not have to import, being rich in coalfields itself, but the miners' yield in Wales and the north-east still had to be transported to London and the south-coast port of Southampton. The only practical means was by sea, to which there was no alternative. From the north-east, the colliers travelled south down the east coast, to Southend, the Thames Estuary and London's docks. Eastern convoys would assemble at Glasgow, making their way south down the west coast, meeting ships from South Wales, chugging across the Bristol Channel, around Land's End, and east to Southampton.

Although there was limited U-boat activity in the comparatively shallow Channel, the greatest threat for merchantmen was from the air, shelling by German batteries around Calais, and E-Boats, fast surface raiders armed with torpedoes. Minefields were another danger. Naturally, convoys were afforded protection by the RN, usually in the shape of two destroyers and half-a-dozen armed trawlers. There was, inevitably, a lack of preparedness, however. No major exercise training in convoy cooperation and protection had been held before the war, the small number of convoy passage exercises were inclined more towards the RN practising operation of its primitive submarine detecting radar. There were no specialist aircraft available and nor was air integrated into any formal convoy management plan. As it happened, keeping the 'Coal Scuttle Brigade' steaming through the Channel

became about much more than just the vital coal the tramps carried – and those aboard the colliers doubtless wished that more thought had been given to their protection.

For the Germans, the priority was now the destruction of British fighters, the objective

Left: Air Gunner Sergeant Albert George Curley, who flew with Pilot Officer Howley (via Elizabeth Callow Wirth).

Below: Me 109s on the prowl over the French coast – the Defiant was no match for this lethal single-seater fighter.

being aerial supremacy for the seaborne invasion of Britain, which Hitler now considered a realistic, albeit unexpected, proposition. First, though, the RAF fighters had to be drawn into battle, and with that foremost in mind, shipping was attacked. On 2 July 1940, the SS *Aeneas* was lost with twenty-one souls, while others were killed and injured on the damaged SS *Baron Ruthven*. By close of play on 4 July 1940, five more ships had been sunk by bombing, two by mines, another by an E-boat, and fourteen more damaged by aerial attacks – sufficient to cause the Prime Minister himself to inquire of the Admiralty what arrangements were being made by the RN and RAF to protect the convoys. In response to this aerial bombardment, the Admiralty closed the Channel to all shipping except the 'Coal Scuttle Brigade'. The RAF fighters, however, consistent with Dowding's policy of carefully shepherding and preserving his limited resources, were not committed to battle *en masse* over the Channel, indeed, sensibly, they never were, no matter what target the enemy prioritised. Instead, the RAF fighters intercepted by flight and individual squadron, more often than not meeting infinitely larger enemy formations comprising both bombers and fighters.

The pattern of enemy air operations during the period 12–19 July 1940, certainly on five out of the eight days, was to operate in strength, deploying formations of mixed bomber types with strong fighter cover. Several of these raids would be incoming on those days, targeting shipping in the Straits of Dover and central Channel. Having rapidly reached their targets, bombers would immediately turn for home, which was a comparatively short distance away. The German fighters would remain, however, ready to pounce on any RAF fighters, which were frequently ambushed while desperately climbing up from the airfields, and fend off any attacks on the bombers. Due to speed, distance and time, the defending fighters generally arrived as independent flight or squadron formations, too late to prevent ships being bombed, but on two occasions out of the eight large-scale raids, German bombers were intercepted while retiring. Invariably, the German fighters, loitering over the sea, eager for action, enjoyed the height advantage, having climbed from their French bases to 10,000–20,000ft, with the bombers approaching their targets some distance below.

On 19 July 1940, *Oberst* Theo Osterkampf's JG 51 was based in the Pas-de-Calais, the Geschwader's various units dispersed around largely temporary airfields inland of Cap Blanc Nez and Wissant, and around St Omer. III/JG 51's *Gruppenkommandeur* was a very experienced fighter leader, *Hauptmann* Johannes Trautloft, who had become an ace in 1936, fighting with Germany's Legion *Kondor*, destroying five republican aircraft before destroying a Polish fighter on 5 September 1939, and two Spitfires over Dunkirk in May 1940. Unlike the RAF, a comparatively

A *Schwarm* of Me 109s.

small peacetime air force, the ranks of which had been substantially swelled by the amateur volunteers of the AAF and RAFVR, *Luftwaffe* personnel were all professional airmen. Trautloft, born near Weimar on 3 March 1912, had learned to fly in 1931, spending four months the following year at the secretly reborn *Luftwaffe*'s training base in Russia. Already an experienced officer, he was one of the first six German pilots to arrive in Spain, and jointly recorded the first German victories in support of Franco. Although he initially flew He-51 biplanes in Spain, these were replaced by the Me 109, which proved itself in Spanish skies. Trautloft, in fact, became responsible for developing fighter tactics with the 109, so all of his experience to date made him a most dangerous foe indeed. Trautloft himself described the scene across the Channel, on the day in question:

> Just as we were sitting down for lunch in our tent, a mission order from the *Geschwader* (Fighter Group 51 HQ) arrived: 'At 1300 hrs [continental time] III *Gruppe* (third wing, comprising three squadrons, of JG 51) will escort, with all available aircraft, a *Zestörergruppe* [destroyer wing] of Me 110s, which will make a dive-bombing attack on a British freighter, equipped with AA guns, north-east of Dover.'
>
> I had the *staffel* (squadron) leaders report to discuss the Gruppe mission. In the meantime, *Hauptmann* Rubensdörffer, commander of the Me 110 *Zestörergruppe Erprobungsgruppe 210* [an experimental precision bombing unit], telephoned and told me how he was going to approach and attack the target. Soon we agreed on measures for the protection of his unit's outward and return flights.
>
> At exactly 1300 hrs, the *Zestörergruppe* appeared over our airfield at St Omer. We took-off and one *Jagdstaffel* [fighter squadron] positioned itself to the left, one to the right and one above the Me 110s.
>
> Immediately after taking-off I could see the English coast. Never before had the weather been as clear as it was that day.

Until reaching the French coast we flew at 500 metres under scattered cloud. At the coast, the clouds cleared and a clear, blue, sky extended before us. We climbed to 3,000 metres and set course for the target, which we could already see from the French coast. When we got closer, the enemy spotted us; the ship began zig-zagging at high speed.

Exactly eighteen minutes after take-off we were over our target, which the *Zestörers* dive-bombed, dropping their bombs at 800 metres before pulling out of their dives and climbing again. They then flew home, so we escorted and shepherded them to safety.

As we still had sufficient fuel remaining, I decided to do some 'free-hunting' with the *Gruppe* – the British fighters must be somewhere. Maybe they had not been alerted quickly enough and were on their way? In anticipation of this, we headed back out over the Channel again. I flew with my *Stabsschwarm* (wing staff section, of four Me 109s) at 3,000 metres. My three *staffeln* were in loose formation, some 1,000 metres higher. Visibility was so good that one could see any aircraft taking-off from the airfields near the coast.

Trautloft knew that a small number of fighters were more likely to effect a successful ambush; the Germans, playing to the technical advantages of their aircraft, often attacking in high-speed diving passes – and away. Several thousand feet above, over thirty Me 109s provided a protective umbrella for their leader.

Thus, the scene was set.

Just after midday, radar stations provided early warning of enemy formations assembling over the Pas-de-Calais, and German dive-bombers were reported attacking shipping off Dover at 1215 hrs. With a surprising delay, it was not until 1220 hrs that the Hurricanes of 111 Squadron's 'B' Flight were scrambled from Hawkinge, led by Squadron Leader John Thompson, to 'intercept enemy aircraft in the

The German ace Johannes Trautloft, pictured later in the war, who led his III/JG51 *Stabschwarm* into attack 141 Squadron's Defiants on 19 July 1940 – thus starting the 'Slaughter of the Innocents'.

Oberleutnant Werner Pichon, who claimed three Defiants destroyed on 19 July 1940, III/JG51's Technical Officer. It is impossible to say who shot down who in this savage melee.

vicinity. Squadron was ordered North, as far as Deal, at 10,000ft'.

At 1230 hrs, 141 Squadron was also scrambled from Hawkinge, with orders 'to patrol twenty miles south of Folkestone at 5,000ft. Three aircraft fail to leave the ground in time, nine only carry out the patrol' (ORB). Correctly, Trautloft had guessed that although the RAF had been slow to react to the attack on shipping, defending fighters would, in due course, arrive on the scene. With the advantage of height and concealed by the sun's dazzling glare, *Oberleutnant* Herbert Wehnelt, the *Gruppe* Communications Officer and Trautloft's wingman, also flying in the *Stabschwarm*, reported to his leader: 'Down below, to the right, several aircraft just crossing the English coast.'

Wehnelt had espied 141 Squadron, shortly after Squadron Leader Richardson had led his Defiants off from Hawkinge.

Trautloft continues:

> I looked towards the spot and located the aircraft, counting three, six, nine of them. They seemed to have only just taken-off. They climbed rapidly, making a large turn towards the middle of the Channel, coming straight at us. They hadn't spotted us yet, so we headed towards them, out of the sun. When I was only 800 metres or so above the formation I noticed the aircraft had turrets behind their cockpits. The aircraft were neither Hurricanes or Spitfires – Defiants – suddenly went through my head, heavily armed two-seaters whose rear-gunner had four heavy machine-guns with enormous firepower [this account, although accurate, was written for propaganda purposes and this is rather an exaggeration: the Defiant's armament was four .303 Browning machine-guns, with which the Hurricane and Spitfire was also armed, and were the same calibre as the Me 109E's pair of nose-mounted machine-guns; the 109, however, had the distinct edge in firepower, considering its two wing-mounted 20mm Oerlikon canons]. They had obviously been sent up to attack our bombers.

Above left: III/JG 51's Stabschwarm; from left: *Oberleutnants* Kath, Pichon and Wehnelt, and their *Gruppenkommander*, *Hauptmann* Johannes Trautloft.

Above right: Squadron Leader Anthony Richardson, CO of 141 Squadron (via Andy Long).

> The enemy formation was still flying tightly together, as if on an exercise, when it suddenly turned back toward England. I didn't understand at all what the manoeuvre was for. After checking once more for signs of Hurricanes or Spitfires, I gave the order to attack. The clock on my instrument panel stood at 1343 hrs. I peeled over and dived towards the rearmost Defiant with my *Schwarmflieger* [fellow section pilots], *Oberleutnants* Wehnelt, Otto Kath (*Gruppe* Adjutant), and Werner Pichon-Kalau von Hofe (*Gruppe* Technical Officer, referred to hereafter as Pichon), following behind. I aimed for the right-hand Defiant.

The commonly accepted narrative is that, having no fixed forward-firing armament, the Defiants, once the Germans recovered from their initial experience and surprise when attacking 264 Squadron from astern, future attacks were made head-on. Clearly, Trautloft's account indicates that, the Defiants having turned north towards home, he attacked from their rear. The fact is that Trautloft had the immeasurable advantages of height, sun – and surprise. In such tactical circumstances, Spitfire and Hurricane squadrons would have also suffered, if not equally certainly with heavy losses, as the outcome of such combats during the Battle of Britain indicates. The fact is that 141 Squadron had been sent off to patrol over the sea at a dangerously low altitude, inviting attack from above – and paid the price.

Above left: Squadron Leader Richardson's gunner, Pilot Officer Anthony Halliwell, who claimed a 109 destroyed on 19 July 1940. Both Richardson and Halliwell survived the war (via Andy Long).

Above middle: Pilot Officer Hugh Tamblyn, a Canadian, whose air gunner, Sergeant Sydney Powell, also claimed a 109 in the action. Of the nine 141 Squadron Defiants engaged, only those of Richardson and Hamblyn later returned to Hawkinge unscathed. Later an ace awarded the DFC, flying Hurricanes with Douglas Bader's 242 Squadron, Tamblyn was killed in action the following year. Powell survived the war (via Andy Long).

Above right: A New Zealander, Pilot Officer Rudal Kidson's Defiant was shot down into the sea. The pilot was never seen again but the remains of his air gunner, Sergeant Fred Atkins, washed up in France and were buried at Boulogne (via Andy Long).

Trautloft continues:

> Suddenly all hell broke loose. The Englishmen had seen us. Defensive fire from a number of turrets flew towards me – fireworks all over the place. I could see bullets passing by on either side and felt hits on my machine, but pressed home my attack. 200 metres, 100 metres – now was the time to fire and my machine-guns and cannon hammered away. The first volley was too high but the second was right in the middle of the fuselage; parts of the Defiant broke away and flashed past me. I saw a thin smoke trail appear below the fuselage and suddenly the aircraft exploded in a huge red ball of flames, which fell towards the sea.

A massacre ensued.

Oberleutnant Pichon claimed three of the hapless Defiants destroyed:

> We dive steeply. My commander attacks the nearest aircraft. Then everything happens at the speed of lightning. I fire a

Pilot Officer John 'Jacko' Kemp, also a New Zealander, also remains missing, along with his air gunner, Sergeant Robert Crombie (via Andy Long).

short burst. The Tommy emits a white stream of leaking fuel. Then it slowly turns over the right wing and descends vertically. I turn around quickly only to see Kath and Wehnelt finish off one enemy aircraft each. I swing in behind the British on the far right and open fire from a distance of 20 metres. My tracer disappears into the fuselage and wings. I give him only a short burst. The same thing is repeated: first, a white stream, and then the plane turns over. I got him! By this time I have shot down four [Pichon claimed three, officially] and still the British cling to their close formation and rearward firepower.

I place myself behind the next aircraft and again fire a short burst. After my second burst the plane drops like a stone. Ten metres next to me, another Me 109 is firing at a Defiant in the next section of three. I see the burst hit one of the enemy's wings, and the next moment the aircraft is torn to pieces in a huge fireball.

Now we had to be careful with ammunition. I selected the plane that flew to the far right. Meanwhile, we had gone down from 3,000 to 1,000 metres. I blast away with all my guns, but he doesn't fall. This is it! I fire with large deflection while turning, and see tracers hit the fuselage and wings. Finally, he goes down. A yellowish-white streak marks his descent, which ends in a frothy water fountain in the Channel, not far from the English coast.

Squadron Leader Richardson (Defiant L6999) later reported that, having initially been ordered to patrol the Channel south of Folkestone at the suicidal height of 5,000ft, at 1235 hrs he was further instructed to:

sweep Cap Gris Nez at 5,000ft. The squadron was attacked out of the sun by twenty – twenty-five Me 109s [which Richardson records as having rained down from 20,000ft]. I immediately

Left: Another air gunner lost during the 'Slaughter of the Innocents' was Pilot Officer Arthur Hamilton, killed with his pilot, Flying Officer Ian Donald, their Defiant crashing near Dover. Tragically, Hamilton, who was buried at Folkestone New Cemetery, had been due to marry later that day. His pilot, Flying Officer Donald, whose father was an Air Marshal, was buried at All Saints', Tilford, Surrey (via Andy Long).

Below: Air-Gunner Sergeant John 'Jackie' Wise (second right, back row, with other air-gunners of 264 Squadron, with which he had previously seen action over Dunkirk) had the most combat experience of all 141 Squadron's aircrew engaged on 19 July 1940 – but was sadly amongst those shot down over the Channel and never found. (via Andy Long).

turned to port, completing a steep turn of 360°. This proved ineffective as aircraft attacked from below and on the outside. I then carried out 'S' turns, turning always towards the attack; this proved effective. After five minutes, Red 2 and myself, Red 1, were the only two Defiants left, so I decided to break off the combat and returned to base.

Squadron Leader Richardson's air gunner, Pilot Officer Antony Halliwell, reported that the:

> Me 109s came down out of the sun. As they came to deliver attack I had one in sights until well within range and opened fire while still astern (slight deflection). Tracer bullets were seen to hit the enemy aircraft, which dived down into the sea, leaving a large, round, patch of foam.

Pilot Officer Hugh Tamblyn (Defiant L7014) was flying to Squadron Leader Richardson's right, in the lead section, when the 109s attacked from astern; his air gunner, Sergeant Sydney Powell, reported that:

> I kept the enemy aircraft in my sight and opened fire at 200 yards. My tracer bullets were seen to hit aircraft which dived into the sea. This aircraft was the same one fired at by Pilot Officer Halliwell. Before this, another Me 109 delivered a similar attack. I was unable to fire as it attacked but as it pulled away to my right I was able to get it in my sight and fired twenty-five rounds. This aircraft dived towards the sea but I was unable to see it go in.

Hauptmann Trautloft, however, had not had everything his own way:

> I had gained speed in my dive and used it to curve into the attack again, to the right. While in the turn I saw another

The names of the missing are commemorated on the Runnymede Memorial – including those of Pilot Officer Richard Howley and Sergeant Albert Curley.

Defiant going down behind me and to my left. By this time all my pilots were attacking, and then suddenly my engine vibrated and began running unevenly. I could smell burning oil in the cockpit and my coolant temperature indicated 120° with oil temperature also rising steadily. For the first time I noticed several hits on my left wing and a trail of smoke underneath it. I felt uneasy – I didn't want to bale out over the Channel.

Then Kath appeared on my left, his aircraft also trailing smoke. 'I've got to make an emergency landing', he told me over the radio, and, like me, headed towards the French coast.

It's a damned uneasy feeling flying so slowly over the sea in a shot-up crate, all the more worrying when one's flying height was diminishing steadily – and all the while the coast didn't seem to be getting any closer. Luckily there weren't any enemy fighters about, otherwise we'd have been easy meat.

At last there was land below and I scraped over Cap Blanc Nez at 200 metres, finally landing on the airfield at St Inglevert with my propeller feathered. I didn't know where Kath had gone – I'd had my hands full during the forced-landing and hadn't been able to follow his progress. During the flight back I'd heard the voices of my pilots over the radio, 'I'm attacking'

On 19 July 2010 – seventy years after the 'Slaughter of the Innocents' – this memorial was unveiled at Rochford Airport, commemorating the role played by Kentish airfields during the Battle of Britain whilst specifically referring to the massacre of 141 Squadron on 19 July 1940 (via Martin Mace).

Above left: Pilot Officer Howley's medals – the coveted Battle of Britain Clasp should correctly be worn on the 1939-45 Star and not the Aircrew Europe Star (Tina Howley Harney).

Above right: 33. In 2014, Pilot Officer Dick Howley's sister, Tina, travelled from Canada to visit the Battle of Britain Monument on Westminster's Embankment, where her brother's name is recorded.

> … '*Abschuss*' [aerial victory], and then I heard '*Achtung, Spitfires!*', from which it was obvious that British fighters had joined the battle.

It was not 'Spitfires' that had suddenly appeared but the Hurricanes of 111 Squadron, and just the three of 'B' Flight's Green Section, to be exact; Flight Lieutenant Stanley Connors DFC:

> Green 2 (Pilot Officer Jack Copeland) saw E/A off the coast after we were ordered on an interception … He informed me on the R/T and I attempted to inform the Squadron Leader, then led my section into the attack. I made an attack from abeam at short range on some Me 109s attacking a squadron of Defiants, and saw my bullets entering cockpit and fuselage of one E/A, which burst into flames and dived into the sea. I made a further attack on a Me 109, which was followed up by Green 2, but was then attacked by several Me 109s, which I shook off by evasive turns and returned to base where I landed at 1330 hrs. I saw ten enemy aircraft dive into the sea, four of them in flames.

Flight Lieutenant Connors, however was mistaken; far from all of the crashing aircraft were enemy.

A proud Tina, wearing her brother's medals, and her niece, Jill Howley, with Dick's name on the Battle of Britain Monument (Tina Howley Harney).

Pilot Officer Copeland:

> I waited until my section leader broke away and then attacked a 109 from astern at 250 closing to 150 yards. I fired 800 rounds into him and saw both wings smoking, and he was obviously seriously damaged. I broke off and returned to base as I was approaching the French coast and had lost contact with the rest of my section.

Pilot Officer Peter Simpson:

> I followed my section leader into a formation of about twenty Me 109s and attacked one from astern. I fired a long burst, the E/A dived and I followed, giving several bursts from short range. Smoke started to pour from the E/A and my windscreen became covered in oil. E/A turned over slowly and started to dive. My section leader saw it fall into the sea.

Without 111 Squadron's intervention, it is likely that none of 141 Squadron would have made it home – thankfully, however, at least Squadron Leader Richardson's and Pilot Officer Tamblyn's Defiants returned to Hawkinge unscathed. The remainder of Squadron Leader Richardson's formation, though, met the following fates:

Pilot Officer Ian MacDougall (Defiant L6983) was crewed that day with Air Gunner Sergeant John Francis Wise, and reported that:

> Owing to the fact that Green 1 and Yellow 2 did not take-off, I assumed Yellow 2's position. I followed the squadron at

5,000ft – I never saw any of the enemy planes at all during the first two attacks, but bullets were being fired from all angles. After the third attack, my engine cut and believing that I had been shot down, ordered the Air Gunner to jump – but as I got no answer assumed him killed, so decided to come down to sea-level to land. On my way down my engine restarted and I was able to proceed to my base, where I found the turret empty, the Air Gunner having obviously baled out previously.

Having previously seen action over Dunkirk with 264 Squadron, 20-year-old Sergeant Wise was the most experienced of all 141 Squadron's aircrew in action this day; he was never found.

Flight Lieutenant Malcolm Loudon's Defiant (L7001) was sufficiently badly hit for him to also order his gunner, Pilot Officer Eric Farnes, to bale out over the sea – Farnes was lucky to be rescued from the waves. Loudon, wounded, managed to nurse his shot-up aircraft back over the Kentish coast to crash-land 200-yards short of Hawkinge aerodrome, coming to rest against a hedge, which caught fire, although fortunately the pilot was rescued from the flames by the local farmer.

Flying Officer Ian Grahame Donald, the son of Air Marshal Sir D.G. Donald, was shot dead in his Defiant (L7009), and crashed, with his air gunner, Pilot Officer Arthur Charles Hamilton, into a cornfield north of Elmsvale Road, Dover. Hamilton, who did not bale out as per certain records, had actually been due to marry later that day.

Pilot Officer Rudal Kidson, a New Zealander from Wellington, and Sergeant Fred Atkins were shot down into the sea (Defiant L7015); Kidson remains missing while Atkins later washed up on the French coast.

Pilot Officer John Rushton Gard'ner, a New Zealander from Dunedin, was flying Defiant L7016, as one of 141 Squadron's four rearmost aircraft. Although shot down almost immediately, Gard'ner's aircraft, unlike the other three Defiants, did not catch fire. Despite being injured, Gard'ner ditched in the sea four miles off Dover and managed to escape the doomed aircraft – which sank, presumably taking his gunner, Pilot Officer Dudley Malins Slatter, to a watery grave, as he was never found. Fortunately, Gard'ner was rescued from the sea just fifteen minutes after he came down.

Pilot Officer John Richard Kemp, also a New Zealander, from Napier, and his air gunner, Sergeant Robert Crombie, crashed into the sea, never to be seen again (Defiant L6974).

Pilot Officer Dick Howley and Sergeant Albert Curley (Defiant L6995) also went down into the Channel – and also remain missing to this day.

Back at Hawkinge, Squadron Leader Richardson immediately flew to RAF Northolt, from where he was conveyed to Fighter Command HQ at Bentley Priory to debrief the disaster – which, appropriately, became known forever more as the 'Slaughter of the Innocents'. The folly of using the Defiant as a day-fighter had been confirmed with tragic consequences. 141 Squadron was released from further operations, and although seven replacement Defiants were delivered on 20 July 1940, the following day the unit was ordered back to Prestwick. The squadron would see no further action during the Battle of Britain, having already lost ten aircrew either killed or missing.

Similarly, on 22 July 1940, the other Defiant-equipped squadron, 264, was withdrawn from Duxford, further north to Kirton-in-Lindsey, where there was likely to be little or no action. On 22 August 1940, with the Battle of Britain at its height, 264, however, returned to 11 Group, operating from Hornchurch. Considering the Defiant's performance to date, this decision is difficult to comprehend. On 1 September 1940, following heavy losses (264 Squadron lost eighteen aircrew during the Battle of Britain), the squadron was pulled out, back to Kirton.

Fortunately, the Defiant played no further part in the day-fighter war, but was found useful as a stop-gap night-fighter, holding the fort, along with the Blenheim, until purpose-built night-fighters, with airborne interception radar, were available in numbers. The story of the Defiant's daylight operations is, therefore, a tragedy of errors indeed – paid for in human life.

With Pilot Officer Richard Alexander Howley and Sergeant Albert George Curley among the missing of 19 July 1940, a period of anguish and uncertainty followed for their families.

On 28 August 1940, Sergeant Curley's father, Major John Curley, wrote to the RAF Records Office at Ruislip:

> Has any further information been obtained concerning my son ... reported missing after air operations on 19 July? If he was taken prisoner of war, surely, we should have had news of him by now. His Squadron Leader seems to think he saw Pilot Officer Howley's aircraft, in which my son was the air gunner, shot down, but surely this does not mean that they had no chance to escape. A sergeant also in the operation said he saw several baling out but unable to state who they were. As these operations were near the coast of France, have we any justification for hoping they were saved on that side?
>
> I would also like to know if I could have the home address of Pilot Officer Howley, or where I could apply for same. No

doubt his relations are suffering the same anxiety as we are, and I would very much like to write to them.

The Air Ministry agreed to forward a letter to Engineer Commander Howley, and Tina Howley Harney confirms that the two bereaved fathers corresponded.

Squadron Leader Richardson's report of 20 July 1940 on the loss of Defiant L6995, Pilot Officer Howley's aircraft, gave no hope however, documenting that the aircraft was 'seen to go down in flames into the sea almost immediately. It is presumed that the pilot was killed prior to the aircraft catching fire.'

Unfortunately, no news having been received confirming that either airman was alive, perhaps a prisoner, six months later, their families were formally notified that their deaths were presumed for official purposes.

There being no known grave, Norah Howley never accepted her son's death and eventually went to hers still clinging to the vain hope that Dick was alive – somewhere. During the war, Norah scoured newspapers for photographs of Allied prisoners of war, desperate to see her son's face among them, but it was not to be.

Today, the sole surviving Boulton-Paul Defiant is preserved at the RAF Museum's Cosford site. Also, a Defiant replica can be seen, appropriately, at the Kent Battle of Britain Museum – situated on the former RAF Hawkinge aerodrome.

On Dick's last leave, popular with the ladies, he brought home his latest girlfriend, Mercy Bailey. Sadly, Dick's younger brother Percy, known universally as 'Jim' (1926–2012), recalled that Mercy's heart would be broken again by the death of subsequent suitors during the war.

Tina Howley Harney:

> Long after the war, Jim applied for Dick's medals, which I treasure, and every 11 November proudly wear the Canadian silver Memorial Cross, which our mother received, along with countless other mothers and widows, commemorating their husbands or sons. Although born in Canada, Dick was listed as a Newfoundlander given our family's long association with 'The Rock', where some of us were born. His name is commemorated on several memorials in Canada, such as the Airman's Memorial at the North Atlantic Aviation Museum in Gander, and in the UK, including the Runnymede Memorial, Battle of Britain Monument, Sir Christopher Foxley-Norris Memorial Wall at the National Memorial to The Few, and in the Book of Remembrance at Westminster Abbey. I do remember that when Dick was lost it just about broke my family, and the fact that neither Sergeant Curley or Dick were ever found was just too much to bear. Our father died in 1945, our mother in 1959, neither ever really recovering from it all.
>
> Dick always signed letters and photographs 'Happy Landings' – a phrase our family has continued using in remembrance of him. We have never forgotten Dick.

As a footnote, the pilots of III/JG 51's *Stabschwarm*, aces all, who began the 'Slaughter of the Innocents', were fortunate indeed to survive heavy fighting on various fronts throughout the war. Johannes Trautloft ended the war as *Inspektor of Tagjäger* (Inspector of Day-fighters) with fifty-eight aerial victories to his name, the majority recorded on the Eastern Front, and decorated with the coveted German Cross in Gold and Knight's Cross. In 1957, he returned to the air force, joining the post-war *Bundesluftwaffe* as a *Brigadegeneral* (Brigadier-General), eventually becoming *Inspektor General* before retiring in 1970 as a *Generalleutnant*. He died, peacefully, on 11 January 1995, at Bad Wiessee, near München.

Chapter Five

Sergeant Bruce Hancock

Today, the picturesque hills, meadows and quintessentially English, biscuit-coloured towns and villages of the Cotswolds, in south-central England, would seem an unlikely place to have been attacked during the Battle of Britain – much less be the location for a still emotive incident occurring on 18 August 1940. Covering nearly 800 square miles, the Cotswolds extends across five counties: Gloucestershire, to the south-west; Oxfordshire to the East, and Warwickshire and Worcestershire to the north-east; it is on the former county that we now focus – to explore what can only be considered an unfair anomaly regarding the coveted Battle of Britain Clasp to the 1939–45 Star...

Gloucestershire, in the West Country, has a rich aviation heritage. In 1910, Sir George White founded the British and Colonial Aircraft Company at Filton, Bristol, made famous during the First Wold War by its two-seater Bristol Fighter. In 1915, the Gloucestershire (later Gloster) Aircraft Company, (GAC) appeared in Cheltenham, producing various military biplane types. The First World War also saw various RFC, followed by RAF, training units based in the county, although this presence decreased after the Armistice. In 1925, another aircraft manufacturer, George Parnall & Co located itself at Yate, north-east of Bristol, and three years later GAC purchased what was previously 7 Group RAF's Air Acceptance Park at Brockworth, near Gloucester. In May 1934, the famous Hawker Aircraft Company took over and expanded a large factory site at Hucclecote, also near Gloucester, initially producing Hart and Audax biplanes before switching to the vitally important new Hurricane monoplane fighter. In 1937, Rolls-Royce and Bristol Aircraft combined to form Rotol Airscrews, handling propeller development and production for both companies, which was originally located in Llanthony Road, Gloucester, but soon moved to Staverton, just outside the city.

During the late 1930s, RAF aerodromes and other facilities were again constructed in Gloucestershire, including those at South Cerney, Kemble, Aston Down and Little Rissington – all of which would play a crucial part

Above left: Sergeant Bruce Hancock – who gave his life during the Battle of Britain, but who is not amongst the Few (via Allan White).

Above right: Similarly, Pilot Officer Alec Bird, a ferry pilot at Kemble, was also killed in action defending England during the summer of 1940, but, like Sergeant Hancock, is not one of the Few.

in the training of RAF pilots. The latter airfield opened on 26 August 1938, playing host to No 6 Service Flying Training School. In June 1940, Home Farm, Sherborne, in the Cheltenham district, became an advance landing ground for Little Rissington (some ten miles to the North), designated RAF Windrush and situated on a plateau just south of the main A40 Cheltenham to Oxford road. With 6 SFTS, pilots, having successfully completed elementary flying training and won their 'wings', would gain experience on the twin-engine Avro Anson.

First flown in 1935, the 'Annie' was originally envisaged as a maritime reconnaissance aircraft, hence being named after British naval hero Admiral George Anson. Upon entering service in 1936, however, it became clear that the Anson was actually a general-purpose aircraft, useful in various roles. By the outbreak of the Second World War, twenty-six RAF units operated the Anson, ten of which were in Coastal Command, although by then it was abundantly clear that the Anson, with a maximum speed of just 188 mph and a ceiling of only 18,000ft, was obsolete and therefore unsuitable for an operational role. The other sixteen Anson units, however, were allocated to Bomber Command. Twelve of these units, including 6 SFTS, belonged to 6 (Operational) Training Group, the job of which was to train crews for Bomber Command. Able to accommodate three or sometimes four aircrew, the training schools provided initial twin-engine air experience before students progressed to the more advanced typesat operational training units, such as the Fairey Battle, Bristol Blenheim, Vickers Wellington, Armstrong-Whitworth Whitley and Handley-Page Hampden bombers. Although the Anson was designed to carry a single forward-firing .303 machine-gun, and another in the dorsal turret, training aircraft were unarmed – which, in the case of Little Rissington's Ansons, considering what a target rich environment Gloucestershire and enemy air activity to date, is perhaps surprising.

The Germans, of course, owing to extensive pre-war aerial reconnaissance over Britain, were aware of all locations of interest, if not the actual significance of certain sites. The West Country, however, escaped the enemy's belligerent attention until 18 June 1940, when the lull following the Dunkirk air-fighting ended: Bristol Aircraft at Filton was attacked by a lone He 111, without damage being caused. On the night of 26 June 1940, 3 SFTS's base at RAF South Cerney was bombed, fortunately without serious damage. On subsequent nights, bombs were dropped fairly randomly across the Cotswolds. In truth, throughout the Battle of Britain the *Luftwaffe* suffered from poor intelligence analysis, failing to grasp how Dowding's System of Air Defence worked, and in particular the crucial importance of both radar and significance of certain buildings at Fighter Command Sector Stations – which accommodated all-important sector operations rooms. That so much effort throughout the sixteen-week conflict was expended by the Germans attacking airfields, such as South Cerney, after

Trainee pilots approach their Avro Ansons ready for an exercise, in a scene reminiscent of the evets at RAF Windrush on the evening of 18 August 1940.

Unteroffizier Herbert Rave with He 111P IG+PT at Dinard (via Allan White).

long and dangerous flights through hostile airspace, which had no direct connection with Fighter Command or the aerial defence of Britain, is a further example of this. Nonetheless, these raids, by lone aircraft, were seen as a means of eroding morale while concurrently causing disruption, including loss of sleep, and although far from a 'knockout blow', represented an increasing investment in collateral damage over time.

On 25 July 1940, a lone daylight raider bound for the aircraft factory at Hucclecote had been brought down near Stroud, having been intercepted by two ferry pilots from Kemble, namely Pilot Officers Alec Bird and Richard Manlove. In fact, Bird had either collided with, or in the opinion of a surviving enemy crewman, deliberately rammed, the Ju 88 intruder. It was a somewhat bittersweet victory, though, given that Bird was killed when his Hurricane crashed close to his victim's bomber at Oakridge Lynch. As explained, in detail, in my *Battle of Britain 1940: The Finest Hour's Human Cost* (Pen & Sword, 2020), Pilot Officer Bird's widow, Marjorie, went to her grave distressed that although her husband's life had been so freely given in the defence of his country during the Battle of Britain, he was not entitled to the Battle of Britain Clasp to the 1939–45 Star, and is therefore not one of the fabled Few. This is, quite simply, because Pilot Officer Bird was not serving with one of the Fighter Command or other associated units officially considered to have fought the Battle of Britain. Similarly, although Bomber Command contributed to victory in the Battle of Britain by, among other things, attacking and disrupting enemy invasion preparations, there would be no Battle of Britain Clasp for those airmen either. Considering that a replacement fighter pilot could qualify for the Clasp by virtue of having flown but one uneventful operational patrol, never having seen the enemy between the official dates of 10 July – 31 October 1940, that airmen from beyond Fighter Command who had seen action, and perhaps made the ultimate sacrifice, but did not receive the Clasp can only be considered both

Above left: A formal portrait of *Unteroffizier* Herbert Rave, the observer/navigator aboard the 'Aldsworth Heinkel' (via Allan White).

Above middle: The He 111's pilot, *Oberfeldwebel* Alfred Dreher, decorated with the Iron Cross 2nd Class, as indicated by the red, white and black ribbon in his buttonhole (via Allan White).

Above right: The He 111's radio operator, *Unteroffizier* Ewald Cohrs (via Allan White).

short-sighted and unfair. Sadly, Pilot Officer Bird would not be the only pilot lost in Gloucestershire during the summer of 1940 and whose name does not appear among the Few.

When Pilot Officer Bird was lost, the Battle of Britain was fifteen days old and in its very early stages, the fighting concentrated over Channel-bound convoys (as explored in previous chapters). As mid-August approached, though, it was clear that the enemy had become emboldened, and was increasingly attacking coastal radar installations and forward airfields in southern England – albeit, again owing to poor intelligence, including bases such as Gosport, Eastchurch and Lympne, which were unconnected with Fighter Command. Tuesday 13 August 1940 was chosen as the date to launch *Reichsmarschall* Göring's great *Adlerangriff* (Attack of the Eagles), the objective of which was the destruction of Fighter Command. For all the Wagnerian rhetoric, however, *Adler Tag* (Eagle Day) was not a huge success owing to poor weather – but it was abundantly clear to the defenders that a new and critical phase of the Battle had begun by day, focused on 11 Group airfields. Over the next few days, heavy attacks were made on all Air Vice-Marshal Park's sector stations, all of which suffered substantial damage, the resulting air fighting intense. On Sunday 18 August 1940, the *Luftwaffe* battered Kenley, Biggin Hill, Tangmere, West Malling, Manston, Hornchurch and Croydon, in addition to lesser targets (although the raid against North Weald was largely turned aside by defending fighters). German aircrews flew some 970 sorties that day, losing sixty-nine aircraft either destroyed or damaged beyond repair; ninety-four German aircrew were killed, forty reported missing, and twenty-five more wounded. Conversely, Fighter Command flew 927 sorties, losing thirty-one fighters, ten pilots killed and twenty wounded. Indeed, the resistance encountered surprised the Germans, to whom it was now abundantly clear that achieving aerial supremacy over southern England would be no 'piece of cake'. As night fell, however, the fighting on what the late British historian Dr Alfred Price famously described as 'The Hardest Day', was not over, and continuing the pattern of operations to date, German bombers prowled over England after dark.

Among the pilots undergoing training at 6 SFTS, Little Rissington, was Sergeant Bruce Hancock, who had been born on 24 June 1914, the youngest of three sons born to George, a travelling jewellery salesman, and Maud Hancock, of 12 Savington Road, Hendon, north-west London. Hendon-born Bruce, a Boy Scout remembered by his family as 'the jolly, carefree, one', attended the town's Algernon Road and William Ellis Schools before joining the staff of Johnston Evans, a local estate agent. On 1 December 1938, Bruce joined the RAFVR, learning to fly at Hendon. After general mobilisation, on 3 September 1939, with the rank of sergeant, after 'square

HEINKEL BOMBER DESTROYED BY ANSON TRAINER

The wreckage of the German Heinkel 111 brought down on Sunday night in a clover field near a small town in the South-West, after being rammed by an unarmed Anson training 'plane.

1. Looking over the bits and pieces of the big German Heinkel bomber. The Heinkel's crew of five were killed.
2. Examining a part of the wing of the Heinkel a quarter of a mile away from the bulk of the wreckage.
3. Mere Heinkel scrap.
4. While our photographer was taking pictures of the

Heinkel a delayed-action bomb dropped by the Heinkel exploded in a field in the distance. Our photographer turned his camera on the column of smoke which shot into the air.
5. One of the Heinkel's engines which landed 50 yards from the burning fuselage.

bashing' at an initial training wing and successfully completing elementary flying training, on 15 June 1940, Bruce was posted to 6 SFTS. On the night of 18 August 1940, Sergeant Hancock was to practise 'circuits and bumps', solo and flying from RAF Windrush. It was to be his last exercise with 6 SFTS, as the following day Bruce was to be commissioned and posted to an operational training unit, on the prior

The aftermath of the He 111 crash at Aldsworth, as it appeared soon afterwards in the *Cheltenham Chronicle*.

The He 111 crash site in January 2022.

leg of his path to a bomber squadron. That final routine flight was to be undertaken in a yellow-painted and unarmed Anson, and at RAF Windrush a row of Glim Lamps had been laid out, to assist pilots' landings and orientation. The problem was that it was not just unarmed, friendly, Ansons active over the Cotswolds that night.

Across the Channel, bitter though the fighting had been during daylight on 'The Hardest Day', not all enemy bomber units had participated in the maximum effort against 11 Group, the brunt of which had been borne by *Luftflotte* 3. *Luftflotte* 2's KG 27 *Boelcke*, based at Dinard, near St Malo on the north-western coast of Brittany had played no part in the fighting that day, and now certain elements of the unit prepared for the usual solo nuisance raids on England after dark. One such crew belonged to 5/KG 27, tasked with bombing RAF Brize Norton, just one of around forty RAF airfields in Oxfordshire. Again, though, this was not an airfield connected to the 'System' or Fighter Command – it was actually home to training and maintenance units, and 110 Squadron of Bomber Command, equipped with Blenheims. A far better target in adjacent Gloucestershire – just ten miles to the west – might perhaps have been RAF Bibury, like Windrush another farm turned advanced-landing-ground, at which, since 7 August 1940, a flight of 87 Squadron's Hurricanes had been based, providing further protection to Bristol and West Country aircraft factories. Nonetheless, at 1740 hrs on 16 August 1940, just two evenings previously, 'Brize' had been attacked by two enemy aircraft, probably He 111s of 3/KG 27, resulting in the largest number of aircraft ever destroyed on the ground. Thirty-two bombs were dropped, 2 SFTS's two hangars being ravaged by fire with forty-six Airspeed Oxford trainers destroyed. In addition, buildings were

A plate from the He 111 discovered during an authorised site investigation in 1986.

damaged and power and water supplies disrupted. Five airmen were injured along with four 'civvies', and a civilian was also killed. Although Brize was not a Fighter Command airfield it was a large airfield and this was a successful attack by any standards, so unsurprisingly the Germans returned to the same target on the night of 18 August 1940.

The pilot of the He 111 concerned (*Werke Nummer* 1408) was *Oberfeldwebel* Alfred Dreher, a 30-year-old from Schwabisch Hall; in German aircraft, unlike the RAF, the observer/navigator is the captain, in this case *Unteroffizier* Herbert Rave, 22, who, together with the 20-year-old flight-engineer and air gunner, *Unteroffizier* Richard Schmidt, hailed from Hamburg. Before the flight, the radio operator, 27-year-old *Unteroffizier* Ewald Cohrs, from Lüneburg, had written home, to his sister, Gertrude. Unusually in such a letter, which typically downplay the dangers faced, Cohrs described the inherent hazards of nocturnal operations, how the stress arising denied him of sleep, and how he craved home leave – all primary evidence of the strain under which enemy aircrews were operating. Collectively, this was an experienced crew, in fact, having previously survived both the Polish and French campaigns. Moreover, unlike many of their RAF counterparts at this time, who were amateur airmen, reservists, like Sergeant Hancock, or auxiliaries, all *Luftwaffe* personnel were full-time professional airmen.

Wartime was, of course, the time of the 'Black Out', with domestic properties, service installations and streets alike cloaked in darkness, no visible light being permitted, for fear of assisting the navigation of enemy aircraft. RAF Brize Norton, however, lay just five miles to the south-east of RAF Windrush, from where, to Rave and his crew, the Glim Lamps of the latter must have literally shone like beacons in the night. It is actually inconceivable, considering the successful attack on Brize only two evenings before, and given the extent of the enemy's assault on RAF airfields for the past five days, that this night-time training, with ground illumination and Ansons with navigation lights switched on, went ahead. Inevitably, the He 111, obviously aware that the Glim Lamps represented a flare path for night landings, was drawn to Windrush – and the opportunity for destruction was presented.

That night, LAC James Walding was Duty Medical Orderly, occupying a tent on Windrush airfield and watching the ongoing flying. The Duty Pilot's green flare, fired from his Very pistol, had soared aloft, signalling the waiting Anson pilots to take-off and begin their exercise. The time was 2250 hrs, Double Summer Time, and night-time proper was rapidly falling. Suddenly, explosions shook the ground, as the He 111's bombs found their mark, straddling the brightly lit flare path. Then, the German machine-guns opened up, raking the airfield. By now, all but one of the Ansons was safely down – only Sergeant Hancock remained airborne, making his approach in Anson N9164, still 'lit up like a Christmas tree', as Walding later recalled. Behind him lurked the He 111, which Walding could see closing quickly on the Anson from astern. The Heinkel's nose-gun opened fire on the defenceless trainer, which, Walding noted, had now extinguished its navigation lights. Still pouring fire on the Anson, the bomber rapidly overhauled its slower target. According to other eye-witnesses, having doused his lights, Sergeant Hancock banked to port, causing the He 111 to overshoot, then, just as the raider passed immediately overhead, the Anson suddenly reared up, crashing into the German. Walding remembered 'a blinding flash', and a 'fiery blob falling to earth'.

Both aircraft, in fact, crashed just two miles or so south-west of Windrush airfield, the He 111, ablaze, at Blackbitch Farm, Aldsworth, near Northleach – killing all aboard instantly. In the next field lay the wrecked Anson – in which LAC Walding and colleagues found the lifeless, and virtually unmarked, body of Sergeant Hancock.

To James Walding, there was no doubt that on that dreadful night he had witnessed a 'signal act of

The dorsal turret on Sergeant Hancock's Anson, found some distance from the main wreckage, and the only known photograph of his crash-site (via Allan White).

The Anson crash site in January 2022, some two miles SW of RAF Windrush, situated between the trees on the horizon.

valour' worthy of a Victoria Cross. Like the case of Pilot Officer Bird, however, it could never be *conclusively* proven that the collision occurred because Sergeant Hancock deliberately rammed his assailant, or whether, perhaps wounded, he had pulled up and collided with the Heinkel. A handwritten minute in Sergeant Hancock's Casualty File, dated 26 August 1940, records that 'Sergeant Hancock was killed while night-flying, and … was shot down by enemy aircraft' – but anecdotal evidence exists from his elder brother, Jim (as he was known in the family, actual name Charles George Hancock) that Bruce had previously told him that should he ever be airborne in an unarmed aircraft and contact an enemy aircraft, he would ram it.

What actually happened, therefore, we cannot be completely certain of, but on balance the available evidence does support the view that Sergeant Hancock did ram his tormentor. This was certainly the view reported by *The Times & Guardian*, Hendon's local read, on 23 August 1940, which headlined: 'Local RAF Hero: Unarmed Sergeant Rammed Enemy Bomber', naming Sergeant Hancock – which was unusual at the time, given the Air Ministry's clear policy of not identifying individuals in the press. Similarly, another newspaper declared 'Rammed Enemy Bomber: Heroic RAF Pilot's Name Revealed', again identifying Sergeant Hancock, and reported that:

> Reliable spectators on the ground believe that the Heinkel, which was on a night-bombing raid, intercepted the Anson, and finding it was an unarmed machine, chased it, firing with machine-guns. When he was found unable to regain his base, Sergeant Hancock, it is believed, resolved to bring down the enemy aircraft. He turned the Anson and rammed the Heinkel, bringing both machines to earth. The planes were completely smashed and the occupants of both – there were five Germans in the Heinkel – were killed.

Above and below: The German crew's military funeral at Northleach Cemetery – astonishingly attended by 200 local people (via Allan White).

Whatever happened in the Cotswold sky that night, Sergeant Hancock left behind a young widow, having married Annie Jayne Sophie 'Cissie' Bingley, a clerk and daughter of a well-known local family living at 42 Bertram Road, Hendon, on 30 March 1940. The happy occasion took place at St John's, the Parish Church of West Hendon, but sadly, less than five months later, on 23 August 1940, Bruce Hancock's funeral was held there, the same church at which he had also been Christened and confirmed. Afterwards, Bruce was buried nearby, at Hendon Park Cemetery.

The previous day, the *Bristol Evening World* had reported upon the Heinkel crew's burial, which took place at Northleach Cemetery:

> Three RAF planes dipped in salute as they flew over a small south-west town, where the funeral took place of five German airmen. The Germans lost their lives on Sunday night, when a 26-year-old sergeant pilot rammed the Heinkel bomber as it flew over a village a few miles away. The Heinkel had attacked with machine-gun fire the defenceless Anson training machine which the Sergeant was flying.
>
> About 200 people gathered in the peaceful country cemetery.
>
> People who might have been victims of the Heinkel's bombs stood for an hour to join with the RAF in paying tribute to the dead airmen of Germany.

A contingent of RAF men from a south-west aerodrome accompanied the cortege through the streets of the town to the cemetery. They acted as bearers, and there was a firing party to fire a volley over the graveside.

At the graveside a service was conducted by an RAF chaplain.

Each coffin bore only a number. That was the only way in which the airmen were identified. The names of two are known, but the others could not be identified.

After the firing party had paid their tribute, a bugler sounded The Last Post, the RAF men saluted and the three planes roaring overhead dipped and turned into the sky.

This report is, for sure, astonishing. Firstly, it is interesting that the enemy airmen are referred to simply as 'German', and not, much more emotively, as 'Nazi', as was typical of Allied wartime propaganda. Moreover, that RAF aircraft and airmen paid such a tribute is as remarkable as the congregation of 200. This was, though, before the West Country had overly suffered as the result of the air war – which, unfortunately, parts of it soon would. This was also before the Germans began the round-the-clock and indiscriminate bombing of London, and the many other British cities which were heavily bombed during the forthcoming night Blitz. All of that said, on 20 April 1944, after years of war and both the main night and 'Baby Blitz', the *Brighton and Hove Herald* reported: 'Nazi Night Raider Crashes in Churchyard of South Coast Town', referring to the loss of *Oberleutnant* Richard Pahl, killed when his Me 410 fighter-bomber, shot down by a Mosquito, crashed into Brighton Cemetery; while there was no large gathering of local, war-weary, people at Pahl's funeral, he was buried with full military honours. Indeed, most enemy airman brought down over Britain were – but without doubt, the large number of people turning out at Northleach was exceptional, even so early in the war when, to a degree, chivalry remained alive and well.

The astute reader may have noticed that while the identities of four crewmen of the He 111 are known, the fifth airman involved has never been identified. Since the war, all have been interred at the *Soldatenfriedhof* – the German Military Cemetery on Cannock Chase in Staffordshire.

The story, however, was far from over…

The advent of air power had put civilians in the front line, all of whom looked to Fighter Command and anti-aircraft defences to protect them. The aircrew were at the sharp end, able to fight the Germans, while the rest were helpless onlookers. In June 1940, however, a Jamaican

The He 111 crew's original grave markers at Northleach Cemetery (via Allan White).

newspaper, the *Gleaner*, cabled the Ministry of Aircraft Production inquiring how much a bomber cost to build. Lord Beaverbrook, the Fleet Street tycoon turned Minister for Aircraft Production responded with a figure of £20,000 – this sum was then rapidly raised by *Gleaner* readers and a cheque despatched to Beaverbrook. Other newspapers from as far afield as Singapore and the Gold Coast followed suit. Beaverbrook's letters of thanks for these donations were published in the press – and by the beginning of July 1940 there were many. Inevitably, an inquiry was received regarding the cost of a Spitfire fighter, which was set at £5,000. The Black Country *Express and Star* newspaper then promoted a 'Spitfire Fund', quickly raising £6,000 and in the process challenging the civic pride and patriotism of other regions.

The *Daily Express* challenged 'Worcester, Gloucester, Greenock, Wigan and Wimbledon', and all other towns with a population exceeding 50,000, to 'buy a "home-town" aeroplane to fight for Britain. An aeroplane built with your money, named after your town.' The *Worcester Evening News and Times* positively responded immediately, the Mayor of Wimbledon acknowledging the 'Faithful City' as his town's 'competitor'. Donations poured in, and by 10 July 1940, the start-date of the Battle of Britain, Worcester had raised its first £5,000, and on that day Lord Beaverbrook issued his first public appeal for aluminium: 'We will turn your pots and pans into Spitfires, Hurricanes, Blenheims and Wellingtons.' Collection centres were set up and the response was overwhelming – even if the alloy used to produce 'pots and pans' was too low grade for aircraft production. The point was, the whole 'Spitfire Fund' and 'pots and pans' initiative had engaged the public in an unprecedented way. What the 'Beaver' had done was provide a means for helpless civilians to feel directly connected with the war effort, and RAF especially, an immeasurable stimulus to morale and a propaganda coup of rare genius – and the people of Hendon, Sergeant Bruce Hancock's hometown, enthusiastically threw themselves into providing every support.

Above left, above right and left: After the war, the He 111 crew were interred at the Soldatenfriedhof, Cannock Chase, and are pictured here by the author on a gloomy Boxing Day 2021. The identity of the fifth airmen has never been established, and whoever he is, he lies buried with *Unteroffizier* Richard Schmidt. The *Leutnant* Herbert Hollstein buried with *Unteroffizier* Ewald Cohrs was the navigator and captain of another German bomber lost over Gloucestershire, namely a Ju 88 reconnaissance bomber which crashed at Coates Manor, Cirencester, and was 308 (Polish) Squadron's first aerial victory, on 24 November 1940.

'The People of Hendon Fighter Four Fund' committed to and succeeded in raising over £20,000 for four Spitfires. On Friday 13 September 1940 – with the Battle of Britain and bombing of London approaching its climax – *The Times & Guardian* reported that the Fund's committee had invited 'Mr and Mrs Geo. Hancock', 'Parents of RAF Hero', to present the second cheque, totalling £4,999, the outstanding £1 having been retained to start the next collection. Considering their loss and the international fervour surrounding, and enthusiasm for, the Spitfire Fund, the pride felt by Sergeant Hancock's parents can only be imagined. The Hendon fund

Sergeant Bruce Hancock's grave at Hendon Cemetery
(Daniel Richards).

ultimately succeeded in achieving its target
and providing four Spitfires: Mk VBs, W3505,
'Hendon Endeavour'; W3332, 'Hendon
Griffon'; W3506 'Hendon Lamb', and W3333,
'Hendon Pegasus'. Perhaps appropriately,
'Hendon Griffon' was taken on charge by 8 MU
at Little Rissington on 28 May 1941, 'Hendon
Pegasus' following on 20 June 1941.

Clearly, Sergeant Bruce Hancock's heroism
was recognised and appreciated by many, but,
like Pilot Officer Alec Bird, because he was not
serving with one of the Fighter Command or
associated units accredited as having fought in
the Battle of Britain, there would be no Battle
of Britain Clasp awarded. Instead of being immortalised among the Few,
these men were simply among millions of casualties suffered globally
during the Second World War, destined to be lost in the murky clouds of
anonymity. Nor would a gallantry medal be forthcoming, probably owing
to the uncertainty around what had actually happened, and overall lack of
eye-witnesses, which was always a problem with air combat.

On 29 August 1940, in fact, Air Vice-Marshal Gossage, Air Member
for Personnel, wrote to the Commanders-in-Chief of all three RAF home
commands – Fighter, Bomber and Coastal Commands, but not Training
Command, informing them that King George VI had expressed surprise
that no fighter pilots had received the VC. On 26 October 1940, Wing
Commander Victor Beamish, commanding RAF North Weald, referring
to an incident occurring on 16 August 1940, recommended a certain
Flight Lieutenant James Brindley Nicolson of 249 Squadron for a DFC.
On that day, 249 had recently arrived at Boscombe Down in 10 Group,
just inland of Southampton, and Nicolson led Red Section to intercept an
incoming formation of enemy bombers. All three Hurricanes, however,
were shot down by German fighters, which ambushed them from above.
The youngest of the Few, Pilot Officer Martyn Aurel King, baled out,
but the 18-year-old's parachute was damaged and he died in the arms of
a Sotonian in a suburban garden; Squadron Leader Eric 'Whizzy' King
crash-landed back at base, but Nicolson, shot down in flames, climbed back
into his blazing cockpit and pressed home his attack on an enemy fighter
before baling out, wounded by enemy fire and badly burnt. Beamish's

The first of four Spitfires presented by the good people of Hendon, under the auspices of the 'Spitfire Fund', this being Mk VB, WW3505, lost in a mid-air collision in 1943. Sergeant Hancock's parents were invited to present the cheque for the second Spitfire, 'Hendon Griffon' (W3332), which was destroyed by enemy action in 1942 but of which no known photographs exist.

recommendation reached Dowding's desk at Bentley Priory, who upgraded the recommendation to the VC – which was approved by the Secretary of State for Air on 7 November 1940. Surprisingly, Nicolson became the only RAF fighter pilot to receive the highest award for gallantry throughout the Second World War. During the Battle of Britain there were countless acts of immense courage that went unrecognised, some equally deserved of a VC, as Nicolson himself knew full-well and at first refused to wear the maroon-coloured ribbon, considering that he did not deserve it when others had done more. One of the problems with recognising a 'signal act of valour' in fighter combat is the speed and height at which events commonly took place, leading to a lack of eyewitnesses – but in Nicolson's case, many Sotonians on the ground watched the dramatic events involved. So the award of a VC during the Battle of Britain was a difficult thing, and clearly it failed to cross Gossage's mind that *Training* Command should be included in his letter's distribution list. Had it been, we can only speculate as to whether the names of Pilot Officer Bird and Sergeant Hancock, who had given their lives in similar circumstances, may have been put forward.

James Walding, however, had never forgotten that fateful night at Windrush, and many years later, during the 1980s, retired to Cheltenham. At that time, the Severnside Aviation Society was actively researching and recording wartime crashes in Gloucestershire, led by the selfless and dedicated researcher Allan White – with whom Mr Walding made contact in 1988. Out then came the story of Sergeant Hancock, and all involved

Air Vice-Marshal Anthony Mason unveils the plaque commemorating Sergeant Hancock outside St Peter's, Windrush, which was dedicated by the Rev'd Colin McCarter in the presence of members of the Hancock family and Allan White (third left), secretary of the former Severnside Aviation Society, who coordinated the initiative (Allan White).

Mr James Walding (third from left), with Allan White and members of the Hancock family, who was the Duty Medical Orderly at Windrush and firmly believed that Sergeant Hancock deliberately rammed the He 111 (Allan White).

became determined to see the Hendon airman commemorated. So it was that on 11 September 1988, over a hundred people filled the church of St Peter at Windrush, to remember him. Among the congregation were proud members of the Hancock family, the commander of the nearby United States Air Force base at Little Rissington, and, appropriately, two serving

TO THE MEMORY OF
SGT PILOT BRUCE HANCOCK R.A.F.V.R
WHO SACRIFICED HIS LIFE
BY RAMMING AND DESTROYING
AN ENEMY HEINKEL BOMBER
WHILE FLYING
AN UNARMED TRAINING AIRCRAFT
FROM WINDRUSH LANDING GROUND
DURING THE BATTLE OF BRITAIN
18TH AUGUST 1940

The plaque set in the wall of St Peter's, Windrush, unveiled on 11 September 1988.

The plaque commemorating Sergeant Hancock on the Watch Office at the former RAF Windrush.

members of what was now 6 Flying Training School, located at RAF Finningley. Outside, set within the ancient church's wall, was a plaque of Cotswold stone, which was unveiled after the service by the Air Secretary, Air Vice-Marshal Anthony Mason. The deeply moving occasion was then concluded by a flypast of Bulldog trainers from Bristol's University Air Squadron. As Allan White said, 'At least Sergeant Bruce Hancock has now been permanently remembered, and his bravery recorded for future generations to wonder at the quality of those young men who paid the price for freedom.'

In 1945, RAF Windrush was decommissioned, and in 1969 the landowner, Lord Sherborne, bought the site back from the MoD. Since then, many of the wartime airfield buildings have been demolished, or screens of trees planted to hide the surviving structures from view. Nonetheless, many installations remain at the site, which was bequeathed by the 7th Baron Sherborne to the National Trust in 1987. The Sherborne Park Estate is now a working one, to which the public have access and can enjoy walks in this

The original blister hangar at Windrush in January 2022. Many decaying wartime buildings survive, but there is no public access to the site.

The Watch Office and an impressive defensive pill box at Windrush in January 2022.

picturesque Cotswold park, so far removed now from the violent events of 1940. Appropriately, on 18 August 2015, the 75th anniversary, a plaque commemorating Sergeant Hancock's loss and bravery was rededicated at the former airfield's surviving Watch Office by the pilot's nephew, Keith Hancock, born three years after his uncle's death: 'I always think of him as my heroic uncle, and wonder what more could a person do, to do their duty in time of war? To my mind, he should clearly have been awarded the VC.'

That Sergeant Hancock has been commemorated locally in Windrush is a great thing. But it is not enough – which is why I chose to include the tale in this book, with a view to raising awareness of such unrecognised sacrifices wider still.

Looking across the old Windrush airfield from within the pill box, towards RAF Brize Norton, in January 2022.

On the cliffs above Folkestone, at Capel-le-Ferne, nestles The National Memorial to the Few, 'Dedicated to the heroic and selfless deeds of the men who won the Battle of Britain, 10 July to 31 July 1940.' There, the Few are commemorated, by name, on the Sir Christopher Foxley-Norris Wall, while the Memorial, a statue of a fighter pilot, sits staring across the Channel towards France. There are busts of the two primary victors of the Battle of Britain, namely Air Chief Marshal Dowding and Air Vice-Marshal Park, and the 'Wing' visitor centre is home to 'The Scramble Experience'. It is a truly wonderful tribute and site – but nowhere will the names of Pilot Officer Alec Bird or Sergeant Bruce Hancock, not being among the actual Few, be found. Now it seems to me, as a great supporter and member of The Battle of Britain Memorial Trust, responsible for the site and which I would urge readers to join, that this is something we, the Battle of Britain community, should address. In 2019, prior to the pandemic, positive initial talks took place on this subject, and I hope very much that as life returns to normal, and awareness of these lesser-known casualties is raised, that these can be resumed – and that ultimately Pilot Officer Alec Bird and Sergeant Bruce Hancock will also be commemorated in some way at this most dignified and appropriate national shrine. That, together with existing local commemorations, would I think, ensure that these important stories are remembered on the widest possible stage – they certainly deserve to be.

Chapter Six

Wing Commander Eric Hugh 'Tommy' Thomas DSO DFC* CdeG

Eric Hugh Thomas was the second of George Frederick and Maude Thomas's three sons, born in Warwick Park, Tunbridge Wells, on 10 October 1917; the couple also had four daughters, Betty, Joan, Celia and Wendy. George Thomas apparently had an adventurous streak, given that – so the story goes – he ran away from school to fight in the Boer War, only to be returned forthwith owing to being underage. After leaving school he studied dentistry in Switzerland, and when the First World War broke out in 1914 was serving as a territorial captain in the 5th Battalion, Royal Sussex Regiment. During the so-called 'Great War', Captain Thomas's lungs were damaged during a gas attack at Ypres – but this did not prevent him, in 1917, transferring to and becoming a pilot in the RFC. After the war, Major George Thomas MC returned to dentistry, practising in his home town of Uckfield and later in Tunbridge Wells. It was not pulling teeth that inspired his three sons, Cecil, known as 'Bobbie', Eric and Bruce, but aviation – and all three would become RAF pilots in the next war.

Eric Thomas was educated at Rose Hill School in Tunbridge Wells before becoming a day pupil in Smythe House at Tonbridge School. With this private education behind him Eric held the key to many doors – and on 6 July 1936 was granted a Short Service Commission, of four years duration, in the General Duties branch of the RAF. On that day, he began elementary flying training with the Bristol civilian flying school based at Yatesbury in Wiltshire, successfully achieving his

Wing Commander EH Thomas DSO DFC* CdeG (all photographs courtesy Sylvia Lewis, unless otherwise indicated).

245

Left: 'Harts and Audax, Penrhos, 1937'.

Below: Gloster Gauntlets of 19 Squadron at Duxford, 1938.

'Pilot's Certificate of Competency for private flying machines, No 10180' on 31 July 1936. Thereafter Pilot Officer Thomas completed service flying training at 6 Flying Training School, Netheravon, and 5 Armament Training Camp at Penrhos, joining 19 Squadron at Duxford on 22 May 1937, to fly Gloster Gauntlet fighters.

Previously in this book we have explored the pre-war RAF scenario, so suffice it to say that this was during the period later described by 19 Squadron armourer Fred Roberts as the 'Strawberries and cream and fruitcake for tea' salad days of the comparatively small between-the-wars air force, which resembled an elite flying club. Although the RAF had started expanding in 1936, in response to the obvious threat posed by Hitler, the focus of spending, owing to the air power doctrine of the time, was largely on the bomber force. Consequently, whereas the *Luftwaffe*'s He 51 biplane fighters had been replaced with the modern, all-metal, Me 109 monoplane fighter by 1937, the RAF's frontline fighter squadrons, including 19, were still equipped with obsolete biplanes, one RAF pilot remarking that Gauntlets were not even fast enough to run away! Nonetheless, the RAF still trained for war, and Pilot Officer Thomas's log book records many such flights in Harts and Gauntlets, including practising Fighter Command attacks, aerobatics, cross-countries, battle climbs, gunnery and formation exercises.

246

Salvation, however, was at hand: on 4 August 1938, Supermarine test pilot Jeffrey Quill delivered the RAF's first operational Spitfire to 19 Squadron at Duxford, an auspicious occasion well-remembered by Pilot Officer James Coward:

> There was great excitement when the first Spitfire arrived... Jeffrey Quill flew the downward leg at 1,000ft, upside down and pumped the wheels down so that they came up above the inverted aircraft. He then slowly rolled round as he turned and landed.

19 Squadron's CO, Squadron Leader Cozens, now had to introduce the Spitfire into service, which he and 19 Squadron did without losing a man – a rare achievement considering how very different the advanced Spitfire was to the comparatively primitive biplanes flown to date.

At 1530 hrs on 15 August 1938, Pilot Officer Thomas flew a Spitfire Mk I, K9792, for the first time, a flight of thirty minutes familiarisation – and the start of a long association with R.J. Mitchell's iconic fighter. Thereafter followed an intensive conversion period for 19 Squadron's pilots as a whole; as Pilot Officer Gordon Sinclair remarked, 'It was hard flying but we were in seventh heaven, everyone wanted the Spitfire and we had it!' And so 19 Squadron, being the RAF's first Spitfire-equipped fighter squadron, earned a unique place in history. Pilot Officer Thomas's log book records 'Intensive flying Spitfire aircraft', throughout the remainder of 1938, by the end of which year 19 Squadron was fully operational by night and day on the new monoplane. On 24 April 1939, however, Eric was posted to the Advanced Training Squadron at RAF Cranwell, but considering that the unit was primarily operating old Audax and Hart biplanes, the young pilot, fresh from flying the incomparable Spitfire, may well have wondered what, in fact, was 'advanced' about it.

At Cranwell, Pilot Officer Thomas practised Fighter Command attacks in the two-seater biplanes, frequently carrying a flight cadet in the air gunner's seat, and flew the twin-engine Airspeed Oxford monoplane, practising 'Lewis gun air to ground attacks'. Eric was there, in fact, on that fateful day, 3 September 1939, when he wrote in his log book '1100 hrs. GREAT BRITAIN DECLARES WAR ON GERMANY.' Although the 'balloon had gone up', as explored in previous chapters, the dreaded 'knockout blow' failed to materialise and little actually changed in the short-term. Life at Cranwell continued as it had pre-war, while the Advanced Air Striking Force flew to operate from French bases, supporting Lord Gort's British Expeditionary Force. Following the German conquest of Norway

Pilots of 19 Squadron at Duxford, 1938. From left, back row: Flying Officer Gordon, Pilot Officer Banham, Squadron Leader Cozens, Pilot Officer Sinclair; middle row, from left: Pilot Officers Ball, Coward, Clouston and Pace; front row, from left: Pilot Officers Robinson, Withall, Mee and Thomas.

and Denmark in April 1940, on 10 May 1940 Hitler attacked the West, and six weeks later it was all over: the BEF evacuated from Dunkirk and France having surrendered. Again as detailed in previous chapters, the Me 109 had achieved total air superiority over the Continental battlefields, outclassing the Hawker Hurricane, although Fighter Command's Spitfires were committed to battle over Dunkirk. There, those squadrons met the 109 for the first time, and began learning fast under combat conditions. After a lull, on 10 July 1940 the Battle of Britain officially began, and on 19 August 1940, Flying Officer Thomas rejoined 19 Squadron, now based at Duxford's nearby Fowlmere satellite airfield.

By that time, things had substantially changed since those heady days of 1938 when 19 Squadron received the first Spitfires. Squadron Leader Cozens had been succeeded in command first by Squadron Leader Geoffrey Stephenson, who had been shot down and captured on 26 May 1940, when 19 Squadron met the enemy over the French coast for the first time. When Flying Officer Thomas returned to the squadron, Squadron Leader Phillip Pinkham was in command, and 'Tommy' joined Flight Lieutenant Brian Lane's 'A' Flight. At this time, 19 was flying the Spitfire Mk IB, armed with just two 20mm Hispano-Suiza cannons, which were proving problematic owing to the Spitfire's thin wing section dictating that the weapon had to be mounted on its side, rather than upright as intended by the manufacturer, causing stoppages. Being located in 12 Group, opportunities to engage the enemy remained comparatively infrequent, although 'A' Flight claimed several Me 110s destroyed on 16 August 1940, and another (probably actually a Do 17) three days later; had cannons functioned properly, however, the damage inflicted upon the enemy would undoubtedly have been greater, frustrating the pilots. On the day he arrived at Fowlmere, Flying Officer Thomas lost no time in flying one of the troublesome Spitfires, R6919, and over the next week flew various routine local sorties. On 21 August 1940, it was practising air-to-ground firing at the Sutton Bridge range, and the following day Eric flew R6958, on patrol with Flight Lieutenant Lane and Sergeant Jack Potter, the threesome forming Red Section. The sortie was uneventful except for one reason: as it was an operational patrol by a Fighter Command squadron, the sortie fulfilled the criteria for Flying Officer Thomas's subsequent award of the Battle of Britain Clasp; he was now one of the Few.

The next day however, 23 August 1940, Flying Officer Thomas was posted away from 19 Squadron, joining 266 'Rhodesia' Squadron at Wittering, also in 12 Group. 266 had re-formed at Sutton Bridge in October 1939; although originally intended to operate the Blenheim, that type was never received, the squadron instead equipping first with the Fairey Battle, then, in January 1940, with the Spitfire. The new squadron saw action over Dunkirk, and on 9 August 1940 had flown to Tangmere, under the orders of Coastal Command, while ground staff moved to Eastchurch. On 12 August, 266 Squadron's Spitfires remained at Tangmere, on readiness, when scrambled to patrol Portsmouth; in the subsequent engagement, Pilot Officer D.G. Ashton was reported missing, and Pilot Officer W.S. Williams forced-landed on the Isle of Wight. That evening, 266 flew to Eastchurch, joining 'B' Flight of 19 Squadron. The reason for the Spitfires' presence, according to the latter's CO, was 'to strafe "E" boats and escort the Battle boys on a beat-up of the other side' – thereby disrupting German invasion preparations. Although this operation did not ultimately take place, the Spitfires' presence was known to the enemy – which bombed Eastchurch accordingly on 13 August 1940, which dawned as *Adler Tag* (Eagle Day). 266 Squadron's hangar was set ablaze, but fortunately only one Spitfire was damaged, with one airman killed and several others injured. Two days later, 266 Squadron proceeded from Hornchurch to operate from the coastal airfield at Manston, and by dusk, three more pilots, including the 30-year-old CO, Squadron Leader Rodney Wilkinson, a Cranwellian, were dead; next day, two more

Above left: Pilot Officer Eric Thomas in pre-war flying kit, outside 19 Squadron's hangar and offices, Duxford 1938.

Above right: Pilot Officer Thomas in pre-war white flying overalls, Gloster Gauntlet and his dog, 'Nimbus I' – with whom, and other pets, he flew many times, each of which had their own log book!

were lost and two others wounded. On 'The Hardest Day', 18 August 1940, Hornchurch, along with other sector stations, was battered, two of 266's Spitfires being destroyed on the ground while five more were damaged by machine-gun and cannon fire. Squadron Leader D.G.H. Spencer, who had served as a supernumerary officer and 'vice' CO since 25 July 1940, was given command on that day, and, seeing no further action from Hornchurch, the squadron retreated back to Wittering on 22 August 1940.

Such, then, was the situation when Flying Officer Thomas and Sergeant C. Sydney, both formerly of 19 Squadron, reported for duty on 24 August 1940. While with 266 Squadron at Wittering, Flying Officer Thomas's log book again records routine training flights, including dogfight, formation, battle climbs and air firing practice, and uneventful patrols. On 7 September 1940, he flew an improved Spitfire Mk IIA, P7327, for the first time, but it would not be a lengthy stay with 266; on 10 September 1940, Flight Lieutenant Thomas, as he had been for a week, was posted to 222 Squadron at Hornchurch, to command 'A' Flight. This was, of course, at the height of the Battle of Britain – and Eric would soon find himself embroiled in bitter air battles over the 11 Group area – and prove himself to be a fine and courageous fighter pilot.

222 'Natal' Squadron had re-formed at Duxford on 5 October 1939, under the command of Squadron Leader Horace 'Tubby' Mermagen, a Cranwellian and gifted aerobatic pilot, equipped with Blenheims and envisioned as a shipping protection squadron. Many years later, Air Commodore Mermagen recalled that in March 1940, 'To our delight the AOC, Air Vice-Marshal Leigh-Mallory, decided to re-equip us with Spitfires. The already enthusiastic pilots faced this conversion from twins to singles with great excitement.' By 17 April 1940, 222 Squadron was fully operational on Spitfires, by day and night. When the shooting began on 10 May 1940, 222 moved to Digby, and a fortnight later to Kirton-in-Lindsey. On 29 May 1940, Squadron Leader Mermagen led his Spitfires to Hornchurch:

> At 6.30 a.m. that day I led the squadron, in fact a wing of several squadrons, on its first patrol over the Dunkirk beaches. The sortie lasted two hours and 45 minutes, a long flight for a Spitfire. The squadron carried out several further sorties, ending on June 3rd when the wretched evacuation appeared completed – no life could be seen either on the beaches or in the country behind. I lost four pilots killed and one missing during that period.

At the end of July 1940, however, 'Tubby' was posted to RAF Warmwell, and was succeeded in command of 222 Squadron by Squadron Leader John Hamar Hill, an experienced pre-war officer who had already lived through quite an adventure when he survived being beaten by French peasants who, when Hill was shot down near Lille, mistook him for a German, and returned home via Dunkirk. It would be Squadron Leader Hill who led 222 Squadron south, to Hornchurch, on 29 August 1940.

Among 'B' Flight's pilots was Sergeant Reg Johnson, who recalled that:

> In the first 48 hours that 222 Squadron was at Hornchurch we lost eighteen aircraft and a number of pilots. We proceeded to go into action in tight formation and our losses were heavy. Eventually we evolved a weaving 'Tail End Charlie' section, Green Section, which weaved about above, below and to the squadron's rear (still in tight formation). It helped.

That was a good job, because 222 Squadron was at Hornchurch throughout the 'Battle of the Airfields', between mid-August and early September 1940, when Hornchurch was among those vital sector aerodromes battered

Pilot Officer Thomas's subsequent dog, 'Nimbus II' and one of 19 Squadron's very first Spitfire Mk Is.

relentlessly by German bombers. 222 Squadron was heavily engaged, not least on 'Black Saturday', 7 September 1940, when the enemy began the round-the-clock bombing of London. It was, therefore, a highly combat-experienced unit with which Flight Lieutenant Thomas made his first flight on 13 September 1940, in Spitfire X4024, a 'Single aircraft Hornchurch patrol' – as Eric took off, however, a stick of bombs was dropped across the airfield, although fortunately he was unharmed. Thereafter, it was often a case of several scrambles and patrols a day, every day, as the enemy continued to concentrate on London.

On Sunday 15 September 1940 – 'Battle of Britain Day' – Flight Lieutenant Thomas fired his guns in anger for the first time, reporting that:

> At approx. 1415 hrs I was patrolling with the squadron over Sheerness @ 20,000ft. Our formation having been broken up by enemy fighters, I dropped to 10,000ft and noticed black anti-aircraft fire about ten miles away at about 10,000ft in the direction of Chatham. By this time I was alone and saw a Do 17 flying alone, due East. I disregarded the AA fire and went in a beam attack out of the sun and managed to get in a short burst at long range, about 400 yards. The E/A then disappeared in a cloud bank. I set my course due east and kept above the clouds, and about four miles further on the Do 17 arrived, flying due east again. I did an astern attack and closed from 300 to 50 yards, firing all the time. I saw pieces of aircraft flying off and rear-gun fire stopped. Just then a yellow-nosed Me 109 got on my tail – I broke off the attack and took cover in cloud. The Do 17 had disappeared when I came up again to look for it.

Eric's attack had been delivered between Chatham and Canterbury, in concert with Pilot Officer 'Raz' Berry of 603 Squadron, also based at Hornchurch. According to the latter Squadron's 'Fighter Command Form "F"', the Do 17 concerned 'crashed near Maidstone', the bomber's destruction shared between the two Spitfire pilots. This aircraft, of 4/KG 3, had actually already been damaged by AA fire, probably explaining why it was straggling alone, and was also attacked by at least three other Spitfire and Hurricane pilots. Eventually, the hapless raider forced-landed at Lower Stoke on the Isle of Grain; the enemy crew were all captured.

Even after the Germans' maximum effort of that great day, there was little respite for both sides. Over the next few days, Eric's log book records patrols by 222 Squadron at high-altitude over the Thames Estuary area, up to 31,000ft. By this time, 11 Group was tending towards using Spitfire squadrons in pairs to provide a high-altitude umbrella, enabling the Hurricanes, which were unsuited to high-flying, to operate lower down. This, however, in unpressurised cockpits, was very demanding physically, but necessary owing to the high altitudes at which enemy fighters were sweeping over south-east England. Fighter sweeps, however, could actually be ignored, a fighter at such a height only being dangerous if defending fighters intercepted. Instead, Air Vice-Marshal Park was largely content to let the German fighters be left unchallenged, burning up fuel unnecessarily on these fruitless incursions over southern England. Or at least that was the case until 20 September 1940…

On that day, for the first time, twenty-two Me 109 fighter-bombers of II/ LG 2, protected by numerous fighters, took off from the Pas-de-Calais bases – London bound. Between Calais and Dover the Germans climbed to 25,000ft before swooping down on the capital. Believing the enemy sweep to be no threat, Fighter Command's squadrons remained grounded, permitting the fighter-bombers to reach London unmolested. Diving to 22,000ft and pressing the bomb release switch, the *Jabo* pilots had already turned for home when their bombs exploded in the City of London and on a rail terminus west of the Thames's great bend. Listening to the British radio frequencies, German intelligence reported a great confusion of orders and counter-orders after the 'fighters' had dropped their bombs.

After the first wave of raiders had caused confusion, a second was reported incoming over the Kent coast at 14,000ft. Unbeknown to the RAF controllers, there were no fighter-bombers in this formation, but the Biggin Hill and Hornchurch Spitfire squadrons were scrambled. 222 and 603 Squadrons were up from Hornchurch at 1055 hrs, but as they desperately climbed for height over the Thames Estuary, the 109s fell on them. Almost immediately, Pilot Officer Laurie Whitbread of 222 Squadron's 'B' Flight

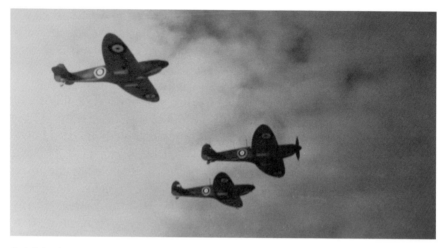

A 'vic' of 19 Squadron's first Spitfires: lead aircraft Squadron Leader Cozens, Pilot Officer Thomas (closest to camera) and Pilot Officer Banham.

was literally blown out of the sky and killed; Flight Lieutenant Thomas reported that:

> At 1115 hrs I was climbing to patrol with five other aircraft when at 25,000ft a squadron of yellow-nosed Me 109s attacked us from the sun in a quarter-attack. I saw tracer shells going past Pilot Officer Edsall and I broke away, getting on the tail of a 109. I opened fire from astern at approximately 200 yards and gave two long bursts of five seconds each. I then saw a trail of white vapour come from the enemy aircraft. I then broke away and carried out a deflection shot at two more Me 109s circling round in tight formation, but saw no result as I had to break away due to being attacked myself.

The enemy fighter was claimed as damaged in the combat, which occurred over Sittingbourne. White smoke, however, is coolant, without which the engine overheats, so it is possible that Eric's target was a machine of 7/JG 53, which forced-landed at Boulogne, having managed to limp back across the Channel. During this combat, however, Fighter Command's pilots claimed two Me 109s destroyed, and a 'He 113' which was actually a 109, in addition to three more damaged; just one Me 109 crashed in England, however, that being *Unteroffizier* Erich Clauser of 9/JG 27 who was killed when shot down by 72 Squadron's Sergeant W.T.E. Rolls at Ospringe. Conversely, Fighter Command lost four pilots killed and several more wounded while reacting to this first 'tip 'n'run' raid. From that raid onwards, no future enemy fighter incursion could be ignored, representing a substantial commitment for Fighter Command. Indeed, Pilot Officer Geoffrey 'Boy' Wellum, an 18-year-old Spitfire pilot with 92 Squadron at Biggin Hill, later recalled to me that this period was the most 'exhausting of all'.

Flight Lieutenant Thomas was now flying operationally every day, often several times a day, and significantly his log book during that last week of September 1940 records two 'wing patrols' of the Maidstone line. Owing to the controversy over 12 Group's so-called 'Big Wing', it is often assumed that Air Vice-Marshal Park never patrolled over 11 Group in strength. While he largely chose to fight the Battle of Britain using small, flexible formations of flight and squadron strength, Park was never averse to patrolling or meeting the enemy in strength when the tactical situation merited such an approach – and German fighter sweeps were invariably made at *Gruppe* or even *Geschwader* strength, the latter comprising over 100 aircraft. Consequently, it made perfect sense to operate Spitfire squadrons in pairs from Biggin Hill and Hornchurch. 222 Squadron, flying from Hornchurch and the forward base at Rochford often found itself, therefore, in company with 41 or 603 Squadrons, with which it shared Hornchurch Sector.

On 28 September 1940, the 222 Squadron ORB states that 'The squadron carried out two patrols during the day, but no contacts were made with enemy aircraft.' Flight Lieutenant Thomas's log book tells a different story, however, recording that 222 Squadron patrolled the Maidstone line and had a 'Fight with about ten Me 109s over Mayfield, Sussex', later reporting that:

> I was patrolling with the squadron at 20,000ft, when the squadron was split up and I found myself alone.
>
> I climbed up into the sun and found myself directly underneath a squadron of Me 109s. I flew along directly beneath them at about 500ft below, pulled the nose up and gave two bursts of about fifty rounds just in front of one enemy aircraft.
>
> I then lost this aircraft in the sun. I transferred my fire to another enemy aircraft and gave a long burst of about 100 rounds from behind and below. This aircraft fell away, just as I was attacked, and that was the last I saw of the enemy aircraft, over Mayfield, Sussex.

On that day, the enemy had made two sweeps towards London, both at or in excess of 20,000ft. 11 and 12 Groups scrambled a total of twenty

Eric Thomas's original pre-war 19 Squadron badge (author).

fighter squadrons to intercept, but only five squadrons engaged each raid, and all resulting combats were with 109s – which were invariably higher than the RAF fighters and therefore, as ever, with the tactical advantage. Consequently, only six German fighters were lost against ten Spitfires and Hurricanes. Flight Lieutenant Thomas's combat, however, appears to have been inconclusive, and consequently no claim was made.

Two days later, 30 September 1940, Flight Lieutenant Thomas flew three patrols and an air test on what was, perhaps surprisingly, the heaviest day of activity for Fighter Command throughout the entire month. The first raid was picked up on British radar screens at 0855 hrs, comprising two formations of twelve and fifty plus respectively, which crossed the coast east of Dungeness five minutes later and struck inland towards Biggin Hill. 11 Group's reaction was slow however, the defending squadrons only scrambling as the raiders crossed the Kentish coast, and consequently only two RAF squadrons engaged the enemy. 222 Squadron patrolled above cloud at 34,000ft but without contact. The next threat was a fighter sweep further West, over Hampshire, dealt with by 10 Group, but then a major raid materialised at 1300 hrs, comprising some 150 'bandits', which crossed the coast between Rye and Folkestone. Initially heading for Kenley and Biggin Hill, the Germans then split up, sub-formations sweeping over the Thames Valley, Dartford and Chatham. Again, for some reason the defending squadrons were given little warning, and it was not until the Germans crossed the coast that 41 and 222 Squadrons scrambled from Hornchurch to patrol the Chatham–Rochford line at 30,000ft, while 603 also left Hornchurch to patrol Maidstone at the same height, where they were met by Biggin Hill's Spitfire squadrons, 66, 72 and 92. Hurricanes from Northolt, Kenley and Croydon were also up, patrolling between 15–20,000ft over Kent. On this occasion, Flight Lieutenant Thomas was leading 222 Squadron:

> At about 1300 hrs, I was ordered on patrol with the squadron. I climbed to 25,000ft and at approx. 1320 hrs sighted four Me 109s in a defensive circle at the same height. I continued climbing to 26,000ft and stayed in the sun. I looked around and

'Before the Blitz': pilots of 19 Squadron pictured at Fowlmere, sometime between 19-23 August 1940; from left: Flight Lieutenant Brian Lane DFC; Sergeants Jack Potter and Bernard Jennings, Pilot Officer Ray Aeberhardt, Flight Sergeants George Unwin and Harry Steere, Pilot Officer Frank Brinsden, Flying Officer Jack Lawson, Flying Officer Leonard Haines, Pilot Officer Arthur Vokes, Flight Lieutenant Wlf Clouston DFC, and Flying Officer Eric Thomas (author).

saw several other formations of Me's milling about and below me and then saw eighteen or twenty-one bombers, flying on a course of 290°. I ordered the squadron into line astern and stayed in the sun and shadowed the bombers. I then ordered the attack and dived down out of the sun through a squadron of Me 109s and attacked the leading vic of three Dorniers. I opened fire, a full deflection quarter attack at 300 yards and held my fire until I passed through the formation. I could see the tracer going into the enemy aircraft. I continued down, as I was chased by Me 109s, to the clouds and went through and found myself in the centre of the balloon barrage. I climbed up quickly into the clouds again but could not see any trace of the enemy aircraft.

Again, though, Eric made no claim, the combat having been inconclusive. The commander of 222 Squadron's 'B' Flight, Flight Lieutenant Geoffrey Matheson, who had also previously served on 19 Squadron, and Pilot Officer E.F. Edsall both claimed Me 109s destroyed, the latter also

Flying Officer Thomas, sitting on stepladder, with other 222 Squadron pilots at Hornchurch during the Battle of Britain (author).

probably destroying another, with Sergeant R.G. Marland claiming two more probables. In response, only Sergeant Iain Hutchinson was shot-up and wounded, but managed to make a safe forced-landing at Denham. 222 Squadron made a further high-altitude patrol that afternoon, without contacting the enemy which again skirmished with British fighters around London. Further West, a feint towards Southampton was followed by a major raid against the Westland Aircraft Factory at Yeovil in Somerset, although owing to cloud obscuring the target, KG 55's He 111s instead virtually obliterated the nearby town centre of Sherborne by mistake. Such were the enemy's losses, however, that it became clear that the He 111 was unsuitable for daylight operations over England and was therefore withdrawn to the nocturnal arena. Indeed, by now it was equally clear to Hitler's OKW that the German bomber force generally was unable to continue sustaining such heavy losses. That being so, with the British aircraft industry now the primary focus of daylight attacks, future raids, it was decided, would be made by Ju 88s of up to *gruppe* strength, heavily escorted by fighters. This was, therefore, a significant day in the Battle of Britain timeline.

Throughout October 1940, 11 Group's fighter squadrons remained mainly troubled by the high-flying fighter sweeps, never knowing whether fighter-bombers were included in enemy formations. Flight Lieutenant Thomas's log book continues to reflect high activity, with numerous 'Squadron standing patrols' over 30,000ft. On 9 October 1940, the Germans, assisted by squally weather which hampered interceptions, concentrated their fighter-bomber attacks on 11 Group's airfields, causing widespread damage. 222 Squadron's first scramble that day was at 1125 hrs, but a patrol over Maidstone at 30,000ft failed to locate the enemy. Then, at 1450 hrs, twelve 222 Squadron Spitfires took-off from Hornchurch with others of

41 Squadron, gaining height over base before once more heading to the Maidstone line. Flight Lieutenant Thomas:

> I was leading the squadron on patrol at 30,000ft, roughly over Chatham. I followed 41 Squadron down to 28,000ft and then saw about five Me 109s directly above at about 29,000ft. I climbed up into them and they made for a layer of cirrus, through which I followed them. I increased revs to 3,000 and gradually outclimbed them and gave a four second burst into the belly of one enemy aircraft. Glycol streamed out of port radiator and he went down in a shallow dive. I followed him down and gave a series of one second bursts at 100 yards, down to 3,000ft. During these attacks glycol came out of the starboard radiator and black smoke from the engine. The enemy aircraft landed with undercarriage up about four miles north of Hawkinge. I circled round, waggling my wings to attract attention. I saw the pilot get out and set fire to his aircraft, which burnt very slowly, a small amount of blue smoke coming out of the cockpit. Civilians then arrived and I saw them approaching the pilot who was standing about thirty yards from his aircraft, holding a white handkerchief and with his arms raised in surrender. The enemy aircraft had a completely yellow nose and rudder.

The enemy pilot was *Feldwebel* F. Schweser of 7/JG 54, who forced-landed and was captured, according to the victor's log book, '4 miles north of Hawkinge' at 1600 hrs. While certain of Flight Lieutenant Thomas's previous combats had concluded inconclusively, there was absolutely no mistaking the outcome this time: one Me 109 destroyed. After this action the days continued much the same, with high-flying patrols either vectored to intercept or in anticipation of German fighters. Flight Lieutenant Thomas would find himself in action again on 25 October 1940, a day of considerable enemy air activity.

The first attack that day was made by three waves of German fighters and fighter-bombers at 0845 hrs, seventy of which reached London, with bombs falling in East Ham, Poplar, and various locations around South London, in addition to Kent and Surrey. At 0930 hrs, 222 was scrambled from Hornchurch to join 92 Squadron patrolling Biggin Hill, Folkestone and Deal, but this sortie passed without event. A second raid of 100 enemy aircraft came in over Dover at 1154 hrs, scattering all over the south-east, bombs exploding in both Kent and Sussex. At 1300 hrs, with yet another threat incoming, 222 Squadron was scrambled and ordered to join Squadron Leader 'Sailor' Malan's 74 'Tiger' Squadron at 10,000ft, but as the 'Tiger'

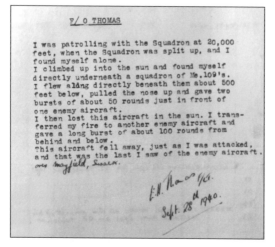

Above left: Flying Officer Thomas's combat report for 28 September 1940, preserved in his log book (author).

Above right: Flight Lieutenant Thomas pictured whilst commanding 'A' Flight of 222 Squadron during the Battle of Britain (author).

sighted enemy aircraft in the meantime, 222 were instructed to climb to 30,000ft, in 74 Squadron's direction. Flight Lieutenant Thomas:

> I was leading the squadron and had gained height to 29,000ft and saw about twelve aircraft in a defensive circle below. I identified these aircraft as friendly and then saw a lot of single-engine aircraft below. I ordered the squadron into line astern and went down onto these aircraft. I got on the tail of a Me 109 and opened fire at 200 yards, closing to about seventy-five yards, when the E/A completed about three downward flick rolls and pulled straight up. I followed and put in another burst and glycol streamed from both radiators. Pilot Officer Edridge also fired at the E/A after this. I got on his tail again and he went straight down. At about 20,000ft the pilot jumped out and I narrowly missed colliding with him. I followed the E/A down and it disappeared in the clouds, vertically. I came below the cloud and recognised West Malling airfield.

Again, there was no mistaking the outcome of this combat: one Me 109 destroyed. The vanquished German pilot was *Feldwebel* J. Gärtner of 8/ JG 26, who was captured, his aircraft crashing at Congelow Farm, Yalding.

260

More skirmishing followed over the next few days, Flight Lieutenant Thomas in action again on 29 October 1940, in a running battle fought between 1330–1345 hrs, over South London and to the coast at Folkestone:

> I was leading the squadron on patrol at 30,000ft and had investigated several formations which turned out to be friendly. I was vectored to roughly the centre of London and then saw a large formation below me flying on a course of 150°. I put the squadron into line astern and dived down and attacked from the rear. While coming into the attack I found about eight Spitfires already engaging from astern. I closed with the enemy, who were flying in a great mass of wide line abreast, stepped up. I manoeuvred so I was 500ft vertically underneath one Me 109, and pulled up and gave a 1½ ring deflection in front. He flew straight through my tracer and then emitted black smoke. I held my fire for three seconds. I then noticed five Me 109s above me so I climbed into the sun and then came into attack again on the right-hand E/A of a small group of five. I closed to dead astern at 250 yards and gave a 3–4 second burst. Streams of glycol came from the radiators and the E/A sheered off to the right. I could not follow him down as I was right underneath about ten E/A which would probably have followed me. Pilot Officer Stuart followed one of the above-mentioned E/A down, and saw it still diving vertically at 200ft.

The 109 attacked by Flight Lieutenant Thomas was seen trailing white vapour by Sergeant John Burgess, who attacked the crippled German fighter after his leader had broken away, firing a seven-second burst while closing to just fifty yards. As Burgess himself broke away, the Spitfire pilot saw the 109's canopy jettisoned and the pilot bale out. Pilot Officer Stuart witnessed the aircraft crash 'ten miles from Dungeness'. The aircraft concerned was a fighter-bomber belonging to the precision-bombing unit 3/ *Erprobungsgruppe* 210, and flown by the *Staffelkapitän, Oberleutnant* Otto Hinze, who baled out and was captured, wounded. Again, there had been no mistake, and the destruction of this Me 109 was shared equally with Sergeant Burgess.

On 31 October 1940, the Battle of Britain is officially considered to have ended, although it is doubtful that 11 Group's fighter pilots noticed much difference until the weather properly closed in and brought things to a natural conclusion in February 1941. Until that time, while the German bombers raided by nights, the fighter and fighter-bomber sweeps actually continued unabated, there being no distinct end to the fighting as, say, the 1969 film *Battle of Britain* portrayed. For 222 Squadron, the patrols and skirmishes continued until 11 November 1940, when the unit was withdrawn to Coltishall in 12 Group. There, in addition to receiving and training replacement pilots, 222 Squadron provided protection to shipping off the east coast, although there was still action to be had with the odd German raider targeting convoys. Indeed, on 28 November 1940, 12 Group HQ signalled 222 Squadron:

> Following received from Flag Officer Yarmouth…. Thanks to your patrol the mine-sweeping and the patrolling trawlers and drifters have not been bombed since it was instituted on 22 November. We are most grateful to you for this protection and hope it will be possible for this to be continued.

Needless to say, Flight Lieutenant Thomas had flown on numerous of these monotonous but essential patrols over the cold North Sea. These maritime protection patrols and training flights became 222 Squadron's norm for the harsh winter of 1940/41, the only excitement for Flight Lieutenant Thomas occurring on 6 March 1941, when a Do 17 was sighted over Southwold but which rapidly disappeared into cloud. There was greater success, however, at 1645 hrs on 4 April 1941, the combat occurring at 5,000ft, fifteen miles north-east of Cromer; Flight Lieutenant Thomas:

> I was leading Red Section on a 'Kipper' patrol, with Pilot Officer Ramsay as Red 2. At about 1630 hrs I was ordered to northern end of patrol line at 6,000ft. I arrived there and was vectored 360° for two minutes, then on 110°. At about 1640 hrs Red 2 called up and reported aircraft at 3 o'clock. I could not see it and so I told Red 2 to lead. This he did and I immediately saw it ahead. I flew up on the port side and Red 2 went in astern. I identified it as a Ju 88. I then went into astern and gave a one second burst from 350 yards. I didn't think he saw us before this, for as soon as I fired he jinked a bit. I closed to 200 yards and opened fire again as the rear gunner started firing at me with red tracer. I kept the button pressed and closed to about seventy yards until I had expended all my ammunition and all rear gunfire stopped. Clouds of black smoke came from both engines and bits of cowling came off the port engine. I found tracer very difficult to see. After I had expended my

ammunition, Pilot Officer Ramsay came into attack and also fired all his rounds from astern, during which attack more bits fell off and Pilot Officer Ramsay's aircraft was covered in oil from the E/A. As Pilot Officer Ramsay finished his attack the E/A managed to stagger into 10/10ths cloud at 7,000ft. I saw most of my rounds enter the E/A's fuselage and port motor.

The E/A was flying at about 230 mph on a course of 090°. It was camouflaged black on top with sky blue underneath and black crosses. I did not notice any black cross on fuselage. Enemy return fire came from lower cupola, machine-gun, red tracer, and very accurate. I sustained two hits in my port mainplane leading edge, one of which went through the main-spar, both boxes of ammo, and finished up in the landing light. E/A climbed steadily for cloud 2,000ft above on being attacked.

The Ju 88 was shared as a 'probable' with Pilot Officer Ramsay.

As explained in previous chapters, the spring of 1941 saw Fighter Command's new chiefs adopt an offensive policy while reorganising the Command around wings of three squadrons, based at each sector station. So it was that on 27 April 1941, 222 Squadron flew from Coltishall to operate

'A' Flight of 222 Squadron, Coltishall, April 1941; from left: Sergeants Ramsay, Marland and Wilson, Flight Lieutenant Thomas, Sergeants Riches and Chipping, Flying Officer Davies, Pilot Officer Logan, Sergeants Scott, Christie and Lewis.

from Duxford, as part of 12 Group's 'Duty Wing', later sweeping locally with the Hurricanes of 310 (Czech) Squadron at 18,000ft. By that time, Flight Lieutenant Thomas had accumulated 1096.45 flying hours, many of them on Spitfires, and recorded in his log book 'Results of engagements to date': three Me 109s destroyed and a shared Do 17, a shared Ju 88 'probable' and a damaged Me 109. Improved weather would soon see that score increase, although Eric had a lucky escape on the night of 11 May 1941, when 'Stick of HE bombs and incendiaries dropped on flare path while taxiing out.' Then, on the first of three patrols on 14 May 1941, a He 111 was sighted over Sheringham, but this too made off into cloud before the Spitfires of Red Section could engage. The third patrol, however, at 1900 hrs off Yarmouth, was more successful, as Flight Lieutenant Thomas reported:

> I was detailed to fly Red 1 with Pilot Officer Laurie as Red 2, to patrol Yarmouth below cloud. On reaching Yarmouth we were immediately vectored 140° and we flew the vector for ten miles. I noticed two trawlers ahead going north and an E/A bombing from low altitude, from astern. Two bombs burst between the trawlers and E/A pulled up, climbing. We went into attack and I delivered a full quarter attack on the

Above left: Eric Thomas's 611 Squadron badge, a unit he commanded in 1941 (author).

Above right: Squadron Leader Eric Thomas whilst attending his DFC investiture with his wife, Eirene (left), and mother, Maude.

port side, opening fire at 300 yards and closing until I passed immediately behind the E/A, which I identified as a He 111. I pulled round and did a series of quarter attacks from each side of about two seconds duration. On my second attack, I saw a full line of my tracer enter E/A at the nose and pass right down to the tail, amid a series of small flashes, and the port engine emitted blue smoke. E/A then jettisoned two large bombs. The E/A then made cloud cover at 18,000ft. I followed into cloud astern and saw the E/A circling to starboard very slowly, blue smoke coming out. I closed to about 200 yards and put in the rest of my rounds from dead astern. Red 2 during this time had been delivering climbing attacks from astern.

The return fire was considerable, tracer, machine-gun, at first from top position. Not very accurate. This ceased completely during the combat, and later when I had exhausted my ammunition and tried to draw his fire there was no reply.

The E/A was camouflaged black with usual white crosses.

Evasive action consisted solely of climbing for cloud cover.

I fired all my rounds with exception of No 2 starboard-gun, which had a stoppage after 100 rounds.

This He 111 was shared as 'damaged'.

At 1615 hrs on 18 May 1941, Flight Lieutenant Thomas received a personal signal at Coltishall:

> Deeply regret to inform you that your brother, Flying Officer Bruce Kentish Thomas, is reported to have lost his life as a result of air operations on 18 May 1941. The Air Council express their deepest sympathy. His mother has been informed.

Bruce Kentish Thomas was Eric's younger brother, born on 27 November 1920, who had also taken a SSC, on 6 March 1939. After elementary flying training at the Civil Flying School, Reading, and advanced service flying training, Pilot Officer Thomas completed an army cooperation course at the School of Army Cooperation, Old Sarum. On 29 January 1940, Bruce reported to 2 Squadron, an army cooperation unit equipped with the Westland Lysander communications aircraft, and based at Abbeville, Drucat, and other airfields in France, supporting the BEF. When the German invasion came on 10 May 1940, 'Shiny Two' was heavily bombed at dawn, thereafter flying tactical reconnaissance and photographic sorties and beginning a somewhat nomadic existence, given the fluid front and speed of the enemy's advance. Nine days later, the squadron was withdrawn to Lympne, on the Kentish coast, from where it continued to fly sorties over the Continent until the Dunkirk evacuation's conclusion. Flying Officer Bruce Thomas remained with 2 Squadron thereafter, until completing a flying instructor's course at the Central Flying School in January 1941, and being posted as an instructor to 12 SFTS on 24 March 1941. Less than two months later, Flying Officer Thomas was up from Grantham on a night-flying exercise with a pupil, LAC C.D. Kenwrick-Cox, in Fairey Battle R7363, when intercepted and shot down by a German Ju 88C night intruder flown by *Oberleutnant* Paul Semrau of 3/NJG 2, based at Glize-Rijen airfield in the Netherlands. The Battle crashed at Little Ponton, two miles south of Grantham; 20-year-old Flying Officer Thomas was killed while his passenger, although injured, survived. Sadly, it would not be the only such tragedy to befall the Thomas family during the Second World War.

For Eric Thomas, operational life after Bruce's death continued much the same, flying from Coltishall and the satellite airfield at Matlask. On 19 June 1941, however, Flight Lieutenant Thomas left 222 Squadron, after nearly a year, and reported for duty with 91 'Nigeria' Squadron, a Spitfire-equipped reconnaissance unit at Hawkinge. In September 1940, 421 Flight had been formed at Hawkinge, the Spitfires of which flew high-altitude reconnaissance flights over the Channel, supplementing the early warning provided by radar. In January 1941, 421 Flight was redesignated 91 Squadron, continuing to fly weather sorties and air sea rescue sweeps. When Eric arrived, the unit was equipped with the new Spitfire Mk VB, and he lost no time in flying one of these improved Spitfires on 20 June 1941 (DL-K), undertaking a local familiarisation flight. Then, it was a matter of daily flights escorting air sea rescue Lysanders over the Channel, dawn patrols and 'Jim Crow' coastal reconnaissance sorties. This was another brief stay, however, as on 27 June 1941, Eric was promoted to acting Squadron Leader and posted to command 611 Squadron at Hornchurch – by which time he was a most experienced fighter pilot and leader.

On the same day that Squadron Leader Thomas left Hawkinge for Hornchurch, 27 June 1941, one of the greatest RAF aces of the early war period, Flight Lieutenant Eric 'Sawn Off' Lock DSO DFC, also arrived at Hornchurch, from 41 Squadron, to command 611's 'A' Flight. 'Tommy' arrived the following day to take command of the squadron, and on the same day Hornchurch received a new Wing Leader, namely Wing Commander F.S. Stapleton, who had previously commanded 611 Squadron. A day later, Fighter Command's new chief, Air Marshal Sholto Douglas, lunched at Hornchurch, after which 611 Squadron's new CO and his flight commanders were presented to him. This was, of course, at the real beginning of Fighter

Command's 1941 offensive, with the improved weather significantly increasing the tempo and frequency of bomber escorts and fighter sweeps over north-west France – and it would certainly be a busy time ahead. Typically losing no time, Squadron Leader Thomas led his new command over enemy occupied France on 30 June 1941, recording the following in his log book:

> Hornchurch Wing providing medium cover, crossed French coast at Gravelines, 16,000ft. Heavy flak to port. 603 Squadron, behind us, engaged by Me 109s. Lost one. Destroyed one. Flew inland 60 miles to Lens via Hazebrouck, Lille, 'Beehive' scored direct hits on power station, returned on reciprocal. Very accurate flak at Hazebrouck. Returned at 10,000ft. Heavy and accurate flak at coast near Gravelines. Saw in all about sixteen Me 109s but could not engage. Result of operation: target successfully bombed. Six Me 109s destroyed. We lost one aircraft.

And so it went on, daily, relentlessly, as these further, selected, log book entries succinctly describe:

3 July 1941:

> Crossed French coast at Gravelines and split into loose fours. Arrived at Hazebrouck with the bombers. Plenty of Me 109s about. Bombers absolutely plastered Hazebrouck. The dust and debris from the attack almost obliterated the town. Saw a Me 109 shot down in flames and break up in the air over the target. Re-crossed coast at Gravelines, 13,000ft. Landfall at Ramsgate. Result of complete operation: target bombed, six Me 109s destroyed, we lost three (red marker flak accurate at Gravelines, heavy flak at St Omer).

9 July 1941:

> Squadron in company with 54 and 603 Squadrons crossed coast at Calais, 24,000ft. Arrived over target at 21,000ft via St Omer. Attacked by Me 109s. Pilot Officer Johnston missing after this attack. Formation split up and came back with bombers via Montreuil, 16,000ft. Crossed French coast between Boulogne and Le Touquet. Saw an aircraft dive into the sea five miles off French coast. Sergeant Townsend, hit by flak and Me 109s, crashed on the front at St Margaret's Bay,

Squadron Leader Eric Thomas DFC, seated, centre, with pilots of his 133 'Eagle' Squadron (author).

uninjured. Result of operation: target bombed from 13,000ft. Thirteen Me 109s destroyed. We lost eight fighters.

14 July 1941:

Squadron in company with 54 and 603 Squadrons crossed coast five miles east of Gravelines at 20,000ft. Bombers bombed target and recrossed French coast five miles north of Hardelot. Crossed English coast at Dungeness, 17,000ft. Flying Officer Dexter DFC collided with another Spitfire over France and baled out? Flight Lieutenant Lock DSO DFC destroyed one Me 109. All bombers home safe.

Sadly, the South African Dexter, another of the Few, had actually been killed, and now lies buried at Samer.

17 July 1941:

Squadron in company with 603 Squadron rendezvoused with torpedo bombers at Beachy Head, 500ft. Crossed Channel, close cover at 100ft. Located ship and torpedoes dropped. All three missed. Accurate and intense flak from ship. Gave the ship a two second burst with cannon and machine-guns from long range at about 800 yards, aiming high. Came home at 50ft behind Beauforts. Saw four Me 109s 4,000ft above – did not attack us.

19 July 1941:

> Rendezvoused with 242 Squadron's Hurricanes, 500ft,
> Manston. Flew with bombers at 0ft to Ostend where bombed
> ship with no result. Ground batteries opened up with a barrage.
> Returned at 300ft and landed at Manston as weather no good
> at Hornchurch. All got back OK. No E/A seen. Good party at
> 'Dog and Duck' in the evening.

24 July 1941:

> Crossed French coast east of Dunkirk, 29,000ft. Smoke
> trails forming. With 603 Squadron. Proceeded to target area
> and rendezvoused with bombers. Escorted bombers back.
> Crossed French coast at Mardyck, 20,000ft. Dived on about
> ten Me 109s but was unable to engage as they were split up
> by 603 Squadron before we got there. Pilot Officer Smith one
> damaged, Wing Commander Stapleton one destroyed.

At the end of the month, Squadron Leader Thomas summarised the
squadron's results: 'During July, the squadron destroyed fourteen Me 109s,
seven probable Me 109s, five damaged Me 109s. Our losses: nine pilots.'

It is now known that throughout the air fighting 'season' of 1941,
Fighter Command's combat claims were enormously exaggerated, not
through any dishonesty by the pilots concerned but owing to the confused
nature of combats over enemy territory, involving hundreds of aircraft.
Indeed, on many occasions Fighter Command's claims bore no semblance
to reality when compared with actual German losses. Since 22 June 1941,
though, the whole 'Non-Stop Offensive', although dubbed the 'Non-sense
Offensive' by the Germans, had
become political following Hitler's
invasion of Russia. The Soviet
leader Stalin was crying out for
Western support, and being in no
position to open the second front as
yet, the air war was the only means
of alleviating pressure on the Soviet

Eric Thomas's 'Eagle' Squadron shoulder
patch (author).

269

Union. As explained elsewhere in this book, the RAF strategy was to tie down *Luftwaffe* units in the west, thus preventing their transfer east, and hopefully see formations from the east sent to reinforce those in north-west France. The strategy was a failure, however, because throughout the war, the Belgian and French coastlines were defended by just two fighter groups, JG 2 and 26, which required no reinforcement. Worse, having started the war on the back foot, lacking combat experience, during the 'season' of 1941, Fighter Command lost many pilots who had become combat veterans during the desperate battles of 1940 – something 611 Squadron was about to experience first-hand.

3 August 1941:

> Flight Lieutenant Eric Lock DSO DFC missing from 'Rhubarb' near Boulogne.

As previously explained, the 'Rhubarb' was a low-level penetration over France, usually by a pair or section of Spitfires, attacking targets of opportunity. During these sorties the RAF fighters were vulnerable to ground fire, and many pilots were lost on these dangerous sorties of questionable value. Indeed, Lock was last seen strafing German troops near Calais, but failed to return to Hornchurch, the assumption being that he was hit by machine-gun fire and crashed in the Channel. Whatever happened, this ace with twenty-six enemy aircraft destroyed and six probables to his name was a pilot Fighter Command could ill-afford to lose. Indeed, as the 611 Squadron ORB recorded, it was 'a ruddy awful waste'.

9 August 1941:

> Led Squadron in company with 403 and 603 Squadrons. Crossed French coast at Dunkirk and proceeded above increasing cloud to Bethune, via St Omer. Jumped by Me 109Fs near St Omer. No result. Came out same way, tailed by Me 109s up-sun, which did not attack. Crossed out at Gravelines, 15,000ft.

That was, in fact, 'Circus 108', during which the Tangmere Wing's leader, Wing Commander Douglas Bader, was brought down in the chaotic fight over St Omer with JG 26's Me 109s – yet another highly motivated and experienced pilot Fighter Command could ill-afford to lose (see Chapter One).

12 August 1941:

> Led Wing. Crossed French coast Le Touquet, 25,000ft. Me 109s above, leaving vapour trails but did not attack us. Went into the sun turned the wing to meet them and came out in a series of full turns via St Inglevert. Squadron attacked here and Pilot Officer Van de Honert attacked by four Me 109Es, sustaining four cannon hits and being slightly wounded in the left arm. Pilot Officer Campbell fired at these and they became frightened and went down into France.

16 August 1941:

> Led Squadron in company with 403 and 603 Squadrons, and North Weald Wing. Crossed French coast east of Dunkirk, 25,000ft. Swept round to St Omer and out at Gravelines. Slight flak at Gravelines. Me 109s followed us out above and up-sun, and made a few dummy attacks. Pilot Officer Lamb lagged behind over Channel and was shot down by Me 109 about ten miles off Gravelines. He went in vertically and did not bale out. Bad show.

24 August 1941:

> By the end of August 1941, Squadron Leader Thomas had led the wing on a number of occasions, and noted in his log book a total of twenty-five bomber escort sorties to 'inland targets', five bomber escorts to 'Shipping Rodeos', and fourteen fighter sweeps over enemy territory – a grand total of 284 hours of operational flying. 611 Squadron's score for month was also recorded: two Me 109s claimed destroyed, along with a probable, offset against four pilots lost.

2 September 1941:

> Led Squadron in company with 54 and two North Weald squadrons. Crossed French coast at Mardyck. No cloud, visibility excellent. Could see all the Dutch islands and whole French coast down to Le Havre at 27,000ft. Swept down to St Omer and out at Hardelot, feeling very fit, did a slow roll over France. No flak and not a single enemy fighter seen or reported.

4 September 1941:

> Led Squadron in company with 54 and 603 Squadrons. Crossed
> French coast 27,500ft at Mardyck. Heavy, accurate, flak at 54.
> 25,000ft, about three miles north of St Omer, sighted eight Me
> 109Es attacking four Spitfires 3,000ft below with ten above
> at our height, attacking head-on. Dived down on the eight Me
> 109s below and they stopped attacking the Spitfires and dived
> down towards St Omer. I followed and fired at two of them with
> cannon and machine-guns. 47 rounds per cannon, 80 rounds per
> machine-gun. Saw a large explosion in one of the 109s, just aft
> of the cockpit, in the fuselage. He fluttered violently but carried
> on down. This was now at 10,000ft, south of St Omer. Broke
> off engagement and came home by myself via Poperinge and
> east of Dunkirk at 5,000ft. Nearly everyone in the squadron
> had a shot. Sergeant Ormiston destroyed one Me 109, Sergeant
> Leigh another, and a few damaged. All pilots back safe, though
> two got shot-up a bit. Result of Wing operation: target bombed,
> eleven E/A shot down, we lost seven Spitfires.

17 September 1941:

> Led Squadron in company with 54 and 603 Squadrons.
> Rendezvoused Dungeness 18,000ft. Crossed French coast four
> miles south of Hardelot and followed bombers to Samer. Heavy
> and accurate flak at bombers all the way in. Over Samer we
> had no other squadrons above us and were well and properly
> jumped by about eight Me 109s, Blue Section being worst off.
> I pulled round to help them but they had all dived away before
> I could get there. However, we all back safely. Sergeant Ingram
> collected a few holes in his tailplane. Squadron Leader Orton
> DFC and Bar, CO 54 Squadron, missing today. Bad show.

A 'bad show' it was indeed. Newell 'Fanny' Orton was among the RAF's
earliest fighter aces, with five confirmed aerial victories even before the
Blitzkrieg began in May 1940. By the time of his death, Orton had at least
seventeen 'kills' to his name, and was another experienced pilot lost to a
questionable offensive.

On 19 September 1941, Squadron Leader Thomas flew a 'Rhubarb' to
the Dutch coast with another Battle of Britain veteran, Flight Lieutenant
George Barclay DFC, now a flight commander on 611 Squadron:

We refuelled at Manston before leaving England, and set off across the North Sea at sea-level. We pulled up to cloud level off Dunkirk, 2,500ft, 10/10ths, and proceeded up the Belgian and Dutch coasts, about three miles offshore, via Nieuport, Ostend, Zeebrugge, Walcheran Island, Noord Beveland and Schouen. We crossed coast inland over Schouen and flew over Haamstede aerodrome where we saw a few Me 109s on the ground. The ground defences opened fire on us. Very inaccurate but we went out to sea again and came in up the estuary between Schouen and Nood Beveland. Flying about half a mile offshore at Colijsplaat was a German naval patrol vessel of about 200 tons. We each dived on this from inshore, opening fire at 800 yards and closing to about 150 yards, fairly raking the whole vessel, explosive bursts being observed in the attack. The vessel replied with green tracer. We then set course for home after a very interesting trip: one patrol vessel damaged.

On 1 October 1941, the Hornchurch and Biggin Hill Wings combined to sweep the French coast at 14,000ft, beneath a complete covering of cloud:

Led squadron of eight in company with 603 and 54 Squadrons and Biggin Hill Wing, all of eight aircraft each. Rendezvoused at Manston ... set course for Gravelines and swept around French coast at 14,000ft to Le Touquet via Cap Gris Nez, three miles off coast. Much flak, and red marker flak from Boulogne and Calais. Patrolled off coast for forty minutes and saw German radial engine single-seater fighter with square wing attacking a Spitfire. Half-rolled down on E/A and opened fire with cannon and machine-guns. Just then a lot of tracer went about three ft above my aircraft from astern. Pulled round to avoid it and lost sight of aircraft I attacked just off Gris Nez. Sergeant Stones, 603, reports seeing an aircraft go in at Gris Nez at this time. Came back via Dover 8,000ft. Very enjoyable party with mostly new pilots as most of experienced pilots in Wing on seven days leave.

611 Squadron ORB:

Beautiful, fine day was too much for the powers that be and a fighter sweep was put on at 1125 hrs. We were to go to

St Omer but at the last moment Bachelor changed his mind [unknown officer] and we just did two of three sweeps off the French coast and came home. The CO had a squirt at one of the new Hun fighters looking like a Curtiss Hawk and swears he would have got it if it hadn't been for another Spit squirting (presumably at it), unpleasantly close to him.

Had the enemy fighter engaged had a comparable performance to the obsolete American Curtiss Hawk, it would have been swiftly despatched by a Spitfire – but it was not. In August 1941, a new shape appeared in the sky, initially misidentified as a Hawk – but rapidly acknowledged as being significantly superior to the Spitfire Mk V. This was a game-changer: the radial-engine, snub-nosed, Focke-Wulf 190, which became known as the 'Butcher Bird' and, in due course, as numbers became available and as Air Vice-Marshal Johnnie Johnson recalled, 'drove us back to the French coast, severely limiting the depth of our penetrations'. Over the Channel on 1 October 1941, the Spitfires had encountered elements of JG 26, although no claims were made or casualties suffered by either side.

Taking advantage of squalls preventing operational flying, on 17 October 1941, Squadron Leader Thomas flew from Hornchurch to Staverton in Gloucestershire, thence to RAF Perdiswell, Worcester, 'to see C.G. Thomas'. This was Eric's elder brother, Cecil George Thomas, known to all as 'Bobbie', who had enlisted on 31 July 1941, volunteering for aircrew. Thereafter Bobbie was sent home to await mobilisation, which came on 23 August 1941 when ordered to report to 7 Initial Training Wing. Then, on 8 October 1941, he was posted to 50 Group Pool, the headquarters of which was at Hindlip Hall (now West Mercia Police HQ), Fernhill Heath, Worcester, just a short distance from Perdiswell, which was home to a Tiger Moth equipped elementary flying training school – where the combat-seasoned Spitfire squadron commander doubtless cut quite a dash. Bobbie was imminently to leave for pilot training overseas, and hence the brief visit, Eric returning to Staverton that afternoon, where he spent the night before flying back to Hornchurch – and the war.

21 October 1941, saw 611 Squadron fly two operational sorties, the first a fighter sweep, taking-off at 1100 hrs:

Led Squadron in company with 54 and 603 Squadrons. Crossed French coast at 21,000ft east of Dungeness where my new helmet gave R/T trouble, and I had to turn back with my No 2. The Wings went on and got jumped between St Omer and Hardelot and got split up. Sergeant McKelvie and Pilot Officer Fawkes collided over France. Sergeant McKelvie baled out and Pilot Officer Fawkes, both with 603 Squadron, flew back to Lympne with 1/3 of his wing snapped off. We lost Pilot Officer Roeper-Bosch, shot down ten miles east of Hardelot.

Sadly, although he called up to say that he was taking to his parachute, Sergeant W. McKelvie was killed and buried at Dunkirk; the Dutch Pilot Officer Johan Willem Yoshitaro Roeper-Bosch was also killed and buried at The Hague. That lunchtime, JG 26's *Kommodore*, *Oberstleutnant* Adolf Galland, claimed Spitfires destroyed west of Samer and west of Hardelot, the latter being his ninety-first victory and undoubtedly 611 Squadron's missing Dutch pilot. The day was not yet over for 611 Squadron, however, which escorted ASR launches off the French coast that afternoon:

> Led Squadron. Left English coast at Dungeness and found fairly thick haze up to 3,000ft in the Channel. Contacted rescue boats and escorted them to four – five miles off Le Touquet, and then four miles off Boulogne. We were in this area for an hour at 2,000–3,000ft, with shore guns firing at us occasionally. Eventually the inevitable happened and we were jumped by six Me 109s and a few FW190s. Charlie Section got it in the neck. Pilot Officer Smith got shot down by a Me 109E and went down streaming glycol and hit the sea vertically, with hell of a splash just behind the rescue launches. All they could find was two oxygen bottles [more likely compressed air, a pair of which cylinders the Spitfire carried, as opposed to a single oxygen bottle] on the surface. Pilot Officer 'Teddy' Reeves got hit and called up to say so and he has not returned to base. It was not being shot down, it was murder of two damn good officers. The squadron's worst day. Three pilots missing for no Huns.

No trace was ever found of either Pilot Officers Norman Jagoe Smith, 24, or John Frederick Reeves, 27, both of whom are commemorated on the Runnymede Memorial. That afternoon, 611 Squadron had been intercepted by JG 26's *Stabschwarm*, *Oberstleutnant* Galland claiming one of the Spitfires lost, while *Unteroffizier* Fast of 2/JG 26 claimed the other, which was his first victory. In total that day, Fighter Command lost twelve Spitfires, nine of which fell to the guns of JG 26, the so-called 'Abbeville Boys and St Omer Kids'.

Above and opposite: Pages from Squadron Leader Thomas's log book whilst commanding 133 Squadron (author).

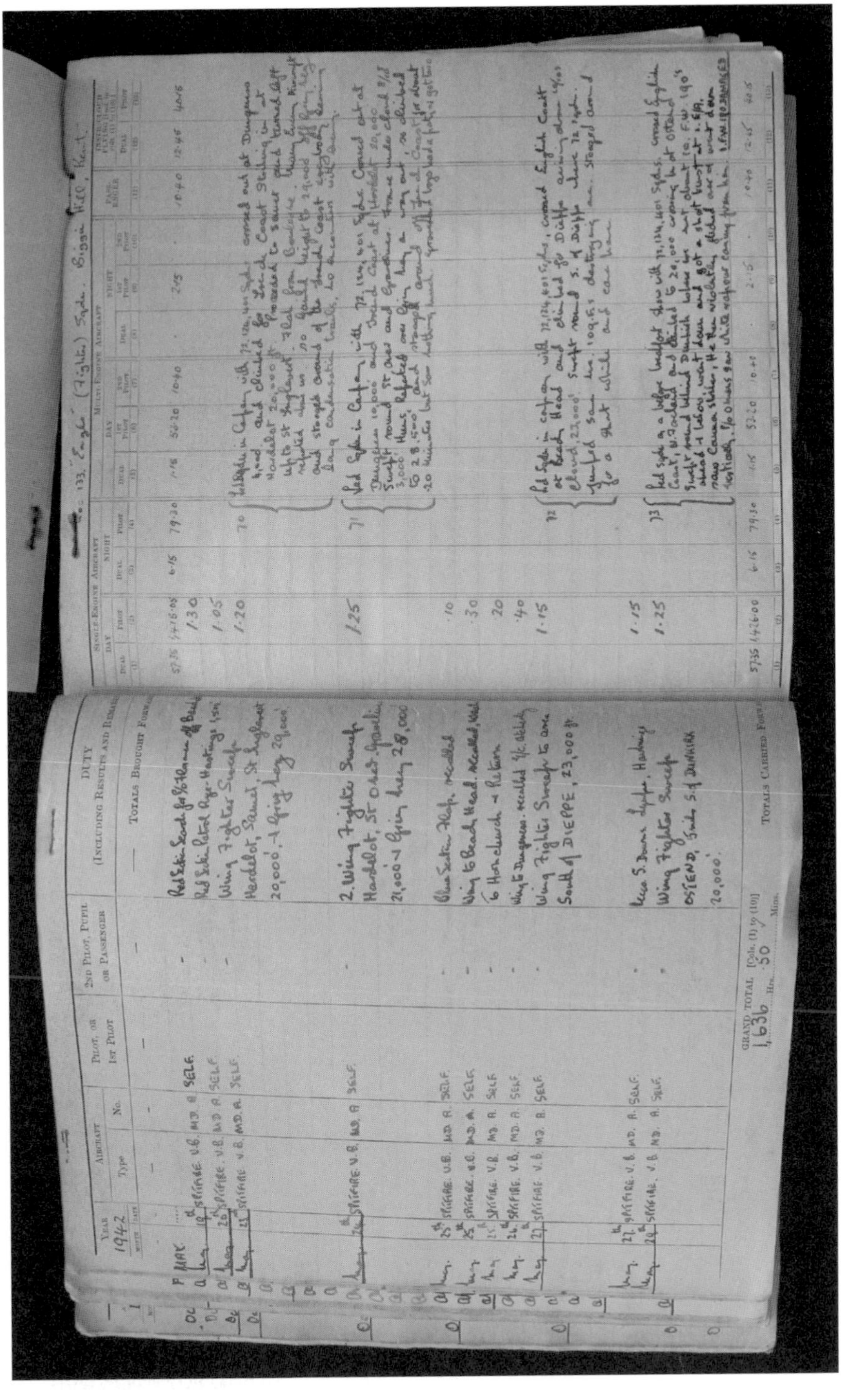

27 October 1941:

> Rendezvoused with Lysander near Hawkinge with four
> Spitfires of 91 Squadron as close escort. Proceeded mid-
> Channel between Calais and Dover, and searched for about
> thirty minutes. Three Me 109s then attacked from about
> 3,000ft above. A combat ensued which lasted about ten
> minutes. I got in a couple of squirts at long range but must
> have missed them. Sergeant Tuckington had a good squirt.
> 91 Squadron got one. We lost Pilot Officer Carey-Hill,
> missing believed killed.

According to the 611 Squadron ORB, regarding Pilot Officer Anthony
Carey-Hill, 'Nobody had seen him in trouble or heard him on the R/T but
we learned later that pilots of 91 Squadron saw a Spitfire dive straight in
at about that time and place and it seems certain that it could have been no
one else.' The 26-year-old, from Kenilworth, had been shot down into the
Channel by a pilot of JG 2, and was later buried at Boulogne.

At the end of October 1941, as the 'season' drew to a close, Squadron
Leader Thomas summarised his combat record: three Me 109s destroyed
and a Do 17 shared; a Ju 88 shared damaged; a Me 109 damaged and a
shared He 111 damaged, and a 'German patrol vessel'. By this time Eric
had flown thirty-one bomber escorts to 'inland targets', six 'Roadstead'
escorts to bombers attacking enemy shipping, and 'Rhubarbs', and
twenty-one fighter sweeps – a total of 320 operational hours and a total of
fifty-nine offensive sorties. His last such sortie with 611 Squadron was on
7 November 1941, an uneventful wing sweep over Boulogne at 20,000ft,
and on 12 November 1941, the squadron was pulled out of the frontline, to
rest and rebuild at Drem in Scotland. Squadron Leader Thomas, however,
would only remain north of the border until 21 November 1941, when
posted to command 133 'Eagle' Squadron, at Eglinton, in Northern Ireland.
It was the end of a relentless period of operational flying for the 24-year-old
Squadron Leader, which included both the Battle of Britain and entire
Non-Stop Offensive of 1941.

On 25 November 1941, a hard-earned and well-deserved DFC was
gazetted for Squadron Leader Eric Thomas:

> This officer has been actively engaged in operational flying
> since August 1940. He fought in the Battle of Britain and
> has participated in sixty sorties over enemy territory since
> the beginning of 1941. He has destroyed at least three enemy

Wing Commander Eric Hugh Thomas DFC* with his personal Spitfire Mk IX, 'EH-T', whilst commanding the Biggin Hill Wing in 1942.

aircraft and shared in the destruction of another; he has also damaged a patrol ship. Assuming command of the squadron (611) in June 1941, Squadron Leader Thomas has consistently displayed great skill and leadership and has contributed materially to its high morale.

133 Squadron could be in no doubt that their new CO was a skilled and highly experienced combat leader. And that was important – because this was the third so-called 'Eagle' squadron raised from American volunteers. This was, of course, just a few days before Japan's infamous attack on the American Pacific fleet at Pearl Harbor, bringing the US into the Second World War on the side of the Western Allies. Previously, America had steadfastly pursued a policy of isolationism from events in Europe, and restricted from providing overt assistance to belligerent nations due to the various Neutrality Acts, which not only extended to materiel but also manpower. Consequently, American flyers wishing to fight for Britain, had first to travel to Canada and clandestinely enlist in the RCAF, before travelling to England (all of which is explained in detail in this author's *Spitfire Down: RAF Fighter Pilots Who Failed to Return*). 133 Squadron

had been formed at Coltishall in August 1941, briefly operating Hurricanes before converting to Spitfires at Fowlmere, thence moving to Northern Ireland in October 1941.

Eglinton, in County Londonderry, was an important airfield on Northern Ireland's northern coast, being well-located for aircraft to patrol over convoys traversing the North Atlantic, and search for U-boats. It was mainly on training flights there that Squadron Leader Thomas was engaged – but on 30 November 1941 he found himself flying two sorties searching for Pilot Officer Roland 'Bud' Wolfe, who had disappeared while returning from a convoy patrol. Although the search for Wolfe and his Spitfire, P8074, *Garfield Weston I*, was fruitless, it later transpired that having suffered engine failure while returning to base, and with no chance of making it home across inhospitable mountain terrain, the American pilot safely baled out over County Donegal, in Eire. The problem was that Eire was neutral, and so Wolfe was interned, only managing to escape and return to England on his ninth escape attempt – by which time the United States had entered the war, enabling him to become a fighter pilot in his own country's air force. Eire's neutrality, however, was not something to trouble 133 Squadron for much longer, as on New Year's Eve 1941, the squadron was posted to Kirton-in-Lindsey in Lincolnshire.

At Kirton, little changed for Squadron Leader Thomas and 133 Squadron in terms of operational flying, the primary features of which remained training and convoy protection patrols. These flights were, however, vital to developing teamwork, which was the cornerstone of Eric Thomas's approach to air fighting and leadership, according to the 'Eagle Squadron' historian Vern Haugland: 'This meant constant practice, concentration on formation flying, rigid adherence to instructions – and more practice and more practice, day after day, usually in deplorably bad flying weather.' Keen for action, certain American pilots volunteered to serve overseas, not least in Malta where the siege was at its height – but Squadron Leader Thomas steadfastly refused all such transfer applications, determined to keep his best men and team together. Nonetheless, one former 'Eagle' recalled that his CO was 'a quiet, reserved, Englishman who through sheer quality of leadership was able to make a cohesive unit out of a bunch of individualistic Yanks'.

There was a personal happy development for Squadron Leader Eric Thomas on 31 January 1942, when the decorated fighter pilot married Kate Eirene Smith at the church of King Charles the Martyr, Tunbridge Wells, the couple having met while swimming at Pembury.

Wartime, however, denied the couple a conventional start to married life, and all too soon Eric was back in a Spitfire cockpit. On 14 April 1942, though, when, as recorded in his log book, Eric was 'Invested with DFC at Buckingham Palace by HM King George VI', his wife, Eirene, as the new Mrs Thomas was known, and mother, Maude, attended what was a proud moment for all.

At lunchtime two days later, after four months of comparatively routine flying, 133 Squadron flew its first offensive sortie over enemy territory. On that day, Squadron Leader Thomas led his Americans to West Malling, joining up with 412 (Canadian) Squadron as the 12 Group Wing, which was led by the ace Wing Commander Peter 'Johnnie' Walker DFC. According to Eric's log book, 'Crossed French coast at Gris Nez, 20,000ft, and went down off coast to Boulogne. A few vapour trails about 8,000ft above us but unidentified. A little flak from Boulogne, very uneventful.' Later that day, at 1750 hrs, 133 and 412 Squadrons were joined by 19 Squadron and again swept over Gravelines and Calais led by Wing Commander Walker, although apart from accurate red marker flak, this patrol was equally uneventful. It was, however, a start.

Although the main night Blitz on British cities had concluded in May 1941, devastating Bomber Command raids on the old German cities Lübeck and Rostock during March 1942 incensed Hitler, who in reprisal ordered 'terror attacks of a retaliatory nature against English cities', approving attacks 'where the greatest possible effect on the civilian population was to be expected'. On 23 April 1942, the first raid of this renewed offensive was mounted against Exeter, the following day a German propagandist, Gustav Braun von Stumm, commenting that 'every building in Britain marked with three stars in the *Baedeker Guide*' would be bombed, referring to the German tourist guidebooks of that name. Von Stumm's reference, however, embarrassed Hitler, keen to present these raids as retaliatory measures, because his comment confirmed that the '*Baedeker Blitz*' deliberately targeted locations of cultural and historic significance, as opposed to those connected with the British war effort. Nonetheless, the raids went ahead, and over the next few weeks Bath, Bristol, Canterbury, Norwich, and York also suffered. On the night of April 28/29 1942, Squadron Leader Thomas found himself an eyewitness to this violence , when he 'Patrolled York from 0245–0400 hrs. Saw many flares, incendiaries and bombs burst in the town, many fires started. Pilot Officer Doorly hit Do 217, and hit by rear gunner had to bale out OK. No 253 Squadron got three.' That night, the old city was badly damaged around its ancient Minster, and eighty-three civilians were killed.

Above left: How the *Evening Standard* reported Eric's appointment to the DSO and loss of his younger brother, Pilot Officer Bruce Thomas (author).

Above right: Squadron Leader Bernard Duperier, commanding 340 (Free French) Squadron in Wing Commander Eric Thomas's Biggin Hill Wing.

This mini-Blitz, however, petered out in August 1942, the fourteen main raids of which had cost the Germans forty more bombers. 133 Squadron, though, would play no further part in the nocturnal defence of 12 Group; on 3 May 1942, the squadron was posted to Biggin Hill.

Arriving at the famous fighter station, known affectionately as 'The Bump', 133 Squadron found the Biggin Hill Wing commanded by Wing Commander Jamie Rankin, who had initially succeeded the first Wing Leader there, namely the South African 'Sailor' Malan, in September 1941, and was recently returned for his second tour as the Station's 'Wing Commander (Flying)'. After local familiarisation flights on 4 May 1942, the following day Squadron Leader Thomas and 133 Squadron covered Bostons bombing Ostend:

> Squadron led by Wing Commander Rankin DSO DFC CdeG rendezvoused at 1,000ft over Clacton and set course for Ostend. After six minutes climbed until 20,000ft was reached

over Ostend. Accurate flak at bombers at 12,000ft, and a few bursts up around us. No enemy aircraft seen. Came back via Deal, quiet show.

It was similarly 'quiet' on 9 May 1942, during a wing sweep in company with 72, 124 and 401 Squadrons, leading Squadron Leader Thomas to conclude that it was 'Difficult to believe there's a war on.' This was not the case on the sweep taking place on 18 May 1942:

> Led Squadron in company with 72, 124, and 401 Squadrons. Flew at 0ft to Beachy Head and then climbed for French coast, passing through 10/10ths cloud over Channel at 16,000ft. No cloud over France. On reaching Dieppe sighted enemy aircraft ahead. 72 leading went for the first four at same level. We engaged two more following behind. I got a burst at 300 yards at two FW190s which turned over and dived vertically down. Pilot Officer Sperry also got a burst in. No claims. Many more enemy aircraft then jumped us and many more seen above them. Wing Commander Rankin then ordered all out and we dived for home. No losses.

Like 1941's offensive, the sweeps and escorts of 1942 continued relentlessly. On 29 May 1942, Squadron Leader Thomas reported that:

> I was leading 133 Squadron. Approximately five miles south of Dunkirk I sighted about ten FW190s flying East. I was at 20,000ft and they were about 1,000ft below me. The E/A passed underneath and turned to the right. I turned to port and dived down. I fired short bursts with cannon and machine-guns from about 300 yards, from the starboard quarter, at one of these aircraft. I saw strikes to the fuselage, and the E/A flicked over twice, violently. I last saw him going down vertically.

This FW190 was credited as damaged.

On the afternoon of 5 June 1942, the Biggin Hill Wing was one of three wings providing a diversionary sweep, during which Squadron Leader Thomas and 133 Squadron 'Jumped the Abbeville "types" over their aerodrome'; officially, Eric reported that:

> I was leading 133 Squadron at 15,000ft south of Abbeville, when I sighted some E/A below. We dived on these, but lost

them before we were able to engage them. I then sighted some more further down, and we went down again. I identified them as Me 109Fs and there were several combats going on in this area at 6,000ft. I got in behind an Me 109 and opened fire from the starboard quarter, from 250 yards, firing a good burst with cannon and machine-gun. The E/A then slumped forward and went down at an angle of 80°. This brought me into dead line astern and I gave the E/A two further bursts, following him down to 4,000ft. He took no evasive action but tended to pull away in the dive. I broke off firing at about 350 yards and last saw him diving vertically into the haze at 2,000ft, with glycol coming from his port radiator. Sergeant Eichar, my No 2, saw the combat and black smoke coming from this E/A. We were south of Abbeville and turned for home in line abreast and came back at 0ft.

I noticed the Me 109 had no yellow on it, but a general camouflage of olive green. I also noticed one squadron from another wing circling Pevensey, which was our rendezvous, at 1,500ft.

This Me 109F was claimed as a 'probable'. At the end of the month, Squadron Leader Thomas again summarised his combat record: three Me 109s destroyed and a Do 17 shared; one Me 109F, and a Ju 88 shared, probably destroyed; one Me 109 and an Fw 190 damaged, and a shared He 111, also damaged.

On the last day of June 1942, 133 Squadron, twenty Spitfires strong, moved from Biggin Hill Sector Station to operate from the coastal airfield at Lympne. From there, the operations continued much the same. On 26 July 1942, Squadron Leader Thomas led the Biggin Hill Wing on a sweep over Gravelines, St Omer and Inglevert, noting that 'Biggin Hill Sector gets three

Fw 190s today making a total of 900 aircraft destroyed since the war began.' On 31 July 1942, the Biggin Hill Wing closely escorted bombers attacking the infamous German aerodrome at Abbeville: 'Aerodrome well-bombed.

Unknown Polish pilots of 306 'City of Torun' Squadron, appearing in Eric's album.

Wing Commanders Eric Thomas (extreme left) and 'Johnnie' Walker with other officers after receiving the Croix de Guerre from General De Gaulle.

Flight Lieutenant King, Pilot Officer Harp and Flight Sergeant Eichar missing. Pilot Officer Barker one Fw 190 destroyed. Pilot Officer Taylor one Fw 190 destroyed, one damaged. Orbited "type" in dinghy until picked up by ASR launch.'

On 31 July 1942, Eric Thomas was promoted to Wing Commander, leaving 133 Squadron to command the Biggin Hill Wing. He had, according to Haugland, 'been an extremely popular leader of 133 Squadron. His pilots sang his praise as the architect of the squadron's rise to eminence in RAF performance categories. They cheered his advancement in early August to Wing Commander, even as they mourned his departure from 133.'

By the summer of 1942, the much-improved Spitfire Mk IX, with its two-stage supercharger and greater power and higher-altitude performance, was beginning to arrive, although the majority of Fighter Command's squadrons remained equipped with the inferior Mk V. On 6 August 1942, Wing Commander Thomas flew one of the new Spitfires (YO-X of 401 Squadron), which were superior to the troublesome Fw 190, for the first time, performing aerobatics at 25,000ft. After several more flights in Mk IXs borrowed from the Canadians, on 11 August 1942, the new Wing Leader flew for the first time an equally new Spitfire Mk IX, with his own initials painted on the fuselage, as was the privilege of Wing Leaders; Spitfire 'EH-T' thereafter becoming Wing Commander Thomas's regular mount. Two days later, he flew this Spitfire, practising 'Jettisoning long-range tanks over base.' The Spitfire, of course, had been designed as a short-range defensive interceptor – not as a long-range offensive fighter. Consequently the Spitfire lacked range for various tasks never envisaged by its designer but which it was now called upon to do. The use of auxiliary, jettisonable, fuel tanks was the only practical means of extending range – which was about to become of vital importance.

17 August 1942 was, as Squadron Leader Thomas recorded in his log book, a significant day: 'First Fortress raid on Europe in the war' – referring to the first strike on enemy occupied Europe by American B-17 bombers of 'The Mighty Eighth'…

On 20 June 1941, the United States Army Air Force (USAAF) was created to oversee and coordinate all US army aviation, with Major General H.H. 'Hap' Arnold in charge. The American air chiefs had, naturally, taken a great interest in the air war over north-west Europe, noting that both the RAF and *Luftwaffe* had failed with daylight bombing, owing to heavy losses, and had traded accuracy for the safety of bombing at night. Consequently, although bomber losses decreased, bombing was infinitely more indiscriminate, owing to the comparatively rudimentary aids available. Arnold, however, believed that daylight bombing was the way forward, and that precision could be achieved through technical advances, especially via the Norden bomb-sight, and the defensive firepower of mass-formations of four-engine bombers – the first of which was the Boeing B-17 'Flying Fortress'. After America entered the war in February 1942, following Pearl Harbor, a delegation of USAAF senior officers, led by Brigadier General Ira C. Eaker, arrived in Britain to prepare for the arrival of Eighth Army Air Force combat units. Like Arnold, Eaker firmly believed in high-altitude precision daylight bombing, and that accurate attacks on vital enemy targets could substantially weaken, or even destroy, Hitler's ability to wage war. Although sceptical, given their own experience of daylight bombing, the RAF gave every support.

The first American bomber units were based in Huntingdonshire, between London and The Wash, with the two squadrons of each bomber group sharing an airfield. The first heavy bombardment group was the 97th, the B-17s of which arrived at Polebrook, west of Peterborough, on 6 July 1942. The first combat sortie by an American crew however, was one embedded in an RAF Boston squadron, attacking the marshalling yards at Hazebrouck on 29 June 1942. On 4 July 1942 – Independence Day – six more American Boston crews joined 226 Squadron, bombing German airfields in the Low Countries. There were American fighter groups in England too, the 31st, having converted to Spitfires at Atcham, flying the first US fighter sweep over France, in company with the Biggin Hill Wing's 401 (Canadian) Squadron, on 26 July 1942. Following several cancellations owing to weather, the 97th Bomb Group was tasked with attacking the Rouen-Sotteville marshalling yards on 17 August 1942.

This, then, was the first raid on enemy occupied Europe by B-17s, Wing Commander Thomas's Biggin Hill Wing being the 'Rear Support Wing', helping protect the twelve Flying Fortresses involved in this historic mission. Colonel Frank Armstrong led the way in his B-17, named *Butcher Shop*, while General Eaker followed in *Yankee Doodle*. German defences were confused, the Abbeville controller misidentifying the 'heavies' as Lancasters, while the Fw 190 pilots of II/JG 26, which intercepted the Allied formation after the 'Castles in the Air' had successfully bombed their target, thought they were

Stirlings. The Spitfires of 401 and 402 Squadrons kept the 'bandits' away from the American bombers, but lost two Spitfires and pilots in the process, while Staff Sergeant Kent West, ball gunner on B-17 *Birmingham Blitzkrieg*, made history by shooting down the Fw 190 of JG 2's *Leutnant* Herbert Horn.

On that day, the Biggin Hill Wing's 133 Squadron had taken-off from Lympne at 1715 hrs, in company with the American Spitfire-equipped 307th Fighter Squadron, which was flying its first offensive operation, reaching Fecamp at 27,000ft. Turning north-east to St Valery, the Spitfires rendezvoused with the 'Forts' and brought them home safely. During II/ JG 26's interception, however, Wing Commander Thomas 'attacked a Fw 190 over Fecamp and got shot up myself. No claim.' Back at Polebrook without loss, the Americans were naturally elated, General Eaker receiving the following signal from Bomber Command's chief, Air Marshal Arthur 'Bomber' Harris: 'Yankee Doodle certainly went to town and can stick another well-deserved feather in his cap.' Going forward, American daylight

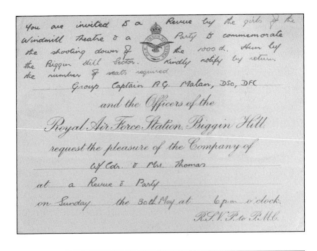

Group Captain Malan's invitation for Wing Commander Thomas to attend the unofficial bachelor party celebrating Biggin Hill's 1,000ᵗʰ aerial victory (author).

Group Captain Malan's official invitation for 'Wing Commander Thomas and Lady' to attend the more formal celebration (author).

losses would be heavy but General Spaatz, commanding the 'Mighty Eighth', stuck to the plan in spite of divided public opinion, and ultimately, after the arrival of purpose-built long-range American fighters, won the day. With the Americans bombing Germany by day, and the RAF by night, Hitler's ultimate fate was sealed on that day when 'Yankee Doodle' went to Rouen – and Wing Commander Thomas was an eye-witness to this historic and inspiring event.

The following day, the Biggin Hill Wing Leader flew to Eastchurch for a conference with Group Captain John Hallings-Pott, Biggin Hill's Station Commander (who had recently taken over from the popular Group Captain 'Dickie' Barwell, tragically shot down and killed in a 'friendly fire' incident on 1 July 1942, and whose death had unsettled the whole Station). Clearly, something else of import was afoot, and indeed it was: Operation JUBILEE.

By this time, the *Wehrmacht* was rolling ever onwards to the Russian Caucasus, having annihilated 300,000 Soviet troops at Kharkov and Kiev. The Japanese were over-running the Far East and even threatening to link up with advancing German forces in Russia. In North Africa, things were also going badly – the British Eighth Army was in headlong retreat. In spite of demands made by the Soviet Dictator Stalin for the Allies to invade France, such an enormous undertaking was still impossible at this time. Yielding to pressure from Stalin, and because ultimately the Allies intended to liberate enemy occupied Europe, it was agreed to probe the enemy's coastal defences on 19 August 1942. Operation JUBILEE, the proposed amphibious landing at Dieppe, represented the largest combined service operation of the war so far.

Dieppe, a thriving French coastal town, was protected by high cliffs, on which were situated heavy coastal batteries. Overlooking the town, it was necessary for commandos to destroy these guns prior to a seaborne assault by two brigades of the Canadian 2nd Army and a Canadian Tank Regiment. Of the 6,000 men involved, 5,000 were Canadian. The Operation's intention was to ascertain whether the harbour town could be seized and held for a day. While on French soil, Allied troops would also destroy installations and any naval vessels moored in the harbour.

Air Vice-Marshal Leigh-Mallory, AOC of 11 Group, which would bear the brunt of the Dieppe aerial fighting, saw JUBILEE as an opportunity to lure the *Luftwaffe* into action on a scale not seen since the Battle of Britain. The fighter force at his disposal comprised fifty-six squadrons, forty-eight of which were Spitfire-equipped – and a total of 750 aircraft. This force would be opposed by just 230 enemy fighters of JGs 2 and 26. Two squadrons of the Biggin Hill Wing, 133 and 401, flew down to operate from Lympne. The American Spitfires of the 'Magic 307' Fighter Squadron were also still there, and, originally omitted from the Battle Order, following protestations from the Americans, were included in the wing's plans. With so many aircraft detailed to participate in JUBILEE, to aid identification in the air, white stripes were painted on all the Spitfires' cowlings and tails, it becoming immediately obvious to all that a 'big show' was in the offing. Briefing by Group Captain Hallings-Pott and Flight Lieutenant 'Spy' de la Torre, Biggin Hill's Intelligence Officer, took place under tight security, and thus the scene was set for the events of 19 August 1942: 'Dieppe Day'.

The plan entailed a naval bombardment, supplemented by RAF fighter-bombers, that would first batter the German coastal defences. Then, RAF Bostons would lay down a smoke screen, under the cover of which the troops, supported by armour, would be landed. The role of the Biggin Hill Wing's squadrons, 133, 222, 401 and 602, in addition to the 307th Fighter Squadron, was to help maintain a protective screen of fighters over Dieppe – and on the big day, the pilots rose at 0300 hrs. At 0550 hrs, 602 took-off from Biggin Hill, followed by 222, then Wing Commander Thomas leading the 307th. The three squadrons flew south, rendezvousing with 133 and 401 Squadrons over Lympne, and swept across the Channel. With the first landing craft having headed for the Dieppe beaches at 0430 hrs, already other squadrons were returning home to refuel, and smoke hung heavily over Dieppe. The Germans were slow to react, but by 0643 hrs, battle had been joined when 5/ JG 26 engaged the Hornchurch Wing, and thereafter German fighters increasingly arrived on the scene, some of which fleetingly clashed with the Biggin Hill Wing's 602 Squadron, the CO of which, Squadron Leader Peter Brothers, and Sergeant Sampson, damaging a 190. The 307th also made its first kill of the war, destroying a 190 but lost Lieutenant Ed Tovrea, who was captured.

Having returned to base and refuelled, the Biggin Hill Wing was up again at 1015 hrs, finding a massive air battle in progress over Dieppe, while German bombers sneaked around the periphery, awaiting opportunities to attack shipping. Into this incredible, whirling, mass of aircraft, the wing sallied forth, all squadrons except 222 scoring heavily. There was less action on the wing's third patrol of the day, by which time the desperate battle on the ground was over, the survivors being withdrawn. On the day's final patrol, only one lone FW190 was encountered, which shot-up a Spitfire which crashed near Hawkinge.

Wing Commander Thomas's log book records the sorties he flew that fateful day, which, interestingly, was not in his personal Spitfire Mk IX but in a 92 Squadron Mk VB, 'QJ-J' – probably so as not to out-pace the remainder of the wing on this important operation:

1: 'Patrol with 307 USAAF Squadron. Dieppe, 3,000ft, after landing had taken place.'
2: 'Patrol with 307 USAAF Squadron. Dieppe, 12,000ft, to cover withdrawal of troops and ships.'
3: 'Patrol with 222 Squadron, 20 miles north of Dieppe, covering withdrawal of ships, 5,000ft.'

In summary:

> Squirt at Fw 190. No claim. Combined operation against Dieppe. Escort cover to Dieppe, over eight destroyers, masses of Assault Landing Craft, Motor Landing Craft, and Tank Landing Craft with sixty tanks. Bostons, Hurricanes, Mustangs, Commandos, 4,000 troops, mostly Canadians. Landing at dawn and withdrawing from 1400 hrs to Beachy Head. Biggin Hill Sector destroyed fifteen enemy aircraft, seven probables, twenty-nine damaged, for loss of six pilots. A most incredible party.

'A most incredible party' it may well have been, but JUBILEE had actually ended in disaster for the Allies. Some 1,096 Allied soldiers were killed, 1,943 captured, and 397 reported missing. None of the intended objectives were achieved. The cynical suggest that this was a deliberate failure intended to prove to Stalin that the Second Front was not an option at this time – if true, the point was made at a high cost of young lives. It is

interesting to note, however, that when the liberation of Europe was eventually mounted, no attempt was made to seize a French port. When the time came, so as to avoid another Dieppe, the Allies towed a prefabricated harbour – 'Mulberry' – in

Wing Commander Eric Thomas and his wife, Eirene, pictured post-war.

sections across the Channel. Disastrous though Operation JUBILEE had been, vital lessons had been learned – of what *not* to do.

From an aerial perspective, 11 Group believed that it had achieved considerable success. Nearly 100 enemy aircraft were claimed destroyed, and 170 probably destroyed or damaged, although actual German losses were forty-eight destroyed and twenty-four damaged. Unpalatable though the thought may be, RAF losses of ninety-seven aircraft to enemy action and three more to flying accidents, with sixty-six others damaged, made Dieppe a victory for the *Jagdfliegern* and German flak gunners. To further confirm the point, the RAF lost forty-seven fighter pilots, as opposed to the *Luftwaffe*'s thirteen. In total, the RAF had flown nearly 3,000 sorties, the enemy 945. The Operation in no way, therefore, provided the success that was intended. Air Vice-Marshal Johnnie Johnson was commanding 610 Squadron and among Fighter Command's most successful pilots that day, destroying a Me 109 and two Fw 190s, and later commented that Dieppe was:

> a bloody tragedy. The Canadians on the ground were slaughtered. Someone said afterwards that it was a seaborne 'Charge of the Light Brigade'. Even the German gunners felt sorry for the Allied soldiers as they pounded them to pieces. Did it achieve anything? As usual we had over-claimed, so although 'LM' hailed it as a great victory, the truth has since come out.

Suffice it to say that Operation JUBILEE was the last time air fighting on this scale would be seen on the Channel coast.

After Dieppe, the 307th was posted to Merston in the Tangmere Sector, while the Biggin Hill Wing continued the now usual round of fighter sweeps and escort sorties over north-west France and to the Dutch coast. On 31 August 1942, Wing Commander Thomas was awarded a Bar to his DFC (gazetted on 18 September 1942):

> Since being awarded the Distinguished Flying Cross, this officer has completed a large number of operational sorties. Throughout, his high qualities of leadership, combined with great courage and skill in the face of the enemy, have set a most inspiring example. He has destroyed at least four hostile aircraft.

By this time, Wing Commander Thomas had flown a total of 750.10 hrs on Spitfires by day, 427.45 of which were operational. A further 26.45 hrs had been flown by night, 16.55 of those being operational. In total, the successful completion of 368 operational sorties made Wing Commander Eric Hugh Thomas DFC and Bar a most experienced fighter pilot indeed.

On 8 October 1942, Wing Commander Thomas flew to Northolt for a conference held by Air Vice-Marshal Leigh-Mallory, and meanwhile Squadron Leader Johnnie Johnson DFC* led his 610 Squadron to Biggin Hill. Something big was in the air again, there being talk of another Dieppe raid, but fortunately this failed to materialise. Instead, the following day, Biggin Hill's Spitfires were to contribute towards escorting American bombers attacking the Lille steel works. On that day, the 92nd, 93rd, 97th and 306th Bomb Groups sent 108 B-17s and B-24 Liberators to Lille, in what was the biggest daylight Allied raid of the war to date. The bombers' depth of penetration, however, remained dictated by that of their escorting fighters, and on this occasion thirty-six squadrons of Spitfires and twin-tailed American P-38 Lightnings were employed as two target support and rear cover wings, in addition to diversionary operations.

Wing Commander Thomas reported that:

> I was leading the wing with 610 Squadron, as rear support for Fortresses bombing Lille. The Wing arrived over Gravelines on time at 25,000ft, just below a thin layer of cirrus. Five bombers came out and then I saw two aircraft coming north over Gravelines. I got in a full quarter attack on the leader, which turned out to be a FW190, and gave a second burst, full deflection, from 200 yards, and a quick squirt at the other FW190, which I am sure I missed. The first one went vertically down followed by his No 2 and I last saw him at about 15,000ft, still going vertically at a phenomenal speed. I had to pull up and around then, but I understand another member of the squadron saw him crash just off Gravelines, into the sea. We patrolled for another ten minutes, watching the bombers come out beneath us, and I saw, just west of Gravelines, four more FW190s in line-astern, flying in much the same formation as a section of Spitfires. I turned in and got on their tails, but they then saw me and put their noses down, and dived vertically away. I gave the No 3 a demoralising squirt from about 800 yards and was much surprised to see him immediately emit volumes of blue smoke from the engine. He continued on vertically down with a trail of blue smoke about 5,000ft long coming from him. Squadron Leader Johnson and my No 3 also witnessed this.

I claim one Fw 190 destroyed, one Fw 190 damaged, and four Fw 190s frightened.

In total, Fighter Command claimed five German fighters destroyed, one probable and three damaged. The American gunners claimed a staggering fifty-six of the enemy destroyed, although this was later reduced to twenty-one destroyed, twelve probables and fifteen damaged. In reality, the Germans only lost two fighters, one of which, probably a JG 2 machine, had to be the Fw 190 Wing Commander Thomas had shot down into the sea, which was seen to crash into the Channel. Four American bombers were destroyed and forty-six damaged – but the raid proved that escorted 'heavies' could reach targets deeper into France with moderate losses. So far as Americans were concerned, this raid represented the greatest effort of 1942, although this is not to say there were no further raids in the short-term, far from it. Soon after the Lille attack however, two bomb and four of five fighter groups were withdrawn to fight in North Africa. Thereafter, newly arrived bomber groups in England needed to be properly trained and increase their experience, and this took time. Nonetheless, the weather was beginning to close in at what was the conclusion of the 1942 'season', so there was little lost as a result of the next raid to match, and indeed exceed, that effort of 9 October 1942 having to wait until 17 April 1943.

Amid these intense operations, again Eric's brother provided a distraction, the fighter ace recording in his log book that on 14 October 1942, he flew 'EH-T' to Chipping Norton in Oxfordshire, 'To see Bob'. 'Bobbie' had been commissioned in August 1942, returning to England in September that year having successfully completed his initial pilot training in America. At the end of September 1942, Pilot Officer Thomas had reported to 6 (Pilot) Advanced Flying Unit at Little Rissington (which 6 SFTS became in April 1942, see Chapter Five), for training on twins. 'Chippy' was used as a satellite airfield for 6 (P) AFU, and there the brothers met before Wing Commander Thomas returned to Biggin Hill. His older brother still had a way to go before finding himself flying a bomber on operations, but would soon complete operational training on Wellingtons at Upper Heyford and convert to 'heavies' the following spring with 1660 Conversion Unit at Swinderby.

Back at Biggin Hill, the war went on. Although a few bombers short of the historic Lille effort, on 21 October 1942, Wing Commander Thomas led a 'Wing fighter sweep, Ile de Batz, Morlaix, Lannion, 16,000ft, while ninety Fortresses bombed Lorient.' This was a particularly important target. Situated on the south coast of Brittany, the port of Lorient became a crucial

What now remains… (author).

U-boat base, with access to the North Atlantic, where the Germans built gigantic concrete submarine pens – which became the focus of many an Allied bombing raid until 1944. On 8 November 1942, Wing Commander Thomas led the wing to closely escort 'thirty-six Fortresses bombing Lille, 26,000ft', noting that the 'wing engaged Fw 190s, damaging one without loss. Good bombing.' A fighter sweep over Hardelot the following day again saw action: 'Wing engaged FW190s, one destroyed and probable, one damaged. No losses.' On 4 December 1942, the wing swept over 'Le Touquet, Boulogne, Calais, 23,000ft', and 'Wing engaged Fw 190s, damaging one. Flight Lieutenant Vancl DFC' (a Czechoslovak pilot). And so it went on, dawn to dusk.

On 20 January 1943, Wing Commander Thomas was appointed to the Distinguished Service Order (gazetted 2 February 1943):

> Since being awarded a Bar to the Distinguished Flying Cross, this officer has led his wing on numerous sorties over enemy territory, in which thirteen enemy aircraft have been destroyed, one of them by Wing Commander Thomas. By his gallant leadership and unfailing devotion to duty, this officer has contributed materially to the success obtained.

'Numerous sorties' was right: 391, to be exact, an incredible record and achievement by any standards. Again, in his log book Eric recorded his combat claims: three Me 109s, one Fw 190 and a shared Do 17 destroyed; one Me 109F probable and a shared Ju 88; one Me 109E, two Fw 190s, and a shared He 111 all damaged, along with the German patrol vessel – the cumulative total exceeded the required five to make Wing Commander Eric Hugh Thomas DSO DFC* officially an 'ace'.

The game, however, was up. Having flown his last operational sortie, a two-wing fighter sweep over Le Touquet, on 29 December 1942, Wing Commander Thomas made his final flight as leader of the Biggin Hill Wing, a weather test in 'EH-T' on New Year's Eve. At the end of January

1943, after yet another long tour of operational flying, and command, Eric was rested and, on 1 February 1943, was sent to the RAF Staff College at Gerrards Cross, London, to attend No 8 War Course. His operational flying days were over, and he knew it, writing in his log book 'I've had it!' There was, however, an uplift on 15 March 1943, when Wing Commander Thomas joined other officers to receive the Croix de Guerre avec Palme from none other than General De Gaulle himself, leader of the Free French – another well-deserved award.

After his staff course, on 7 May 1943, Wing Commander Thomas was posted to 10 Group HQ at Colerne in Wiltshire. Three weeks later, however, Eric was back in a Spitfire, having somehow managed to get command of the Ibsley Wing, in Hampshire! There Eric found 129, 504 and 616 Squadrons, all, perhaps surprisingly at this time, still flying the Spitfire Mk V. Typically, the new 'Wingco' lost no time in getting airborne, in BM532, and on the morning of 29 May 1943, led the Ibsley Wing on 'Close escort to Whirlwind bombers – shipping strike Barfleur – Cherbourg', and that afternoon provided 'Close escort to about 160 Fortresses and Liberators bombing St Nazaire' – another U-Boat base. On 30 May 1943, Wing Commander Thomas was off to a party, however, to celebrate 'the shooting down of Biggin Hill's 1,000th Hun aircraft by Pilots of the Sector' at Biggin Hill, having been invited by the Station Commander, Group Captain A.G. 'Sailor' Malan – the 'thrash' featuring 'a revue by the girls of the Windmill Theatre' and was a male-only affair. Not so was the formal party thrown by Malan to celebrate the 1,000th victory at the Grosvenor Hotel in London's Park Lane on 9 June 1943, to which 'Wing Commander E.H. Thomas DSO DFC and Lady' were invited. Having flown to Biggin Hill for the occasion on 8 June, Eric returned to Ibsely three days later, and after practice wing flights was back in action on 13 June 1943:

> Wing escort to twelve Venturas, St Brusiac viaduct ...
> Engagement with four FW190s west of Guernsey at sea-level.
> One Ventura shot down in flames.

On 17 June 1943, Wing Commander Thomas flew his personal Spitfire Mk VC, another 'EHT', 'Practice bombing, four 11½lb. Chesil Bank'. As we have seen, the likes of Wing Commander 'Billy' Burton had worked hard to pioneer RAF close air support in the western desert, and which would soon come of age in Sicily and Italy – before becoming the devastating weapon it was in Normandy in 1944. That RAF fighter squadrons were looking to and training for the fighter-bomber role at this time, speaks volumes.

By this time, the American bomber offensive had similarly matured, as indicated by Wing Commander Thomas's log book entry of 22 June 1943: 'Wing escort to 240 Fortresses, Sliedrecht, Rotterdam, 16,000ft: raid on Huns' synthetic rubber factory. First American raid on the Ruhr.'

Attacks also remained ongoing against German airfields, such as on 24 June 1943: 'Wing close escort to twelve Mitchells, Maupertus aerodrome, 12,000ft: Excellent bombing of aerodrome and dispersals. One Mitchell exploded, direct hit by flak. Engagement with Fw 190s.'

On 29 June 1943, the Ibsley Wing provided 'Withdrawal support, eighty Fortresses, Argentan, Caen, Le Havre, 11,000ft: Fortresses met over Argentan and escorted to Beachy Head.'

13 July 1943: 'Escort Cover Wing to twelve Mitchells bombing Brest aerodrome 15,000ft. Diversion for 120 Lancasters bombing Turin: Bombs seen to burst near target. Heavy flak. About 20 Lancasters seen returning from Italy.'

Having provided 'close withdrawal support' to '240 Fortresses bombing Villacoublay and Le Bourges' on 14 July 1943, the 27th saw the Ibsley Wing escorting twelve Bostons attacking Schiphol aerodrome: 'Engagement with many Me 109s inside the Dutch coast.' The following day, a similar commitment saw the Fokker aircraft factory near Amsterdam attacked: 'Heavy accurate flak all the time over enemy territory. Good bombing.'

On the last day of July 1943, the Ibsley Wing escorted 'twenty-one Marauders bombing Merville aerodrome; in Hardelot, out Gravelines: Bombs seen to burst on aerodrome. Running engagement with Fw 190s and Me 109s from Merville to Gravelines. Accurate flak.' By that day, Wing Commander Thomas's operational sorties had increased to 412. 8 August 1943, however, would be his last operational flight, providing close support to 'Bostons bombing U-Boat stores, Rennes.' Two days later, it was all over again, and Eric was posted to command Fighter Command's School of Tactics at Charmy Down; considering his extensive and distinguished operational record, dating back to the RAF's first ever Spitfires back in 1938, it would be hard to imagine a more qualified officer. Upon leaving, 'Tommy' received a letter from Middle Wallop's Station Commander, Group Captain Stephen Hardy:

> I was very sorry your tour in this Sector was so quickly cut short. Under you, the wing fully maintained the excellent standard they had under Tom Morgan. Your leading was always admirable, and it was a great pleasure for me to feel that one with your great experience was looking after the flying operations.

> I hope that you will be happy in your new job and that we
> shall serve together at some later date.

The Fighter Command School of Tactics also used the airfield at Aston Down, near Stroud, home to a Spitfire operational training unit, and Wing Commander Thomas was soon using various Spitfire Mk IIs and Vs to get about. On 22 August 1943, a somewhat unusual type for a fighter pilot features in his log book: an Avro Lancaster II, the '1st Pilot' of which was 'Flying Officer Thomas', the '2nd Pilot, Pupil or Passenger' being 'Self and crew'. The sortie was a night-flying test, the pilot, of course, being Eric's brother, 'Bobbie', who had flown Lancasters operationally since being posted to 49 Squadron at Fiskerton on 2 June 1943. It must have been a great moment for the two surviving brothers, one a decorated fighter ace, the other a veteran of eight raids on Germany and another on Milan. For Eric, life at the fighter school was less exciting than it was now for his elder brother, although he did still fly on several escort operations. On 5 November 1943, however, Eric's log book records that 'Night of 3-4. Bob missing from night raid. Dusseldorf.'

Flying Officer Bobbie Thomas had flown his first raid on the night of 14/15 June 1943, when Oberhausen was attacked by 197 Lancasters; the starboard side of his aircraft's cockpit was hit by flak, seriously wounding the flight engineer. Two nights later, Bobbie flew his usual ED438, EA-R, among over twenty Lancasters bombing Cologne. On the night of 21/22 June 1943, he had to contend with not only the mid-upper turret going unserviceable, but equally so the starboard engine. Pressing on, Bobbie and crew nonetheless bombed Krefeld, returning an hour late. Then it was Wuppertal, Essen, Hamburg, Mannheim, Nuremburg, Milan, Munchen Gladbach, Hannover, Bochum, Munich, and the 'Big City' – Berlin. Then came that fateful raid on Dusseldorf, on the night of 3/4 November 1943. By then, Bobbie was a flight lieutenant and captain of an experienced crew on their twentieth operation, a 589 strong raid by Lancaster and Halifax bombers. Eighteen bombers failed to return, and sadly ED438 was among the eleven Lancasters lost – shot down near Cologne by *Oberleutnant* Ludwig Meister in an Me 110G-4 night-fighter of 1/NJG 4 based at Florennes, in Belgium. Although initially the entire crew was reported missing, it was later established via the International Red Cross that three of the crew had safely taken to their parachutes, becoming prisoners of war – but the other five, including Flight Lieutenant Thomas, were killed when their aircraft exploded near Koln. After the war, the remains of those killed in the explosion were identified by the Missing Enquiry Research Unit and buried at Rheinberg British Military Cemetery in Germany. For the Thomas family, having already lost Bruce to a German night-fighter, Bobbie's loss was a bitter blow.

At the Fighter Leaders' School, Wing Commander Thomas's logbook records that his personal Spitfire Mk VB also carried his initials on the fuselage, the flights involved being largely of a training and evaluation nature. On 10 December 1943, a daughter, Diana Jill, known as Jilly, was born to Eric and Eirene Thomas, but there was little respite for the new father: on 15 December 1943, he flew a practice attack on base at 'low-level', a 'wing patrol', and three days later flew with another unidentified wing covering the withdrawal of Flying Fortresses from enemy occupied France. Interestingly, on 25 January 1944, Eric flew a Hurricane Mk IV, practice-firing eight 25lb rockets at a beach target. Many subsequent sorties involved dive-bombing and other fighter-bomber related exercises, indicative of the changing war: although far from spent as yet, the *Luftwaffe* was being drained away resisting the full fury of the American daylight assault on Germany, and the RAF by night, in addition to the massive commitment of the Eastern Front. Gone were the dark days of 1940, as the Allies ruled the skies, and minds were increasingly focused on the forthcoming Second Front, which was clearly now not far away, and the need to provide close air support to troops on the ground. The fighter pilot's role was changing, although as Air Vice-Marshal Johnnie Johnson commented, 'I could never get that excited at the sight of bombs hanging off my graceful Spitfire.'

D-Day, the long-awaited Allied invasion, Operation OVERLORD, came on 6 June 1944. Wing Commander Thomas did not fly that momentous day, and the following day was posted away from the Fighter Leaders' School, then located at Millfield, to 85 Group HQ at Uxbridge. Eric's log book records many flights visiting fighter stations in southern England and liaising with the squadrons. On 10 June 1944, he flew down to Lympne in an Oxford, and borrowed a Spitfire Mk IXB, 4D-G:

> First patrol in beach-head area. Flew as Red 3 to Squadron Leader JCF Hayter DFC, 74 Squadron. Fair amount of broken cloud ranging 500–5,000ft. Heavy and light flak from Caen area. Masses of ships offshore, and gliders, parachutes of all colours in the fields. Ground pock-marked with bomb and shell holes. However, seemed strangely quiet everywhere, somehow, to what one had expected.

To get about, Wing Commander Thomas generally flew an obsolete Spitfire Mk I, K9936, an old aircraft built at Southampton by Supermarine and test-flown by George Pickering at Eastleigh on 18 April 1939. Three days later the aircraft was taken on charge by 72 Squadron, suffering a minor flying accident in July 1940. Thereafter the Spitfire survived several years with various operational training units before allocation to 85 Group HQ on 10 May 1944; its ultimate fate is unknown but was presumably scrapped post-war. On 11 June 1944, Eric flew a very different Spitfire, the new Mk XIV, for thirty minutes. Unfortunately his impressions of this machine are unrecorded, but this was incomparable to the dainty Mk I, being a growling Rolls-Royce Griffon-engine variant with a top speed of nearly 450 mph and a service ceiling of 43,500ft. A new threat was about to appear on the Channel front, however, and the Mk XIV's performance would be required to help deal with it: the *Vergeltungswaffe* 1 'Vengeance Weapon', jet-powered, pilotless, flying bomb.

The first V1s were launched against London on 13 June 1944, provoked by the successful Allied landings in Normandy, launched from ramps located in the Pas-de-Calais. When the fuel ran out the engine cut and the device dived to earth, exploding upon impact. At the peak of this new offensive, over 100 'Doodlebugs' or 'Buzz-bombs', as they were popularly known, were launched against south-east England daily, and until the launch-sites in the Netherlands were taken in October 1944, over 10,000 of these frightening missiles were hurled at Britain. 2,400 V-1s fell on Greater London, the resulting death-toll reaching 6,000, with 18,000 more Londoners being seriously injured. To the defences, the V-1 – officially codenamed 'Diver' – was a problem, flying at over 400 mph at 2,500ft, meaning few RAF fighters could catch them. Spitfire XIIs, XIVs and the Hawker Tempest Mk V were the primary fighters able to outpace the V-1, although some were brought down by Spitfire Mk IXs, Mustang IIIs, Mosquitos and, towards the offensive's conclusion, the RAF's first jet fighter, the Gloster Meteor. Balloons and AA guns also played their part in combating this menace. Collectively, these defences destroyed 4,261 'Divers', RAF fighters the majority by a small margin. Destroying the V-1 was difficult, however, because of the resulting violent explosion. To shoot them down, fighters had to fly to such a close range that damage from flying debris in the event of a successful hit was a real hazard. Some pilots devised a method of catching and formating on the 'Diver' before tipping it over with a wingtip, throwing the missile's all-important gyroscope into confusion and causing it to crash – hopefully exploding harmlessly in the sea or countryside.

On 17 June 1944, Wing Commander Thomas patrolled between Dover and Beachy Head for forty minutes in a 91 Squadron Spitfire Mk XIV, hoping to intercept a 'Diver' but without sighting one of the deadly missiles.

Two days later, Eric flew a Tempest Mk V, which could also exceed 400 mph, on an 'Anti-"Diver" Patrol off coast: Sighted "Diver" over Beachy

Head but Spitfire Mk XIV engaged just before I was in position. Saw this Spit destroy "Diver" at 1830 hrs ten miles north of Beachy.'

On the afternoon of 27 June 1944 Wing Commander Thomas flew a Tempest Mk V, leading 3 Squadron's Yellow Section: 'Anti-"Diver" patrol to six miles off coast, Dungeness to Hastings, 4,000ft: one pilotless aircraft destroyed. Confirmed by Pilot Officer Slade-Betts, No 3 Squadron, two miles north of Rye. Crashed in orchard and blew up after three second burst.' The official report stated that the 'Type 16 "Diver"' had been sighted two miles off Rye, incoming at 300 mph on a course of 330° and at 2,500ft. After a short pursuit, Yellow 1 fired three short bursts, causing the flying bomb's port wing to drop and emit grey smoke before exploding at Peasmarsh. This was quite an achievement to add to an already impressive combat record.

That 'Diver' victory proved to be Wing Commander Thomas's final operational sortie and combat success. Indeed, his last flight in a Spitfire, the aircraft with which he had been so connected for six years, was a thirty-minute transit flight from Southend to Heston on 3 July 1944. Perhaps appropriately, it was made in the old Mk I, K9936, the very same type young Pilot Officer Eric Thomas had flown when 19 Squadron received the very first Spitfires back in 1938. A week later, Wing Commander Thomas was posted to 484 Group Control Centre at Goodwood, for 'General Duties Operations', and a week later to the Personnel Holding Unit at Morecambe as supernumerary. He was not, however, a well man: on 24 July 1944, Eric was admitted to the RAF Hospital, Halton, suffering from Tuberculosis – possibly brought on, it has been suggested, by comparatively primitive and unhygienic aircraft oxygen supply systems. On 22 September 1944, Wing Commander Eric Thomas relinquished his commission and was invalided out of the service; he would never pilot an aircraft again. As Eric concluded in his log book: 'Finis'.

On 4 April 1945, Eric's mother, Maude, died of cancer, having been nursed by his sister, Celia. Aged 16 when war broke out, Celia joined the Women's Royal Naval Service, more commonly known as the 'Wrens', at 18, later finding herself engaged in highly secret work for nine months connected with code-breaking at Bletchley Park's Stanmore outstation. With her mother's illness, however, this came to an end with a compassionate discharge enabling her to care for Maude. The experience left a lasting mark, because Celia subsequently trained to be a doctor. Her august and only surviving brother, however, was still not a well man.

1948 found the retired Wing Commander employed as Mess Secretary at HQ No XI Fighter Group, at Hillingdon, Uxbridge, and living locally in Sweetcroft Lane. Eric even managed three flights that year, two jollies in a 'Dominie', although this was not the later jet of that name but a de Havilland Dragon Rapide biplane, flown by a Flight Lieutenant Crone DFC, and another in an Anson piloted by one Squadron Leader Primavesi, a former wartime Mosquito pilot. On 3 August 1950, Eric flew as a passenger in an Anson from Bovingdon to Manston and return, the pilot on that occasion being Group Captain Rupert 'Lucky' Leigh, who had commanded 66 Squadron during the Battle of Britain. It was the last time Eric ever flew.

In 1951, the Thomas family suffered another tragedy, when Eric and Eirene's son Guy, born in 1948, died of a rare cancer. At that time, the bereaved father was working as an administration officer for the Middlesex Territorial Association, the family having moved to the Windsor area. In the years that followed, son Timothy and second daughter Sylvia arrived, Eric then being employed to manage the car parks at Royal Ascot Racecourse.

Having survived so many incredibly dangerous operational flights during the war, on 21 April 1959, Wing Commander Eric Hugh Thomas DSO DFC* CdeG RAF (Ret'd), a husband and father, succumbed to TB and died, aged just 41, at the King Edward VII Sanatorium, Easebourne, near Midhurst.

It was a sad end indeed to someone who had so much to live for, and had done so much for his country – a 'Forgotten Hero' indeed.

Epilogue

Every book is a journey, for author and reader, and in this one we have gone back in time to the pre-war 'salad days' of the peacetime RAF, then joined our heroes fighting over Dunkirk, during the Battle of Britain and well beyond. Of Fighter Command, 544 aircrew perished in the summer and autumn of 1940, in addition to more from other commands; by the war's end, over 700 more of the Few had lost their lives.

For some, killed in action during the Battle of Britain, it was all over in a flash. For others who survived the summer of 1940, the western desert awaited, or other tumultuous events, such as the 'Non-stop Offensive' of 1941, the 'Channel Dash', the Fw 190 menace, daylight bomber escort missions and fighter sweeps, Dieppe, D-Day, and even defending England against flying bombs. This book, therefore, is about much more than the actual Battle of Britain.

The book is, I suppose, a forensic reconstruction of the lives of those in it, and to a degree their families. Our heroes speak to us through previously unpublished memoirs, log book entries, and much more. Unique snapshots allow us to peer through time at their long-gone world, and, perhaps, get a feel for how it was back then.

Hopefully those who stories are recorded, in detail, in this book, will be better-known as a result. It is said that unless things are written, they are forgotten. If that is so, at this, the end of our journey, those featured in are forgotten no more – which is as it should be.

Acknowledgements

This book would not have been possible without the kind cooperation and support of the families of the airmen concerned, namely:

Wing Commander H.F. Burton: The late Jean and Keith Allom; The Baroness Hodgson CBE of Abinger, to whom I am also indebted for contributing such a moving foreword.

Group Captain T.P. Gleave: Angela and Tim Lodge.

Wing Commander R.G. Kellett: The Kellett family, collectively.

Wing Commander E.H. Thomas: Sylvia and Nigel Lewis, and Tim Thomas.

Pilot Officer R.A. Howley: Tina Howley Harney.

Sergeant A.G. Curley: Elizabeth Callow Wirth.

Sergeant Bruce Hancock: Keith Hancock.

The following are relatives of either air or ground crew mentioned in the book, who also provided unique assistance:

Squadron Leader Peter Starr Mills; Lynn and Stephen Reglar; Stuart MacKenzie; Judith Bambrough.

The following individuals and their organisations:

Group Captain Patrick Tootal OBE, Honorary Secretary Battle of Britain Fighter Association and Battle of Britain Memorial Trust.

Bob Marchant, Honorary Secretary, The Guinea Pig Club.

Kevin Barnes and the Commonwealth War Graves Commission.

Hazel Crozier, College Curator, RAF College Cranwell.

Dr Rachael Abbiss and Joseph Hall at the Battle of Britain Bunker, Uxbridge.

Edward McManus, Battle of Britain London Monument.

Alan Thomas, MoD Air Historical Branch.

Linda Duffield, Tony Adams and Neil Broughton of the Kenley Revival Project.

Simon Nicholas, Countryside Manager, Cotswolds, National Trust.

The following fellow authors and researchers also provided freely given and invaluable assistance:

Allan White, for selfless sharing of his own pioneering research into wartime aviation incidents occurring in Gloucestershire; Andy Long, whose knowledge of the Defiant's operational history was invaluable; Glenn Gelder, Gordon Lawley, Nick Willey and Daniel Richards for helping with photographs of graves; Paul Gentleman; John Slater; Paul Heys, and Richard King.

As always, Martin Mace went above and beyond, assisting in all kinds of ways, and the team at Pen & Sword are always a pleasure to work with.

Bibliography

Pilots' Flying Log Books

Group Captain T.P. Gleave
Wing Commander H.F. Burton
Wing Commander R.G. Kellett

The National Archives

The Operations Record Books of the following units:
AIR27/252   19 Squadron
AIR27/598   66 Squadron
AIR27/738   91 Squadron
AIR27/764   96 Squadron
AIR27/866   111 Squadron
AIR27/945   133 Squadron
AIR27/969   141 Squadron
AIR27/1371   222 Squadron
AIR27/1511   253 Squadron
AIR27/1558   266 Squadron
AIR27/1663   303 Squadron
AIR27/2058   600 Squadron
AIR27/2109   611 Squadron
AIR27/2126   616 Squadron.
AIR26/315   239 Wing
AIR29/558/1   6 Service Flying Training School

Pilots' Combat Reports of the following units:
AIR50/26   66 Squadron
AIR50/55   133 Squadron
AIR50/61   141 Squadron
AIR50/51   222 Squadron
AIR50/97   253 Squadron

AIR50/117	303 Squadron
AIR50/167	603 Squadron
AIR50/173	611 Squadron
AIR50/176	616 Squadron

Casualty Files

AIR81/2929	Squadron Leader T.P. Gleave.
AIR81/2910	Squadron Leader H.M. Starr.
AIR81/2896	Pilot Officer D.N.O. Jenkins.
AIR81/2158	Sergeant G. MacKenzie.
AIR81/2889	Sergeant J.H. Dickinson.
AIR81/3976	Flying Officer D.M. Robertson, Pilot Officer E.W. Blackwell, and Kapral F. Skrzypczak.
AIR81/2986	Sergeant J.F.C. Wise.
AIR81/1145	Flight Lieutenant M. Loudon and Pilot Officer E. Farnes.
AIR81/1146	Pilot Officer R. Kemp and Sergeant P. Crombie.
AIR81/1147	Pilot Officer J.R. Gard'ner and Pilot Officer D.M. Slatter.
AIR81/1148	Pilot Officer R. Kidson and Sergeant F. Atkins.
AIR81/1149	Pilot Officer R.A. Howley and Sergeant A.G. Curley.

Unpublished Sources

Memoir of Group Captain T.P. Gleave, original manuscript of *Eagles of Nemesis* and Gleave papers.
Memoir of Wing Commander R.G. Kellett and Kellett family papers.
Correspondence and papers, Dilip Sarkar Archive.

Published Sources

'AHE', 'Cranwell and its Traditions', *Journal of the Royal Air Force College*, 1930, pp. 12-15
Alcorn, J., Battle of Britain Top Guns, *Aeroplane Monthly*, September 1996
Alcorn, J., Battle of Britain Top Guns Update, *Aeroplane Monthly*, July 2000
Allen, Wg Cdr H.R., *Fighter Squadron 1940-1942*, Granada, London, 1982
Anon., *RAF Middle East: The Official Story of Air Operations in the Middle East, from February 1942 to January 1943*, HMSO, London, 1945
Balfour, H., *Wings Over Westminster*, Hutchinson & Co Ltd, London, 1973
Bishop, E., *McIndoe's Army: The Story of the Guinea Pig Club and its Indomitable Members*, Grubb Street, London, 2001
Boot, H., and Sturtivant, R., *Gifts of War: Spitfires and Other Presentation Aircraft in Two World Wars*, Air Britain, Tonbridge, 2005

BIBLIOGRAPHY

Branson, N., & Heinemann, M., *Britain in the Nineteen Thirties*, Weidenfeld & Nicolson, London 1971

Brickhill, P., *Reach for the Sky*, BCA, London, 1952

Clapson, M., *The Routledge Companion to the Twentieth Century*, Routledge, London, 2009

Cornwell, P., *The Battle of France, Then & Now: Six Nations Locked in Aerial Combat, September 1939 to June 1940*, Battle of Britain Prints International Ltd, Harlow, 2007

Cox, S., and Gray, P. (Eds), *Air Power History: Turning Points From Kitty Hawk to Kosovo*, Frank Cass, London, 2005

Cull, B., *First of The Few: 5 June – 9 July 1940*, Fonthill, Stroud, 2013

Cull, B., *Battle for the Channel: The First Month of the Battle of Britain, 10 July – 10 August 1940*, Fonthill, Stroud, 2017

Delve, K., *Fighter Command 1936-1968: An Operational Record*, Pen & Sword, Barnsley, 2007

Delve, K., *The Desert Air Force in World War II: Air Power in the Western Desert 1940-1942*, Pen & Sword, Barnsley, 2017

Douglas, MRAF Lord Douglas of Kirtleside, with Robert Wright, *Sholto Douglas: Years of Command, a Personal Story of the Second War in the Air*, Collins, London, 1966

Dundas, Grp Capt Sir H.S.L., *Flying Start: A Fighter Pilot's War Years*, Stanley Paul & Co Ltd, London, 1988

Fellowes, Air Cdre P.F.M. (Ed), *Britain's Wonderful Air Force*, Odhams Press Ltd, London, 1942

Fenton, Air Cdr H.A., *Aquarius: The Man Who Holds the Watering Pot. A Flying Memoir 1928-1945*, privately published, Le Vallon, Jersey, 1992

Foreman, J., *RAF Fighter Command Victory Claims of World War 2, Part One 1939-1940*, Red Kite, Walton-on-Thames, 2003

Franks, N.L.R., *Royal Air Force Fighter Command Losses of the Second World War, Volume 1, Operational Losses: Aircraft and Crews 1939-41*, Midland Publishing, Hersham, 2008

Franks, N.L.R, *Air Battle for Dunkirk: 26 May – 3 June 1940*, Grubb Street, London, 2006

Freeman, R.A., *The Mighty Eighth: A History of the US 8th Army Air Force*, Doubleday & Co Ltd, New York, 1973

Gladman, B.W., *Intelligence and Anglo-American Air Support in World War Two: The Western Desert and Tunisia, 1940-43*, Palgrave Macmillan, Basingstoke, 2009

Gleave, Grp Capt T.P. (published under pseudonym 'RAF Casualty'), *'I Had A Row With A German'*, Macmillan & Co Ltd. London, 1941

Goss, C, *Bloody Biscay: The History of V Gruppe/Kampfgeschwader 40*. Crecy Publishing Ltd, Manchester, 1997

Haig-Brown, A.R., *The OTC in the Great War, Country Life Publications*, London, 1915

Hall, D.I., *Strategy For Victory: The Development of British Tactical Air Power 1919 – 1943*, Praeger Security International, Westport, Connecticut, 2008

Haslam, Grp Capt E.B., *The History of RAF Cranwell*, HMSO, London, 1982

Haugland, V., *The Eagle's War: Saga of the Eagle Squadron Pilots, 1940-45*, Jason Aronson Inc Publishers, Maryland, 1992

Ishoven, A van, *The Luftwaffe in the Battle of Britain*, Ian Allen Publishing Ltd, Shepperton, 1980

James, J., *The Paladins: A Social History of the RAF up to the Outbreak of World War 2*, Futura Publications, London, 1990

James, T.C.G., *The Battle of Britain: RAF Official Histories*, Frank Cass, London, 2000

Jenkins, S.C., *Oxfordshire at War Through Time*, Amberley Publishing, Stroud, 2014

Johnson, AVM J.E., *Wing Leader*, Chatto & Windus London, 1956

Kellett, R, *Wearhead to Washington: A Collection of Sketches, Portraits, Memoirs, Transcripts and Associations Relating to the Kellett Family From Weardale*, York Publishing Services Ltd, York, 2017

Kent, Wg Cdr J.A., *One of The Few: A Triumphant Story of Combat in the Battle of Britain*, History Press, Stroud, 2008

King, R, *303 (Polish) Squadron: Battle of Britain Diary*, Red Kite, Walton-on-Thames, 2010

Lisiewicz, Sqn Ldr M. (ed), *Destiny Can Wait: The Polish Air Force in the Second World War*, Willian Heinemann, London, 1949

Longworth, P., *The Unending Vigil: The History of the Commonwealth War Graves Commission*, Pen & Sword Ltd, Barnsley, 2010

Mason, F.K., *Battle Over Britain*, Aston Publications, Bourne End, 1990

Mason, P.D., *Nicolson VC: The Full and Authorised Biography of James Brindley Nicolson*, Geerings of Ashford Ltd, Ashford, 1991

McKee, A., *The Coal Scuttle Brigade*, Souvenir Press Ltd, London, 1957

Morgan, E.B., and Shacklady, E, *Spitfire: The History*, Key Publishing, Stamford, 1987

Mowatt, C.L., *Britain Between the Wars 1918-40*, Taylor & Francis Books Ltd, London, 1968

Neil, Wg Cdr T.F., *Gun Button to Fire*, William Kimber, London, 1987

Orange, V., *Dowding of Fighter Command: Victor of the Battle of Britain*, Grub Street, London, 2008

Overy, R.J., *The Air War 1939-45*, Europa Publications Ltd, London, 1980

Oxspring, Grp Capt R.O., *Spitfire Command*, Cerberus, Bristol, 2004

Pope, R., *War and Society in Britain: 1899-1948*, Longman, London, 1991

Price, Dr A, *Battle of Britain: The Hardest Day, 18 August 1940*, MacDonald & Jane's Publishers Ltd, London, 1979

Priestly, J.B., *English Journey*, Willian Heinemann Ltd, London, 1934

Probert, Air Cdre H., and Cox, S. (eds), *The Battle Re-Thought: A Symposium on the Battle of Britain*, Airlife Publishing, Shrewsbury, 1991

Rennison, J., *Wings Over Gloucestershire*, Piccadilly Publishing, Cheltenham, 1988

BIBLIOGRAPHY

Shores, C., and Williams, C, *Aces High*, Grubb Street, London, 1994

Simpson, A., and Simpson, G (eds), *Aircrew Casualties of the Battle of Britain, 1940*, Battle of Britain Memorial Trust, West Malling, 2014

Simpson, G., *A History of the Battle of Britain Fighter Association: Commemorating the Few*, Pen & Sword, Barnsley, 2015

Stevenson, J., *British Society 1914-45*, Penguin, London, 1984

Toliver, Col R.F., and Constable, T.J., *Fighter Aces of the Luftwaffe*, Schiffer Books, Atglen, PA, 1996

Wallace, G., *RAF Biggin Hill: The Immortal Story of one of the Battle of Britain's most famous fighter stations*, Putnam & Co Ltd, London, 1957

White, A., *Unsung Heroes: A Story of Wartime Incidents in the Cotswolds*, Severnside Aviation Society, Chepstow, 1989

White, A., The Last Casualties of The Hardest Day, *Aeroplane Monthly*, October 1989

Wynn, K., *Men of the Battle of Britain: A Biographical Directory of the Few*, Frontline Books (Pen & Sword Ltd), Barnsley, 2015

Websites

Battle of Britain Memorial to the Few:
https://www.battleofbritainmemorial.org
Battle of Britain London Monument:
http://bbm.org.uk
East Grinstead Museum/Guinea Pig Club:
https://www.eastgrinsteadmuseum.org.uk/guinea-pig-club/the-guinea-pig-club/
Kenley Revival Project:
https://www.kenleyrevival.org
TV Programmes
This Is Your Life, Group Captain T.P. Gleave CBE, broadcast in January 1991, and available on YouTube: https://youtu.be/-UAKIcv62Eo

Other books by Dilip Sarkar

Spitfire Squadron: No 19 Squadron at War, 1939-41
The Invisible Thread: A Spitfire's Tale
Through Peril to the Stars: RAF Fighter Pilots Who Failed to Return, 1939-45
Angriff Westland: Three Battle of Britain Air Raids Through the Looking Glass
A Few of the Many: Air War 1939-45, A Kaleidoscope of Memories
Bader's Tangmere Spitfires: The Untold Story, 1941
Bader's Duxford Fighters: The Big Wing Controversy
Missing in Action: Resting in Peace?
Guards VC: Blitzkrieg 1940
Battle of Britain: The Photographic Kaleidoscope, Volumes I-IV
Fighter Pilot: The Photographic Kaleidoscope
Group Captain Sir Douglas Bader: An Inspiration in Photographs
Johnnie Johnson: Spitfire Top Gun, Part I
Johnnie Johnson: Spitfire Top Gun, Part II
Battle of Britain: Last Look Back
Spitfire! Courage & Sacrifice
Spitfire Voices: Heroes Remember
The Battle of Powick Bridge: Ambush a Fore-thought
Duxford 1940: A Battle of Britain Base at War
The Few: The Battle of Britain in the Words of the Pilots Spitfire Manual 1940
The Last of the Few: Eighteen Battle of Britain Pilots Tell Their Extraordinary Stories
Hearts of Oak: The Human Tragedy of HMS Royal Oak
The Sinking of HMS Royal Oak In the Words of the Survivors (re-print of Hearts
    of Oak)
Spitfire Voices: Life as a Spitfire Pilot in the Words of the Veterans
How the Spitfire Won the Battle of Britain
Spitfire Ace of Aces: The True Wartime Story of Johnnie Johnson Douglas Bader
Fighter Ace: The Extraordinary Life of Douglas Bader, Battle of Britain Hero
    (re-print of above)
Spitfire: The Photographic Biography Hurricane Manual 1940
River Pike
The Final Few: The Last Surviving Pilots of the Battle of Britain Tell Their Stories
Arnhem 1944: The Human Tragedy of the Bridge Too Far

OTHER BOOKS BY DILIP SARKAR

Spitfire! The Full Story of a Unique Battle of Britain Fighter Squadron
Battle of Britain 1940: The Finest Hour's Human Cost
Letters from The Few: Unique Memories of the Battle of Britain
Johnnie Johnson's 1942 Diary: The War Diary of the Spitfire Ace of Aces
Johnnie Johnson's Great Adventure: The Spitfire Ace of Ace's Last Look Back
Spitfire Ace of Aces – The Album: The Photographs of Johnnie Johnson
Sailor Malan – Freedom Fighter: The Inspirational Story of a Spitfire Ace
The Real Spitfire Pilot
Bader's Big Wing Controversy: Duxford 1940
Bader's Spitfire Wing: Tangmere 1941
Spitfire Down: Fighter Boys Who Failed to Return
Arise to Conquer (by Wing Commander IR Gleed, introduced by and with extra
historical commentary by Dilip Sarkar)

Index